MW00627494

SHRI GURU GRANTH SAHIB

THE AWAKENER

ੴ

SHRI GURU GRANTH SAHIB

THE AWAKENER

BS MANDER

White Falcon
Publishing

www.whitefalconpublishing.com

Shri Guru Granth Sahib – The Awakener
BS Mander

www.whitefalconpublishing.com

ISBN - 978-1-63640-274-1

DEDICATION

This book is dedicated to you, the readers, who are walking the spiritual path. May this book help you speed up your spiritual journey and also motivate you to explore the depths of *Shri Guru Granth Sahib*.

ACKNOWLEDGEMENTS

I express my sincere gratitude to the following:

Lt Gen BPS Mander (Retd) for his deep interest in the book, and for recommending many quotes that have enriched the content. He was ever-willing to share his views on any aspect, and we spent many long hours discussing various topics.

Gp Capt Ajit Singh, SC, VM (G) (Retd) for critically analyzing the draft and making many useful recommendations.

My nephew Aakarshan, a highly motivated and devout Amritdhari Sikh, for his critical views and reviews which I found immensely useful.

My daughter Manka and son Samar who, despite their busy schedules, went through the script with a fine-tooth comb and offered many meaningful suggestions, most of which were incorporated. Samar was also a great help with the final proof reading of the book.

My wife Jasmeet, a sincere devotee of *Shri Guru Granth Sahib*, for her encouragement and full support throughout.

White Falcon Publishing headed by Ms Navsangeet Batth and the team comprising Akshit Bagai, Priya Sahu, Sukhdeep Singh and Shrikesh Kumar, for their ever willing co-operation and professional approach resulting in high quality of work.

Thank you all. Without your help this book would not have eventuated as it has.

FOREWORD

This book was ideated some fifteen years ago after I had read *Shri Guru Granth Sahib* several times and was convinced that it is a supreme spiritual guide for living an enriched and purposeful life. The lessons contained in the Holy Scripture are the collective wisdom of thirty-six saintly people and their advice is as relevant today as it was during the time it was written – perhaps more so now, because of the troubled times the world is going through.

I feel that the rich philosophy and wisdom contained in the Holy Book needs to be shared with more and more people. This is my humble effort towards that end, and I am sanguine it would serve that purpose.

Let me say this, I neither have any special qualification for writing this book nor have I had any special insight, vision or any other spiritual experience that pushed me on. However, I do feel that besides my own motivation, it was God's will that made me hold the pen and write.

May be I have studied the *Granth Sahib* a little more than the average reader. Otherwise, I am just another co-traveler with you on this wonderful journey called life.

CONTENTS

CONTENTS

INTRODUCTION

ੴ

Shri *Guru Granth Sahib* (SGGS) is a divine and highly revered scripture. Though it is the sacred text of the Sikhs, its teachings are not confined to any one sect or religion. It encourages people of every faith to read and follow it, without asking them to compromise with their own religious or spiritual beliefs. Its verses are often heard in the homes of many non-Sikhs too. Numerous devotees, belonging to different religions offer prayers in *gurdwaras* (Sikh temples), where SGGS is kept with reverence and its verses are sung & recited every day. It does not condemn or denigrate any religion, nor does it seek other people to convert to Sikhism. The wisdom contained therein is for anyone seeking spiritual awakening.

Many believers cherish a desire to read and understand SGGS but for most it only remains a desire that's never fulfilled. This is so because it is a lengthy text with 1430 pages and is written in languages not easily understood. Even Punjabi language, written in *Gurmukhi* script, is dated and is not easily grasped by the present-day Punjabis. Also, there is no universally accepted translation available, and there are many variations in different translations that we do come across. There is a bigger problem with parts written in other languages (in *Gurmukhi* script) such as Sanskrit, Brijbhasha, Arabic, Persian, Hindi, Sindhi, Lehndi, Dakhni, Bengali and Marathi. For better comprehension one also needs to have knowledge of ancient Indian scriptures, mythology and beliefs. However, these problems are not so un-surmountable as to hinder our understanding the true wisdom of SGGS.

The contents of SGGS are written in verse and are known as *gurbani*, (Guru/God's word), or simply *bani*. What most Sikhs read daily are extracts from SGGS published in small booklets known as *gutkas*. However, most people do this as a mere ritual of uttering the *gurbani* without any real understanding. The true value of SGGS lies in studying it, understanding it, and then applying the lessons in our daily lives. Reading *gurbani* a million times will serve no purpose if it is not imbibed and the teachings not practiced.

Guru Nanak Dev (1469-1539) laid the foundation for creation of SGGS with his own poetry. Whenever he was in commune with God he would receive *gurbani* verses and would start singing, while his companion Bhai Mardana would play the *rabaab*, a string instrument. The only person other than Bhai Mardana who understood and memorized Guru Nanak's hymns was Bhai Lehna, a devout follower of Guru Nanak. Bhai Lehna realized the significance of Guru Nanak's poetry and did not want to leave it to the oral tradition to spread and pass down. Punjabi till then was not an advanced language and did not even have a script. Bhai Lehna therefore created the *Gurmukhi* script, which till now is the script for Punjabi in India – Pakistan has Arabic based *Shahmukhi* script for Punjabi.

Because of Bhai Lehna's devotion and wisdom, Guru Nanak passed down his *Guruship* to him, even at the cost of annoying his sons and other members of the family. Bhai Lehna became Guru Angad Dev, the second Sikh Guru.

Poetry of Guru Nanak was handed down to successive gurus who made their own contributions. In 1604 the earlier version of SGGS called the *Adi Granth* was compiled by Guru Arjan Dev (1563-1606), the 5th Guru, which contained the writings of first five gurus and other holy saints & bards. It was dictated by Guru Arjan Dev and was handwritten by Bhai Gurdas, a Sikh scholar and maternal uncle of Guru Arjan Dev.

One of the reasons for Guru Arjan Dev to compile SGGS was that Meharban, grandson of Guru Ram Das, the 4th Guru, had begun writing his own unenlightened verses under Guru Nanak's name, in the same style as adopted by Sikh Gurus. The followers were often confused and were at a loss to differentiate true *bani* from Meharban's compilation.

Many spiritual writers of the time approached Guru Arjan Dev to have their works included in SGGS but he was very selective and approved only those writings which conformed to Sikh ideals and values.

The *Adi Granth* was later expanded by Guru Gobind Singh, (1666-1708), the 10th Guru, who added the writings of his father, Guru Teg Bahadur (1621-1675), the 9th Guru. However, this was not an easy task. The original version of *Adi Granth* was in possession of Dhir Mal, son of Baba Gurditta and grandson of Guru Har Gobind, the 6th Guru. When Guru Gobind Singh approached Dhir Mal to get the original text, he refused, and taunted the Guru saying, "If you are a guru, then prepare your own." Guru Gobind Singh then dictated the entire *Adi Granth* from his memory to Bhai Mani Singh. The great task of re-writing the scripture was finally completed in 1705 at Damdama Sahib (Talwandi Sabo).

Though Guru Gobind Singh wrote beautiful poetry, he did not include it in SGGS, but created a separate text titled *Dasam Granth.*

Something unique about SGGS is that it has original writings of the founders; unlike most other religious scriptures, which were written by the followers/disciples of the founders. Also, the writings are not only of Sikh Gurus, but also include those of Hindu and Muslim spiritual leaders. It is a symbol of real secularism. Details of authors of SGGS are at Appendix A.

Another uniqueness of SGGS is that, unlike other religious scriptures, its teachings are not based on any significant stories. In Hindu scriptures we have the epics Ramayana and

Mahabharata, in the Bible its Adam & Eve, David & Goliath among others. In Quran too there are many stories including those of Prophets Eesaa (Jesus) and Moosa (Moses). SGGS, however, is all 1430 pages of hymns of divine wisdom.

For the Sikhs, SGGS is the 11th and the eternal Guru, a status given to it by Guru Gobind Singh, the 10th and last living Guru. In October 1708 he proclaimed at Nanded, Maharashtra:

"Aagya Bhaee Akaal Ki Tabhi Chalayo Panth.
Sabh Sikhan Ko Hukam Hai Guru Manyo Granth.
Guru Granth Ji Maneyo Pragat Gura Ki Deh.
Jo Prabh Ko Milbo Chahay Khoj Shabad Mein Leh."

(With the authority of the Timeless One this religious path is established.
All Sikhs are directed to accept *Granth* as their Guru.
Trust that *Guru Granth* has emerged as embodiment of the Guru.
Whosoever desires to meet God should search for Him in the word - of *gurbani* in SGGS.)

Though Sikhism is the fifth largest organized religion of the world, not much is known about it, even in countries with sizeable Sikh population. In 2015 a study was conducted in USA where 1800 Americans were shown several pictures of Sikh men and women in different attires. They were then asked to give their views/comments about the people in the pictures. Their replies indicated:

Only a few had heard the word 'Sikh' somewhere.

They thought these people were from middle-east area.

They believed they are not civilized, they beat their women.

They said their religion had something to do with Islam.

Later when briefed about Sikh values and principles enshrined in SGGS they all changed their opinions and said

Sikhs were a wonderful people and they would love to have them as their neighbours and friends.

Another survey in 2016 in Great Britain found that 1 in every 7 Sikhs was discriminated against at work and 1 in 5 in public places - despite being economically the most successful people. A recent report says that hate crime against Sikhs in UK rose by 7.3 percent during the year 2019-20, while there was a decline in overall cases. The main reason has been their mistaken identity as Islamic terrorists. There is indeed a vast gap in information about Sikhism in the world, as well as within India, which needs to be bridged so that Sikhism and Sikhs are better known and understood.

The aim of this book is to give an overview of SGGS to those, who have not had the time or the motivation to read the complete holy book; as also, to introduce them to important and recurring themes contained therein. It is hoped that this will lead to a greater interest in reading the complete holy book that I am sure will result in spiritual growth of the reader. Even if you do not read the complete SGGS but follow the teachings contained in this book on a regular basis you would be a far better person than someone who reads the holy book daily, but does nothing to make himself an enlightened human being - the real purpose of SGGS.

SGGS forms the basis of Sikh philosophy which shows a practical path for human endeavour towards awakening. It has immense universal appeal but needs greater effort to make it known to the world at large. This book is my humble effort to make Sikhs and non-Sikhs aware of Sikh values and beliefs. It is my hope and expectation that it reaches the hands of those living in India and abroad who can serve this purpose.

It is a matter of great pride for the followers of SGGS, that three quotations from the holy book have been incorporated in a United Nations' official document, for the first time ever. In

2017 UN launched a 'Faith for Rights' initiative, by the office of the High Commissioner, United Nations Human Rights, to include mutually enriching connections between religions of the world, by including suitable quotations from all major religious texts. Proposals from various religions were made by nation states practicing those religions. Since there is no Sikh nation state, there was no one to represent Sikhism. However, UN Advisory Committee member Dr Iqtidar Karamat Cheema, a UK based Muslim historian, took the initiative and had three quotes included in UN document. These quotations with English translation are given at Appendix B.

I mentioned in the beginning that SGGS is a spiritual scripture. What does that mean? What is spirituality? Well, spirituality is the belief that beyond our physical world, there are other realms or domains which are not visible to us because they are vibrating at different frequencies. We experience these realms after death, before we are reborn, as also after our final liberation from the physical world. The soul (*atma*) within us is from the spiritual world that is connected to Supreme Soul (*Param-atma*) which is also in the spirit form. All religions believe in spirituality, though there are differences in detail.

Some of the important issues a spiritual guide should deal with are:

Is there God?

If so, what is the concept of God?

How did the universe come into being?

Who created it?

Is there a purpose in our life?

How should we live our life?

Is there life after death?

If so, what kind of life is that and how is it determined?

In the chapters that follow, we shall look at these questions, as well as other teachings covered in the holy book. I have focused more on the lessons and wisdom contained in SGGS, and not so much on technical detail or facts & figures.

"Shri Guru Granth Sahib is a source book, an expression of man's loneliness, his aspirations, his longings, his cry to God and his hunger for communication with that Being. I have studied the scriptures of other great religions but I do not find elsewhere the same power of appeal to the heart and the mind as I find here in these volumes."

Pearl S Buck (1892-1973)
US Nobel Laureate
Pulitzer Prize Winner

READING NOTES

ੴ

There are several quotations from SGGS given in every chapter and each quotation follows a fixed pattern, as given in the example below:

ਨਾਨਕ ਸਭੁ ਕਿਛੁ ਤੁਮਰੈ ਹਾਥ ਮੈ ਤੁਮ ਹੀ ਹੋਤ ਸਹਾਇ॥

Nanak sabh kichhu tumrai haath mai tum hee hoat sahaaye.

नानक सभु किछु तुमरै हाथ मै तुम ही होत सहाइ॥

Nanak, everything is in your hands, only You can help me.

M9/1429/7

The first part of the quotation is in Punjabi (*Gurmukhi* script), as it appears in SGGS, then the Roman script, followed by Hindi (*Devanagri* script) and finally the translation/explanation in English. While converting the *Gurmukhi* quotations into Roman script I have not used any fixed pronunciation key – it was difficult to work out a proper standardized scheme.

As per the style of that time all writers mentioned their names in most of their poetry but the Sikh Gurus used only Guru Nanak's name, because they all carried his *jyot* (divine light/flame). For example, the above quote mentions that Guru Nanak is saying it, but the actual author is Guru Teg Bahadur (9th Guru).

At the bottom right of each quotation are the following details; first the writer's name, then the page number of SGGS, followed by the line in which the quotation begins. Names of

Sikh Gurus are not mentioned, instead we have the *Mahalla* (House) numbers. *Mahalla* 1 (or M1) means 1st Guru which was Guru Nanak, M2 means 2nd Guru, which was Guru Angad Dev and so on. Thus, M9/1429/7 written at the bottom right of above quote means it is written by Guru Teg Bahadur, the 9th Guru, at page No 1429 and starts at line No 7. Names of writers other than Sikh Gurus are given as actual.

Also note that the way the quote is written gives the impression that the reader is praying to Guru Nanak for help, but actually it is Guru Teg Bahadur (using Guru Nanak's name) who is praying to God. Sometimes the quote starts with *Kahu Nanak* (Nanak says), while other times it simply starts with Nanak, even though it implies 'Nanak says.' Same applies to other writers.

In spiritual literature like SGGS you sometimes come across statements that seem conflicting and contradicting. This is so because it is the language of the enlightened saints which comes from their hearts. It is the language of love and truth. We are more accustomed to the language of logic and reasoning which comes from the head. Because of this we don't always clearly understand the language of these holy people – we have to rise to their level to fully grasp their utterances. People are still trying to de-codify many statements of Jesus made over two thousand years ago. Ancient Chinese philosopher Lao Tzu had rightly said, "The words of truth are always paradoxical."

CHAPTER 1

GOD

ੴ

There are many descriptions of God and His attributes in SGGS and we get to know Him in many different ways. But as we shall see, He cannot be fully comprehended or explained. We can properly explain something only if it is within our intellectual capability to grasp. God Almighty is too great and therefore not in our power to grasp accurately. Yet for people to get an idea something has to be said. Though not fully describable He is certainly perceivable. Saying nothing about God doesn't help.

I have referred to God as He/Him, but that is only for the sake of convenience. He is not confined to any class, race or gender.

The first two opening lines of SGGS, written by Guru Nanak to describe God are:

ੴ ਸਤਿ ਨਾਮੁ ਕਰਤਾ ਪੁਰਖੁ ਨਿਰਭਉ ਨਿਰਵੈਰੁ
ਅਕਾਲ ਮੂਰਤਿ ਅਜੂਨੀ ਸੈਭੰ ਗੁਰ ਪ੍ਰਸਾਦਿ॥

Ekoankaar, Sat Naam, Karta Purakh, Nirbhao, Nirvair,
Akaal Moorat, Ajuni, Saibhang, Gur Parsaad.

ੴ सति नामु करता पुरखु निरभउ निरवैरु
अकाल मूरति अजूनी सैभं गुर प्रसादि॥

ੴ(Ekoankaar) - There is one creator God.

Sat naam - His name is true.

Karta purakh - He is the creator.

Nirbhao - He is without fear.

Nirvair - He is without enmity.

Akaal moorat - He is timeless.

Ajuni - He doesn't come into the cycle of death and rebirth.

Saibhang - He is His own creator.

Gur parsaad - He is attained by the grace of the Guru/God.

M1/1/1

This is called the *Mool Mantar*, or the principal statement. It is pertinent to note that the first thing written in the *Mool Mantar* is the symbol ੴ *Ekoankaar*. It has three components, *Ek* (One), *Oan* (God), and *Kaar* (creation), which means there is but one God who has created everything.

Now Guru Nanak is not the first person who espoused the concept of one Supreme God. That credit, it is believed, goes to Akhenaten, an Egyptian Pharaoh who ruled as far back as 1350 BC. He is known to be the first ruler in the world who believed in monotheism and taught the same to his citizens. He believed in one universal God named *Aten*. So when we say there is one creator God it is nothing new.

Most religions believe in one Supreme God. In Hinduism also where people worship many deities, they do believe in one Supreme God called *Brahaman*, also referred to as *Parmeshwar, Ishwar, Bhagwaan, Parmatma* and so on.

However Hindus as well as Muslims, believed that *theirs* was a superior God. Guru Nanak said there was no question of *your* God or *my* God, there is only One God for all. The first words he spoke after his enlightenment were, "*Na ko Hindu na Musalmaan*" (There is neither Hindu nor Muslim) meaning that all humanity is one, thus same One God is common to all.

Guru Nanak's statement in *Ekoankaar* is even more profound. If we look deeper, we realize what he is saying is, that not only is there one God for all, but that at some level, there is Oneness of everything in the creation. Prof Sahib Singh, the renowned Sikh scholar says, 'Oan' means that entity like which there is no other, and in which is contained the entire universe. Since everything in the universe is component of the whole, everything is interconnected. There is Oneness, not only of humanity but of *everything*. Even science tells us today that at the sub-atomic level everything in the cosmos is interconnected and is sub-part of the whole. Thus *Ekoankaar* means there is Oneness of the whole creation - there is no separateness. Adi Shankara, the eighth century sage had said, "Where there is duality by virtue of ignorance, one sees all things as distinct from the Self. When everything is seen as the Self, there is not even an atom other than the Self..."

We find it difficult to conceive this Oneness because of our strong individualized and self-limiting personalities. If a wave in the ocean sees itself as an independent entity, it is nothing more than just a wave. But when it sees itself as an integral part of the ocean, it becomes the mighty ocean. When we accept Oneness of the cosmos we begin to see ourselves as part of the Whole, we awaken. We become One, we are part of God. What is preventing us from seeing our Oneness? It is our ego. We'll see more on ego and Oneness in later chapters.

Let us now see quotations from SGGS where the authors attempt to define God but finally express their inability to do so. Even an enlightened person like Guru Nanak who has described God in many ways, finally says that even if one knows God, He can't be written or spoken about:

ਜੇ ਹਉ ਜਾਣਾ ਆਖਾ ਨਾਹੀ ਕਹਣਾ ਕਥਨੁ ਨ ਜਾਈ॥

ਗੁਰਾ ਇਕ ਦੇਹਿ ਬੁਝਾਈ॥

ਸਭਨਾ ਜੀਆ ਕਾ ਇਕੁ ਦਾਤਾ ਸੋ ਮੈ ਵਿਸਰਿ ਨ ਜਾਈ॥

Jay hao jaana aakha nahi kehna kathan na jaayee.

Gura ik deh bhujaayee.

Sabhna jia ka ik Daata so mai visar na jaayee.

जे हउ जाणा आखा नाही कहणा कथनु न जाई॥

गुरा इक देहि बुझाई॥

सभना जीआ का इकु दाता सो मै विसरि न जाई॥

Even if one knows God, He cannot be fully spoken of and written about.

Guru has explained this one thing.

There is only One Lord of all souls, may I never forget Him.

M1/2/9

Expressing the same inability to describe God, Bhagat Ravidas says:

ਜੋਗੀਸਰ ਪਾਵਹਿ ਨਹੀ ਤੁਅ ਗੁਣ ਕਥਨ ਅਪਾਰ॥

ਪ੍ਰੇਮ ਭਗਤਿ ਕੈ ਕਾਰਨੈ ਕਹੁ ਰਵਿਦਾਸ ਚਮਾਰ॥

Jogisar paveh nahi tua gunh kathan apaar.

Prem bhagat kai kaarnay kahu Ravidas chamaar.

जोगीसर पावहि नही तुअ गुण कथनु अपार॥

प्रेम भगति कै कारणै कहु रविदास चमार॥

Even the great yogis cannot understand (You). Your virtues are beyond words.

Because of my love and devotion, I the shoemaker Ravidas, say this.

Ravidas/346/8

Now some quotations in SGGS on One God for all.

Guru Nanak says:

ਸਾਹਿਬੁ ਮੇਰਾ ਏਕੋ ਹੈ॥ ਏਕੋ ਹੈ ਭਾਈ ਏਕੋ ਹੈ॥

Sahib mera eko hai; eko hai bhaayee eko hai.

साहिबु मेरा एको है॥ एको है भाई एको है॥

My Lord is One, He is the One O brothers, He is the only One.
M1/350/5

Guru Nanak again:

ਏਕੋ ਰਵਿ ਰਹਿਆ ਸਭ ਠਾਈ॥ ਅਵਰੁ ਨ ਦੀਸੈ ਕਿਸੁ ਪੂਜ ਚੜਾਈ॥

Eko rav reheya sabh thaayee; awar na deesai kis pooj charaayee.

एको रवि रहिआ सभ ठाई॥ अवरु न दीसै किसु पूज चड़ाई॥

The One is pervading every place, I can't see any other, whom I could offer my worship.
M1/1345/4

Guru Amar Das, the third Sikh Guru, says:

ਨਾਨਕ ਦਾਤਾ ਏਕੁ ਹੈ ਦੂਜਾ ਅਉਰੁ ਨ ਕੋਇ॥

Nanak Daata ek hai dooja aur na koye.

नानक दाता एकु है दूजा अउरु न कोइ॥

O Nanak, the Giver is only One, there is no other.
M3/65/19

With his belief in one God, Guru Nanak says, he follows only God's path without wavering, and does not think of worshipping any other entity:

ਦੁਬਿਧਾ ਨ ਪੜਉ ਹਰਿ ਬਿਨੁ ਹੋਰੁ ਨ ਪੂਜਉ ਮੜੈ ਮਸਾਣਿ ਨ ਜਾਈ॥

Duvidha na parho Har bin hor na poojao, marhai masaan na jaayee.

दुबिधा न पड़उ हरि बिनु होरु न पूजउ मड़ै मसाणि न जाई॥

I do not waver, and do not worship anything, or anyone, other than God; I do not visit graves or cremation grounds.

M1/634/8

Where is God to be found? He is everywhere, as also He is within you. Guru Teg Bahadur tells us:

ਕਾਹੇ ਰੇ ਬਨ ਖੋਜਨ ਜਾਈ॥
ਸਰਬ ਨਿਵਾਸੀ ਸਦਾ ਅਲੇਪਾ ਤੋਹੀ ਸੰਗਿ ਸਮਾਈ॥

Kaahay ray bun khojan jaayee.
Sarab niwaasi sada alepa tohi sung samaayee.

काहे रे बन खोजन जाई॥
सरब निवासी सदा अलेपा तोही संगि समाई॥

Why go looking for Him in the forests?
He is omnipresent, always untarnished, He resides within you.

M9/684/14

The renowned Swami Parmahansa Yogananda once asked his guru Sri Yukteswar to allow him to go to the Himalayas to seek God. The guru replied, "Many hill-men live in the Himalayas, yet possess no God perception. Wisdom is better sought from a man of realization than from an inert mountain." Swami Yogananda did go to the Himalayas, but returned empty handed. He attained God-realization back home under the guidance of his guru.

God is perceived differently by different people depending upon their level of awareness and spiritual understanding. Guru Gobind Singh said, *"Aap Apni Budh Hai Jeti, Barnat Bhin Bhin Tohay Teti"* (As per their own level of understanding, people describe Him differently.) Hence, our level of consciousness determines our concept of God. As we advance spiritually so does our understanding of God. Every day we learn something new. Guru Nanak says:

ਸਾਹਿਬੁ ਮੇਰਾ ਨੀਤ ਨਵਾ ਸਦਾ ਸਦਾ ਦਾਤਾਰੁ॥

Sahib mera neet nava, sadaa sadaa daataar.

साहिबु मेरा नीत नवा सदा सदा दातारु॥

My Lord is new every day, He is the Giver forever and ever.

M1/660/2

Guru Arjan Dev expresses similar views:

ਗੁਣ ਨਿਧਾਨੁ ਨਵਤਨੁ ਸਦਾ ਪੂਰਨ ਜਾ ਕੀ ਦਾਤਿ॥
ਸਦਾ ਸਦਾ ਆਰਾਧੀਐ ਦਿਨੁ ਵਿਸਰਹੁ ਨਹੀ ਰਾਤਿ॥

Gunh nidhaan navtan sadaa pooran ja ki daat.
Sadaa sadaa aaraadheeyai din visroh nahi raat.

गुण निधानु नवतनु सदा पूरन जा की दाति॥
सदा सदा आराधीऐ दिनु विसरहु नही राति॥

He is full of virtues and ever new, his gifts are complete.
Worship Him all the time, don't forget Him neither during day nor night.

M5/47/4

The above two verses say, God is, *neet nava* (is new everyday) and *navtan sada* (always in new form). This means, like His entire creation, He is also evolving and moving ahead with time. He is not stuck in any old time-frame.

We cannot fully understand God unless we raise our spiritual understanding to His level. Guru Nanak says:

ਏਵਡੁ ਉਚਾ ਹੋਵੈ ਕੋਇ॥ ਤਿਸੁ ਉਚੇ ਕਉ ਜਾਣੈ ਸੋਇ॥

Evad oocha hovai koye, Tis oochay kao jaanai soye.

एवडु ऊचा होवै कोइ॥ तिसु ऊचे कउ जाणै सोइ॥

You have to rise to His high level, to know that
High Lord.

M1/5/10

Another attribute of God is that He is permanent and indestructible, while everything else, yes everything, will come to end one day, God survives forever. Guru Nanak says:

ਨ ਸੂਰ ਸਸਿ ਮੰਡਲੋ॥ ਨ ਸਪਤ ਦੀਪ ਨਹ ਜਲੋ॥
ਅੰਨ ਪਉਣ ਥਿਰੁ ਨ ਕੁਈ॥ ਏਕੁ ਤੁਈ ਏਕੁ ਤੁਈ॥

Na soor sas mandlo, na sapt deep nah jalo.
Ann paun thir na kuee, ek tuee ek tuee.

न सूर ससि मंडलो॥ न सपत दीप नह जलो॥
अंन पउण थिरु न कुई॥ एकु तुई एकु तुई॥

Neither the sun, nor the moon, nor the planets, nor the seven
continents, nor the oceans.
Nor food, nor the wind; nothing is permanent. You alone are
Lord, You alone.

M1/144/2

God has control over every living being says Guru Arjan Dev:

ਜੀਅ ਜੰਤ ਤੇਰੇ ਧਾਰੇ॥ ਪ੍ਰਭ ਡੋਰੀ ਹਾਥਿ ਤੁਮਾਰੇ॥

Jia jantt teray dhaaray, Prabh dori haath tumaaray.

जीअ जंत तेरे धारे॥ प्रभ डोरी हाथि तुमारे॥

All forms of living beings are under your control.
O Lord, the string of their lives is in your hands.

M5/626/19

Guru Nanak says however much effort we may put in, it is finally God that makes everything happen:

ਸਭਨੀ ਛਾਲਾ ਮਾਰੀਆ ਕਰਤਾ ਕਰੇ ਸੁ ਹੋਇ॥

Sabni chhaala mariya Karta karay so hoye.

सभनी छाला मारीआ करता करे सु होइ॥

Everyone jumps around (makes all sorts of effort), but only
that happens which the Creator wills.

M1/469/5

Guru Arjan Dev has same view on finality of God:

ਮਤ ਕੋਈ ਜਾਣਹੁ ਅਵਰੁ ਕਛੁ ਸਭ ਪ੍ਰਭ ਕੈ ਹਾਥਿ॥

Mut koyee jaanoh awar kachh sabh Prabh kai haath.

मत कोई जाणहु अवरु कछु सभ प्रभ कै हाथि॥

Do not believe anything else, everything is in Lord's hands.

M5/814/4

Most of us do accept that God is all-powerful and controls everything in our life, but we just don't care about Him; unless, of course, we land into some serious trouble. We will do anything for our religion, not for God. If God is abused or insulted by someone, nothing is likely to happen to him. At best such a person may be called a fool or a non-believer. But try saying something against a religion or its founder. The reaction is always sharp and could easily lead to disharmony, even riots. We give much greater importance to the founders of religions who teach us about God, but care little about the Supreme Almighty. God's love connects us with each other, but religion often separates. More wars have been fought and millions killed for the sake of religion, than for any other cause. Understand the difference between religion and God and focus on worshipping God, who is our real Creator and Provider.

Though the word religion actually means 'sacred duty', but that is not how it is practiced. It is often misused to spread hatred and enmity.

In this chapter we have seen some attributes of God, as given in SGGS. As I have said, it is difficult to fully comprehend the Creator, but we will continue to learn about Him as we go along.

"Where can we go to find God if we cannot see Him in our own hearts and in every living being?"

Swami Vivekananda (1863-1902)
Indian Mystic

CHAPTER 2

CREATION

ੴ

There are remarkable references in SGGS regarding creation of the cosmos, which include things that even science did not know at the time this holy book was compiled. Till as late as the beginning of 20th century the scientific community widely believed that the universe had no beginning, that there was no moment in time when it was created and therefore, there was no creator. Science did not believe in God because it could not grasp or measure Him in a laboratory - a condition science puts on proving the existence of anything. However, many scientists now believe in God, and the fact that He created the universe. Einstein said, "The more I study science, the more I believe in God."

Modern science tells us that mass and energy cannot be created or destroyed - it can only change form, from one to the other. What this means is that all creation happened in one go and nothing has been added or removed ever since, though mass and energy keep appearing in different forms. Let us now see what SGGS says on these issues.

How did the universe come into existence? Guru Nanak says:

ਕੀਤਾ ਪਸਾਉ ਏਕੋ ਕਵਾਉ॥ ਤਿਸ ਤੇ ਹੋਏ ਲਖ ਦਰੀਆਉ॥

Keeta pasaao eko kavaao, tis tay hoye lakh dariyaao.

कीता पसाउ एको कवाउ॥ तिस ते होए लख दरीआउ॥

God created everything with one sound. Thenceforth
hundreds of thousands of rivers began to flow.

M1/3/16

The creation took place with one sound. Nanak said this in
15th, or at best in the 16th century, while the theory of 'big
bang' was propounded only in 1930 by Belgian astronomer
Georges Lemaitre.

On creation happening in one go, Guru Nanak says:

ਆਸਣੁ ਲੋਇ ਲੋਇ ਭੰਡਾਰ ॥ ਜੋ ਕਿਛੁ ਪਾਇਆ ਸੁ ਏਕਾ ਵਾਰ ॥
ਕਰਿ ਕਰਿ ਵੇਖੈ ਸਿਰਜਣਹਾਰੁ ॥ ਨਾਨਕ ਸਚੇ ਕੀ ਸਾਚੀ ਕਾਰ ॥

Aasan loye loye bhandaar, jo kichhu paayeya su eka vaar.
Kar kar vekhai Sirjanhaar, Nanak saachay ki saachi kaar.

आसणु लोइ लोइ भंडार॥ जो किछु पाइआ सु एका वार॥
करि करि वेखै सिरजणहारु॥ नानक सचे की साची कार॥

God's presence and his storehouses are everywhere,
whatever He put into them was done in one go.
He created the creation, and watches over it, O Nanak,
true is the creation of the True Lord.

M1/7/4

What was the state before creation took place with the big
bang? No one knows. However, Guru Nanak who lived from 1469
to 1539 visualized and described that state in the following verse:

ਅਰਬਦ ਨਰਬਦ ਧੁੰਧੂਕਾਰਾ ॥ ਧਰਣਿ ਨ ਗਗਨਾ ਹੁਕਮੁ ਅਪਾਰਾ ॥
ਨਾ ਦਿਨੁ ਰੈਨਿ ਨ ਚੰਦੁ ਨ ਸੂਰਜੁ ਸੁੰਨ ਸਮਾਧਿ ਲਗਾਇਦਾ ॥

Arbad narbad dhundukaara, dharan na gagna hukam apaara.
Na din rayan na chand na suraj, sunn samaadh lagaayeda.

अरबद नरबद धुंधूकारा॥ धरणि न गगना हुकमु अपारा॥
ना दिनु रैनि न चंदु न सूरजु सुंन समाधि लगाइदा॥

For un-measurable period of time, there was only utter
darkness, there was no earth no sky, there was only the
infinite command of God.
There was no day or night, no moon or sun, God sat
in silent meditation.

ਖਾਣੀ ਨ ਬਾਣੀ ਪਉਣ ਨ ਪਾਣੀ॥ ਓਪਤਿ ਖਪਤਿ ਨ ਆਵਣ ਜਾਣੀ॥
ਖੰਡ ਪਤਾਲ ਸਪਤ ਨਹੀ ਸਾਗਰ ਨਦੀ ਨ ਨੀਰੁ ਵਹਾਇਦਾ॥

Khaani na baani paun na paani, opat khapt na aavan jaani.
Khand pataal sapt nahi saagar nadi na neer vahaayeda.

खाणी न बाणी पउण न पाणी॥ ओपति खपति न आवण जाणी॥
खंड पताल सपत नही सागर नदी न नीरु वहाइदा॥

There was no source of life, no sound, no air, no water, there
was no growth, no consumption, no coming or going.
There were no continents or nether regions, no seven seas,
and no rivers of flowing water.

M1/1035/9

Till as late as mid 18th century it was believed that
creation took place around 10,000 years ago. With many
refinements in the study of the universe, it is now estimated
that it came into being about 13.7 billion years ago. How
accurate or how true this is we cannot be sure, because the
theory of creation is just that, a theory. A very recent report
says the universe is perhaps two billion years younger than
earlier estimates.

Guru Nanak says it is impossible to determine when the
creation took place and only God knows:

ਕਵਣਿ ਸਿ ਰੁਤੀ ਮਾਹੁ ਕਵਣੁ ਜਿਤੁ ਹੋਆ ਆਕਾਰੁ ॥
ਵੇਲ ਨ ਪਾਈਆ ਪੰਡਤੀ ਜਿ ਹੋਵੈ ਲੇਖੁ ਪੁਰਾਣੁ ॥
ਵਖਤੁ ਨ ਪਾਇਓ ਕਾਦੀਆ ਜਿ ਲਿਖਨਿ ਲੇਖੁ ਕੁਰਾਣੁ ॥

Kavan si ruti maah kavan jit hoa aakaar.

Vel na paaya pandati jay hovai lekh Puraan.

Vakht na paaya qadia jay likhan lekh Quran.

कवणि सि रुती माहु कवणु जितु होआ आकारु ॥
वेल न पाईआ पंडती जि होवै लेखु पुराणु ॥
वखतु न पाइओ कादीआ जि लिखनि लेखु कुराणु ॥

What was that season, and what month, when the universe was created?

The pandits do not know the time, for if they knew, it would have been written in the *Puraanas*.

That time is not known to the *qazis*, for if they knew, it would have been written in the Quran.

ਥਿਤਿ ਵਾਰੁ ਨਾ ਜੋਗੀ ਜਾਣੈ ਰੁਤਿ ਮਾਹੁ ਨਾ ਕੋਈ ॥
ਜਾ ਕਰਤਾ ਸਿਰਠੀ ਕਉ ਸਾਜੇ ਆਪੇ ਜਾਨੈ ਸੋਈ ॥

Thiti vaar na jogi jaanay rut maah na koyee.

Ja Karta sirathi kau saajay aapay jaanai soyee.

थिति वारु ना जोगी जाणै रुति माहु ना कोई ॥
जा करता सिरठी कउ साजे आपे जाणै सोई ॥

The day and the date are not known to the yogis, nor is the month or the season. He who created the universe, Himself knows.

M1/4/16

Many modern scientists believe that the universe is in a constant state of expansion and contraction. This means, having started from a state of non-existence it keeps expanding for billions of years and having attained full size it starts contracting. After billions of years it contracts back to nothingness - and the cycle continues. These words of Guru Arjan Dev point in the same direction:

ਕਈ ਬਾਰ ਪਸਰਿਓ ਪਾਸਾਰ॥ ਸਦਾ ਸਦਾ ਇਕੁ ਏਕੰਕਾਰ॥

Kayee baar pasreo paasaar, sadaa sadaa ik ekankaar.

कई बार पसरिओ पासार॥ सदा सदा इकु एकंकार॥

Many times, He created His creation, forever and ever He is the One Creator God.

M5/276/13

Commenting on the vastness of the universe, at a time when not much was known about it, Guru Nanak says:

ਧਰਤੀ ਹੋਰੁ ਪਰੈ ਹੋਰੁ ਹੋਰੁ॥ ਤਿਸ ਤੇ ਭਾਰੁ ਤਲੈ ਕਵਣੁ ਜੋਰੁ॥

Dharti hor parai hor hor, tis tay bhaar talai kavan jor.

धरती होरु परै होरु होरु॥ तिस ते भारु तलै कवणु जोरु॥

There are many planets beyond and further beyond. What power is supporting their weight? (It is God he infers).

M1/3/14

Here are some references on creation by Guru Arjan Dev (1563-1606):

ਕਈ ਕੋਟਿ ਸਸੀਅਰ ਸੂਰ ਨਖਜਤਰ॥

Kayee kot sasiyar soor nakhyatar.

कई कोटि ससीअर सूर नक्ष्यत्र॥

There are millions of moons, suns and stars.

M5/275/19

ਕਈ ਕੋਟਿ ਖਾਣੀ ਅਰੁ ਖੰਡ ॥ ਕਈ ਕੋਟਿ ਅਕਾਸ ਬ੍ਰਹਮੰਡ ॥

Kayee kot khaani aur khand, kayee kot aakaas brahmand.

कई कोटि खाणी अरु खंड ॥ कई कोटि अकास ब्रहमंड ॥

There are millions of forms of growth, in millions of divisions/ parts. There are millions of skies and galaxies.

M5/276/11

Remember, in the SGGS, the above lines about presence of millions of planets and stars were written by Guru Arjan Dev prior to the year 1606 - he was martyred that year. This was the time when science in the west was still struggling with limited knowledge of only a few planets of our solar system and was debating whether or not earth was at its centre. Though Nicolaus Copernicus, the Polish astronomer, had published his theory in 1543 (the year he died) stating it was the Sun that was at the centre of the solar system, it wasn't given much attention. Galileo Galilei reinforced the Copernician theory but in 1633 was summoned before the Inquisition, and forced to recant his belief in that theory.

In 1610 Galileo had used a telescope to study the milky-way to discover that it was composed of a huge number of faint stars. Much later, in the 1920s, observations by astronomer Edwin Hubble showed that the milky-way was just one of around 200 billion galaxies in the observable universe.

I have highlighted the above theories only to signify the importance of the contents of SGGS. I do not suggest that this holy book can be used as a science book. A Sikh zealot put out a story some time ago that NASA keeps a copy of the SGGS in their office and whenever they get stuck on any issue they refer to the holy book and get their answers. Such fabricated and false stories only cause more harm than good. Obviously the story was denied by NASA.

It is incorrect to compare a holy book to a science book, because they deal with totally different issues. Holy books explore the spiritual domain and suggest ways for truthful living, while science deals with material things. Science says things have to be seen to be believed, but spirituality says there are things that you have to first believe before you can see them. Science does not believe in God because it cannot see Him. But if you first believe in God you will see Him everywhere, in everything. For science, He is too great to be grasped. However, now there is some convergence between spirituality and science.

Notwithstanding the science's point of view on how or who created the universe, the pertinent question remains - how can there be a creation without the Creator? A famous song by Nusrat Fateh Ali Khan says, *"Koyee To Hai Jo Nizaam-E-Hasti Chala Raha Hai. Wohi Khuda Hai Wohi Khuda Hai."* (There has to be someone who is running the show, of cosmic order. He is God, He indeed is God.)

Guru Arjan Dev says:

ਜੋ ਕਿਛੁ ਹੋਆ ਸੁ ਤੁਝ ਤੇ ਹੋਗੁ ॥ ਅਵਰੁ ਨ ਦੂਜਾ ਕਰਣੈ ਜੋਗੁ ॥

Jo kichhu hoa su tujh tay hoag; avar na dooja karnai joag.

जो किछु होआ सु तुझ ते होगु ॥ अवरु न दूजा करणै जोगु ॥

Whatever exists has been created by You, no one else is capable of doing it.

M5/176/15

And what a creation He has created! It is impossible to conceive anything better. You only need to look at things around you with some attention and you will marvel at His work. Can you think of more beautiful flowers, trees, birds, animals, seas, beaches, mountains, rain, clouds, snow; everything is made to perfection. Look at the human body; we can't conceive anything more beautiful, or more capable of learning and performing. Isn't it amazing that among billions and trillions of people born on this planet no two people were/ are ever exactly alike, despite having same form and features?

Guru Amar Das says:

> ਮੇਰੈ ਪ੍ਰਭਿ ਸਾਚੈ ਇਕੁ ਖੇਲੁ ਰਚਾਇਆ ॥ ਕੋਇ ਨ ਕਿਸ ਹੀ ਜੇਹਾ ਉਪਾਇਆ ॥
>
> Merai Prabh saachai ik khel rachaaya, koye na kis hee jeha upaaya.
>
> मेरै प्रभि साचै इकु खेलु रचाइआ ॥ कोइ न किस ही जेहा उपाइआ ॥
>
> **My True Lord has staged a play, He created no one like anyone else.**
>
> **M3/1056/10**

Same holds true for the animal and plant worlds. Then there are so many planets, stars and other bodies in the universe. We have no idea as yet, of other forms of life that may exist there.

Guru Arjan Dev again says:

> ਨਾਨਕ ਰਚਨਾ ਪ੍ਰਭਿ ਰਚੀ ਬਹੁ ਬਿਧਿ ਅਨਿਕ ਪ੍ਰਕਾਰ ॥
>
> Nanak rachna Prabh rachi bahu bidh anik prakaar.
>
> नानक रचना प्रभि रची बहु बिधि अनिक प्रकार ॥
>
> **Says Nanak, God has made the creation, in so many different ways.**
>
> **M5/275/11**

Guru Arjan Dev continues:

ਹਰਨ ਭਰਨ ਜਾ ਕਾ ਨੇਤ੍ਰ ਫੋਰੁ॥ ਤਿਸ ਕਾ ਮੰਤ੍ਰ ਨ ਜਾਨੈ ਹੋਰੁ॥

Haran bharan ja ka neytr phor, Tis ka mantr na jaanai hor.

हरन भरन जा का नेत्र फोरु॥ तिस का मंत्रु न जानै होरु॥

**He can destroy or create with the wink of an eye
(instantaneously).
No one knows of His secret ways.**

M5/284/2

Guru Nanak speaks of only one command pervading the entire creation:

ਏਕੋ ਹੁਕਮੁ ਵਰਤੈ ਸਭ ਲੋਈ॥ ਏਕਸੁ ਤੇ ਸਭ ਓਪਤਿ ਹੋਈ॥

Eko hukam vartai sabh loyee, ekas tay sabh opat hoyee.

एको हुकमु वरतै सभ लोई॥ एकसु ते सभ ओपति होई॥

**One single command (of the Creator) prevails in all
the worlds.
From the One, all were created.**

M1/223/7

It is now believed that the origin of the universe was a single point, which contained in itself the blueprint of the entire universe. Besides all stars and planets in the cosmos, the blueprint also included all forms of life, including you and me. This is just like a small seed which contains in itself the blueprint of a massive tree.

Guru Amar Das amazingly makes a similar comment on creation when he says:

ਕਹੈ ਨਾਨਕੁ ਸ੍ਰਿਸਟਿ ਕਾ ਮੂਲੁ ਰਚਿਆ ਜੋਤਿ ਰਾਖੀ ਤਾ ਤੂ ਜਗ ਮਹਿ ਆਇਆ ॥

Kahai Nanak sristi ka mool racheya joyt raakhee ta tu jug meh aayaa.

कहै नानकु स्रिसटि का मूलु रचिआ जोति राखी ता तू जग महि आइआ ॥

Says Nanak, He created the blueprint, the seed, of the Universe, and put His light into it, and thence you came into the world.

M3/921/16

God has created the universe which is not only unimaginably vast but also amazingly precise. Deepak Chopra, in his book, 'Life After Death', writes, "If the expanding universe, moving at millions of miles per minute, had been off by a fraction of a second, the formation of stars and galaxies would have been impossible, because the momentum of the explosion would have exceeded the ability of gravity, the weakest force in nature, to halt it. Only the most delicate balancing act kept the push-pull of two forces so close together that they can dance together instead of tearing each other apart." Only God could have done it.

"It is impossible to account for the creation of the universe without the agency of a Supreme Being."

George Washington (1732-1799)
First US President

CHAPTER 3

PURPOSE OF LIFE

ੴ

Why do we come into this world? Why are we born? Is it a random happening or is it in accord with some plan? Are we to waste this life in meaningless pursuits or is there a more specific higher purpose?

Sheikh Farid raises this question in SGGS:

ਫਰੀਦਾ ਚਾਰਿ ਗਵਾਇਆ ਹੰਢਿ ਕੈ ਚਾਰਿ ਗਵਾਇਆ ਸੰਮਿ ॥
ਲੇਖਾ ਰਬੁ ਮੰਗੇਸੀਆ ਤੂ ਆਂਹੋ ਕੇਹੇ ਕੰਮਿ ॥

Freeda chaar gavaaya handd kai chaar gavaaya summ.
Lekha rabb mangesiya tu anho kehray kumm.

फरीदा चारि गवाइआ हंढि कै चारि गवाइआ समि ॥
लेखा रबु मंगेसीआ तू आंहो केहें कमि ॥

Farid says, you spend day hours wasting around,
and night hours in sleep.
God will ask you to explain, what did you come into this
world for?

Farid/1379/17

This question by Sheikh Farid is on the mind of everyone who looks at life more deeply.

There indeed is a purpose, and that purpose is to rise high spiritually, to the level of godhood and merge with God, become one with God. To become God. In his bestseller book, 'The Road Less Travelled', M. Scott Peck, MD, says, "God wants us to become Himself. We are growing towards godhood. God is the goal of evolution. It is God who is the source of the evolutionary force and God who is the destination."

Yes, God is the destination and He is reachable. According to *Mundakya Upanishad* (3-2-9), "He who knows *Brahman* (God) verily becomes *Brahman*."

Every soul was once part of God, the Supreme Soul. He separated each soul from Himself for its individual journey to experience various realms in different reincarnations. After the experience is complete, God reunites each soul with Himself. The soul, after a journey of thousands of reincarnations, attains salvation and returns to an ever blissful home - not to be born again. However, some highly evolved souls may be reborn as *Avtars*, when ordained by God for a specific purpose on earth.

On separation of soul from God and its reunification, Guru Ram Das says:

ਸਭ ਤੇਰੀ ਤੂੰ ਸਭਨੀ ਧਿਆਇਆ ॥ ਜਿਸ ਨੋ ਕ੍ਰਿਪਾ ਕਰਹਿ ਤਿਨਿ ਨਾਮ ਰਤਨੁ ਪਾਇਆ ॥
ਗੁਰਮੁਖਿ ਲਾਧਾ ਮਨਮੁਖਿ ਗਵਾਇਆ ॥ ਤੁਧੁ ਆਪਿ ਵਿਛੋੜਿਆ ਆਪਿ ਮਿਲਾਇਆ ॥

Sabh teri tu sabhni dhiaaya, jis no kripa kareh tin naam ratan paaya.
Gurmukh laadha manmukh gavaaya, tudh aap vichhoreya aap milaaya.

सभ तेरी तूं सभनी धिआइआ ॥ जिस नो क्रिपा करहि तिनि नाम रतनु पाइआ ॥
गुरमुखि लाधा मनमुखि गवाइआ ॥ तुधु आपि विछोड़िआ आपि मिलाइआ ॥

> All belong to You, all meditate on You. Those You bless receive the jewel of Your Name.
> The God-oriented people obtain it, and the self-oriented lose it.
> You detach them from Yourself, and You make them reunite with You.
>
> M4/11/15 & M4/365/14

The words 'gurmukh' and 'manmukh' mentioned above are frequently referred to in SGGS. Let's digress a little to see what they mean. *Gur* means guru/God and *mukh* means face. *Gurmukh*, therefore, is someone whose face (mind orientation) is towards God. He is a selfless person who thinks of God and His creation all the time. On the other side *manmukh* is the one who is *munn* (own mind) oriented, who is self-centered, always thinking of himself. *Gurmukh* is an enlightened person while *manmukh* is way down. One should seek company of *gurmukhs* and shun *manmukhs*.

We originated from a different world, at a different spiritual plane, where everything is ideal and perfect. In such a state the soul knows that everything is great, but doesn't realize how great it is because there is nothing to compare with. Beauty can be appreciated only when compared with ugliness. Value of love can be known only if there is hatred around. Significance of truth is realized only when you experience falsehood. You can't know light if you haven't seen darkness. We live in a world of duality where it is long vs short, sweet vs bitter, high vs low, tall vs short, good vs bad and so on. This duality can be experienced only in our material world which God created for us. He sends us as individual souls into the material world to realize our own goodness. Our job is complete only when we have gone through all experiences of good & bad, and of pain & pleasure. At the culmination of this experience we reunite with God and remain merged thereafter. The cycle of birth and death ceases. How soon this cycle will end depends on how quickly we learn about the purpose of our life and work towards it. But it is not entirely in our control because we can only do our best - the final outcome depends on God's grace.

During our life we get so attached to material things (*maya/duality*) that we forget the real purpose of our life, which is the spiritual awakening, or God-realization. If we die with inadequate experience, God gives us another chance in rebirth. Depending upon our balance-sheet of good or bad karma at the end of one life, the spiritual masters determine what kind of life we will have in the next one. This continues till our final liberation, after which there is no rebirth.

To be born as a human being is a great opportunity for spiritual growth. Guru Arjan Dev tells us not to miss this opportunity:

ਲਖ ਚਉਰਾਸੀਹ ਜੋਨਿ ਸਬਾਈ ॥ ਮਾਣਸ ਕਉ ਪ੍ਰਭਿ ਦੀਈ ਵਡਿਆਈ ॥
ਇਸੁ ਪਉੜੀ ਤੇ ਜੋ ਨਰੁ ਚੂਕੈ ਸੋ ਆਇ ਜਾਇ ਦੁਖੁ ਪਾਇਦਾ ॥

Lakh chauraasi joan sabaayee, manas ko Prabh deeyee
vadeaaayee.
Is pauri tay jo nar chookai so aaye jaaye dukh paayeda.

लख चउरासीह जोनि सबाई ॥ माणस कउ प्रभि दीई वडिआई ॥
इसु पउड़ी ते जो नरु चूकै सो आइ जाइ दुखु पाइदा ॥

There are 8.4 million forms of life, but it is only the humans on whom God has bestowed greatness.
Whosoever falters on this step (of life), shall continue to suffer the pain of coming and going (life & death).

M5/1075/14

As human beings we are greatly blessed. It is the highest form of life, because only as humans can we appreciate the spiritual side of life - of sharing, caring, helping, praying, worshipping, and evolving. Enjoying material benefits does not distinguish us much from lower forms of life. Even animals can enjoy good food, drink, sex, good environment etc. Only humans can experience the joys of spiritual growth which leads us to godhood. Even the angels do not have this blessing - they must be born as humans to attain godhood.

This is what Bhagat Kabir says on significance of human life:

ਗੁਰ ਸੇਵਾ ਤੇ ਭਗਤਿ ਕਮਾਈ॥ ਤਬ ਇਹ ਮਾਨਸ ਦੇਹੀ ਪਾਈ॥
ਇਸ ਦੇਹੀ ਕਉ ਸਿਮਰਹਿ ਦੇਵ॥ ਸੋ ਦੇਹੀ ਭਜੁ ਹਰਿ ਕੀ ਸੇਵ॥

Gur seva tay bhagat kamaayee, tabb ih manas dehi paayee.
Is dehee kau simreh dev, so dehi bhaj Har ki sev.

गुर सेवा ते भगति कमाई॥ तब इह मानस देही पाई॥
इस देही कउ सिमरहि देव॥ सो देही भजु हरि की सेव॥

By serving the Guru and worshipping, you have attained this human form.
Even the angels worship (and yearn for) this form; use this body for worship and service to the Lord.

Kabir/1159/7

A very popular verse by Guru Arjan Dev on the subject:

ਭਈ ਪਰਾਪਤਿ ਮਾਨੁਖ ਦੇਹੁਰੀਆ॥ ਗੋਬਿੰਦ ਮਿਲਣ ਕੀ ਇਹ ਤੇਰੀ ਬਰੀਆ॥
ਅਵਰਿ ਕਾਜ ਤੇਰੈ ਕਿਤੈ ਨ ਕਾਮ॥ ਮਿਲੁ ਸਾਧਸੰਗਤਿ ਭਜੁ ਕੇਵਲ ਨਾਮ॥

Bhayee prapat maanukh dehuriya, Gobind milan ki ih teri bareeya.
Avar kaaj terai kitai na kaam, mil sadhsangat bhaj kewal naam.

भई परापति मानुख देहुरीआ॥ गोबिंद मिलण की इह तेरी बरीआ॥
अवरि काज तेरै कितै न काम॥ मिलु साधसंगति भजु केवल नाम॥

> You have attained human body, this is your only chance to meet God.
> No other deed is of any use to you; join the company of the holy and meditate on Lord's Name.
>
> M5/378/1

The last line of the above verse which says no other deed is useful, applies to usefulness for spiritual advancement. It does not mean that you do not work to fulfill your duties and responsibilities of the physical world. More on this later, in the chapter on 'Seeker as Householder'.

Guru Teg Bahadur highlights here how difficult the journey was before you attained the human form, and urges you to start worshipping:

> ਫਿਰਤ ਫਿਰਤ ਬਹੁਤੇ ਜੁਗ ਹਾਰਿਓ ਮਾਨਸ ਦੇਹ ਲਹੀ ॥
> ਨਾਨਕ ਕਹਤ ਮਿਲਨ ਕੀ ਬਰੀਆ ਸਿਮਰਤ ਕਹਾ ਨਹੀ ॥
>
> Firat firat bahutay jug haareyo manas deh lahee.
> Nanak kehat milan ki bariya simrat kahaa nahee.
>
> फिरत फिरत बहुते जुग हारिओ मानस देह लही ॥
> नानक कहत मिलन की बरीआ सिमरत कहा नही ॥
>
> Wandering around through so many ages, you were defeated and exhausted, and then obtained this human body.
> Nanak says, this is the opportunity to meet the Lord, and you are not meditating on Him.
>
> M9/631/16

The purpose of life should be to worship God and do good deeds with which the sins of this life, as well as of previous lives, are paid for and we get out of the cycle of birth & death. We are then on our way to godhood. Don't waste this golden opportunity.

Guru Nanak warns us here:

> ਰੈਣਿ ਗਵਾਈ ਸੋਇ ਕੈ ਦਿਵਸੁ ਗਵਾਇਆ ਖਾਇ ॥
> ਹੀਰੇ ਜੈਸਾ ਜਨਮੁ ਹੈ ਕਉਡੀ ਬਦਲੇ ਜਾਇ ॥
>
> Rayan gawaayee soye kai divas gavayaa khaaye.
> Heeray jaisa janum hai kaudi badlay jaaye.
>
> रैणि गवाई सोइ कै दिवसु गवाइआ खाइ ॥
> हीरे जैसा जनमु है कउडी बदले जाइ ॥
>
> The nights are wasted in sleep, and the days in eating.
> Human life is like a precious jewel, but it is being lost in
> exchange for a cowry (a small sea-shell of little value).
>
> M1/156/17

On living a life without purpose, Guru Nanak says:

> ਫਿਟੁ ਇਵੇਹਾ ਜੀਵਿਆ ਜਿਤੁ ਖਾਇ ਵਧਾਇਆ ਪੇਟੁ ॥
> ਨਾਨਕ ਸਚੇ ਨਾਮ ਵਿਣੁ ਸਭੋ ਦੁਸਮਨੁ ਹੇਤੁ ॥
>
> Phit iveha jeeveya jit khaaye vadhaaya pait.
> Nanak sachay naam vin sabho dushman hait.
>
> फिटु इवेहा जीविआ जितु खाइ वधाइआ पेटु ॥
> नानक सचे नाम विणु सभो दुसमनु हेतु ॥
>
> Shame on such living where you eat only to enlarge your belly.
> Nanak says, without the True Name, everyone is your enemy.
>
> M1/790/18

Bhagat Kabir makes a similar comment:

ਪੇਟੁ ਭਰਿਓ ਪਸੂਆ ਜਿਉ ਸੋਇਓ ਮਨੁਖ ਜਨਮੁ ਹੈ ਹਾਰਿਓ ॥

Pait bhareo pasua jiu soeyo manukh janam hai haareyo.

पेटु भरिओ पसूआ जिउ सोइओ मनुखु जनमु है हारिओ॥

You fill your belly, sleep like an animal, you have lost this human life.

Kabir/1105/15

You indeed are a loser in this life if you eat and live like an animal. Your purpose in life is much greater.

Guru Amar Das also cautions us not to waste this life:

ਭਾਈ ਰੇ ਭਗਤਿਹੀਣੁ ਕਾਹੇ ਜਗਿ ਆਇਆ ॥
ਪੂਰੇ ਗੁਰ ਕੀ ਸੇਵ ਨ ਕੀਨੀ ਬਿਰਥਾ ਜਨਮੁ ਗਵਾਇਆ ॥

Bhaayee ray bhagat-heen kaahay jug aaya.
Pooray gur ki sev na keeni birtha janam gwaaya.

भाई रे भगतिहीणु काहे जगि आइआ॥
पूरे गुर की सेव न कीनी बिरथा जनमु गवाइआ॥

O brother, why have you come into this world without devotion to God?
You have not served the True Lord and have wasted this life.

M3/32/6 & M3/64/16

Here is Bhagat Kabir's plea to God to help him attain life's purpose by releasing him from the cycle of death and rebirth. He sees life in human form to be like swimming in a terrifying ocean:

ਕਹੈ ਕਬੀਰੁ ਸੁਨਹੁ ਰੇ ਸੰਤਹੁ ਖੇਤ ਹੀ ਕਰਹੁ ਨਿਬੇਰਾ॥
ਅਬ ਕੀ ਬਾਰ ਬਖਸਿ ਬੰਦੇ ਕਉ ਬਹੁਰਿ ਨ ਭਉਜਲਿ ਫੇਰਾ॥

Kahai Kabir sunho ray santoh khet hi karo nibera.
Ab ki baar bakhs banday ko bahur na bhaujal phera.

कहै कबीरु सुनहु रे संतहु खेत ही करहु निबेरा॥
अब की बार बखसि बंदे कउ बहुरि न भउजलि फेरा॥

Says Kabir, listen O holy people, resolve all your bodily
desires/issues now.
Spare me O Lord this time, so that I don't return to this scary
ocean any more.

Kabir/1104/11

Another quote by Guru Arjan Dev on attainment of life's
purpose and rejoining with our Maker:

ਜਿਉ ਜਲ ਮਹਿ ਜਲੁ ਆਇ ਖਟਾਨਾ॥ ਤਿਉ ਜੋਤੀ ਸੰਗਿ ਜੋਤਿ ਸਮਾਨਾ॥
ਮਿਟਿ ਗਏ ਗਵਨ ਪਾਏ ਬਿਸ੍ਰਾਮ॥ ਨਾਨਕ ਪ੍ਰਭ ਕੈ ਸਦ ਕੁਰਬਾਨ॥

Jiu jal meh jal aaye khataana, tiu jyoti sung jyot samaana.
Mit gaye gavan paaye bisraam, Nanak Prabh kay sadd
kurbaan.

जिउ जल महि जलु आइ खटाना॥ तिउ जोती संगि जोति समाना॥
मिटि गए गवन पाए बिस्राम॥ नानक प्रभ कै सद कुरबान॥

As the water merges with water, the individual soul merges
with the Supreme Soul.
The wanderings are over and you attain an ever restful state,
Says Nanak, I'm ever ready to sacrifice myself for God.

M5/278/4

The soul, from its detachment from the Supreme Soul to its salvation and re-merger with Supreme Soul, undertakes a very long journey. Our one lifetime on earth is a very small portion of the overall experience. In the following verse Guru Nanak calls earth as temporary resting place:

ਰਾਤੀ ਰੁਤੀ ਥਿਤੀ ਵਾਰ ॥ ਪਵਣ ਪਾਣੀ ਅਗਨੀ ਪਾਤਾਲ ॥
ਤਿਸੁ ਵਿਚਿ ਧਰਤੀ ਥਾਪਿ ਰਖੀ ਧਰਮ ਸਾਲ ॥

Raati ruti thiti vaar, pavan paani agni paataal;
Tis vich dharti thaap rakhi dharam saal.

राती रुती थिती वार ॥ पवण पाणी अगनी पाताल ॥
तिसु विचि धरती थापि रखी धरम साल ॥

(God has created) nights, seasons, dates and days;
air, water, fire and lower realms.
Amongst these He has established earth as temporary
resting place.

M1/7/11

Remember, the earth is a temporary resting place. Do not think of making it a permanent residence - you can't. You have to move on. Though we have a brief stay here but it is the most crucial one, because it is here that you can spiritually learn and gain the maximum. That's why it is called the 'earth school' for the souls.

To achieve life's real purpose we must shed our heavy burden of materialism because that has got us badly entangled and is a great hindrance. The story below illustrates this:

A tourist from USA once visited the famous Polish Rabbi Hafez Hayyim. He was astonished to see that the Rabbi's home was only a simple room filled with books. The only furniture was a table and a bench.

"Rabbi, where is your furniture?" asked the tourist.

"Where is yours?" asked Hafez in return.

"Mine? But I'm only a visitor here."

"So am I," said the Rabbi.

We are all visitors here on a brief journey, but we tend to live in a manner as if we shall be here forever. A good principle of happy and successful journey is to travel light. Don't be burdened with heavy loads of materialism. Carry with you the rewards of God's worship and love of the people you come across. You will not meet your possessions in the afterlife, but you will meet the ones you loved. Keep this thought in mind while charting the course of your life.

Make purpose of your life a life of purpose.

"We are not human beings having a spiritual experience. We are spiritual beings having a human experience."

Pierre Teilhard de Chardin (1881-1955)
French Philosopher

CHAPTER 4

ENLIGHTENMENT

ੴ

As we have seen, the purpose of life as per SGGS is to attain enlightenment, which leads us on to godhood. Enlightenment has many names like awakening, enhanced awareness, higher consciousness, liberation, attainment, self-realization, God-realization, salvation, *moksh, nirvana, mukti, nistaara* and so on. What does all this mean?

Steve Taylor, a British author and lecturer on psychology & spirituality, has done extensive research on enlightenment. He has closely interacted with dozens of enlightened people and has published his findings in various books and essays. He says there is a marked change in the psychological framework and perceptions of enlightened people. Here are some common signs he observed in such people:

Are aware of Divine presence.

Live more in the now than in past or future.

Believe in oneness and connectedness of the universe.

Have inner quietness.

Are happy being alone and inactive.

Have reduced or no fear of death.

Have universal outlook.

Are high on moral values.

Feel this world is a very beautiful place.

Are beyond accumulation and attachment.

Have more authentic relationships.

Are open to new things.

Let us now see what SGGS says about enlightenment. The names used for enlightened people in SGGS are *gurmukh, saadhu, saadh, sant, brahm giani, guru, mukt,* etc. Though some people try to differentiate between these titles, in actual fact they all mean the same, i.e., a person who has reached a higher level of spiritual awareness and has arrived at the door of godhood. This is also referred to as opening of *dasmdwar* (the tenth gate).

In SGGS the attributes of an enlightened person are given at different places, but mostly in *Sukhmani Sahib* (Pages 262-296). It is interesting to note how attributes mentioned by Steve Taylor are quite in line with those of SGGS, as shown below:

Aware of Divine Presence

ਬ੍ਰਹਮ ਗਿਆਨੀ ਕੈ ਏਕੈ ਰੰਗ ॥ ਬ੍ਰਹਮ ਗਿਆਨੀ ਕੈ ਬਸੈ ਪ੍ਰਭ ਸੰਗ ॥

Braham giani kai ekai rung, braham giani kai basai Prabh sung.

ब्रहम गिआनी कै एकै रंग ॥ ब्रहम गिआनी कै बसै प्रभु संग ॥

The enlightened one loves the One Lord alone,
Lord is always with him.

M5/273/6

Belief in Oneness and Connectedness of the Universe

ਉਰਿ ਧਾਰੈ ਜੋ ਅੰਤਰਿ ਨਾਮੁ ॥ ਸਰਬ ਮੈ ਪੇਖੈ ਭਗਵਾਨੁ ॥

Ur dhaarai jo antar naam, sarab mai pekhai Bhagwaan.

उरि धारै जो अंतरि नामु ॥ सरब मै पेखै भगवानु ॥

He who keeps Lord's name in his heart,
sees God in everything.

M5/274/2

Have Inner Quietness

ਬ੍ਰਹਮ ਗਿਆਨੀ ਕੈ ਧੀਰਜੁ ਏਕ ॥ ਜਿਉ ਬਸੁਧਾ ਕੋਉ ਖੋਦੈ ਕੋਉ ਚੰਦਨ ਲੇਪ ॥

Braham giani kai dheeraj aik, jiu basudha kou khodai kou
chandan lep.

ब्रहम गिआनी कै धीरजु एक ॥ जिउ बसुधा कोऊ खोदै कोऊ चंदन लेप

Enlightened one is calm, like the earth, which doesn't get
perturbed, whether you dig it up (cause hurt) or apply
sandalwood paste (to mitigate pain).

M5/272/13

Have Reduced or No Fear of Death

ਜਨਮ ਮਰਨ ਕਾ ਭ੍ਰਮੁ ਗਇਆ ਗੋਬਿਦ ਲਿਵ ਲਾਗੀ ॥

Janam maran ka bhram gaya Gobid liv laagi.

जनम मरन का भ्रमु गइआ गोबिद लिव लागी ॥

Birth and death have no meaning as I am now attuned
to the Lord.

Kabir/857/10

Have Universal Outlook

ਹਰਖੁ ਸੋਗੁ ਜਾ ਕੈ ਨਹੀ ਬੈਰੀ ਮੀਤ ਸਮਾਨਿ ॥

ਕਹੁ ਨਾਨਕ ਸੁਨਿ ਰੇ ਮਨਾ ਮੁਕਤਿ ਤਾਹਿ ਤੈ ਜਾਨਿ ॥

Harakh soag ja kai nahi bairee meet samaan.

Kahu Nanak sunn ray mana mukt taahe tai jaan.

हरखु सोगु जा कै नही बैरी मीत समानि ॥

कहु नानक सुनि रे मना मुकति ताहि तै जानि ॥

He who is not affected by happiness or sorrow, and for whom
friend and foe are the same, says Nanak, know him to
be liberated.

M9/1427/6

Beyond Accumulation and Attachment

ਜਿਹਿ ਮਾਇਆ ਮਮਤਾ ਤਜੀ ਸਭ ਤੇ ਭਇਓ ਉਦਾਸੁ ॥

ਕਹੁ ਨਾਨਕ ਸੁਨੁ ਰੇ ਮਨਾ ਤਿਹ ਘਟਿ ਬ੍ਰਹਮ ਨਿਵਾਸੁ ॥

Jih maya mamta tajee sabh tay bhaiyo udaas.

Kahu Nanak sunn ray mana tih ghat Braham nivaas.

जिहि माइआ ममता तजी सभ ते भइओ उदासु ॥

कहु नानक सुनु रे मना तिह घटि ब्रहम निवासु ॥

He who gives up his attachment to *maya*, and is
detached from everything,
Says Nanak, God resides in his heart.

M9/1427/9

High on Moral Values

ਮਿਥਿਆ ਨਾਹੀ ਰਸਨਾ ਪਰਸ ॥ ਮਨ ਮਹਿ ਪ੍ਰੀਤਿ ਨਿਰੰਜਨ ਦਰਸ ॥
ਪਰ ਤ੍ਰਿਅ ਰੂਪੁ ਨ ਪੇਖੈ ਨੇਤ੍ਰ ॥

Mithya naahi rasna paras, munn meh preet Niranjan daras.
Per triya roop na pekhai netar.

मिथिआ नाही रसना परस ॥ मन महि प्रीति निरंजन दरस ॥
पर त्रिअ रूपु न पेखै नेत्र ॥

He does not speak falsehood.
His mind is filled with love for vision of the Pure One.
His eyes do not look at another's woman.

ਕਰਨ ਨ ਸੁਨੈ ਕਾਹੂ ਕੀ ਨਿੰਦਾ ॥ ਸਭ ਤੇ ਜਾਨੈ ਆਪਸ ਕਉ ਮੰਦਾ ॥

Karan na sunai kahoo ki ninda, sabh tay jaanai aapas
kao manda.

करन न सुनै काहू की निंदा ॥ सभ ते जानै आपस कउ मंदा ॥

His ears do not listen to ill of anyone, he doesn't consider
himself to be worthy (is modest).

ਇੰਦ੍ਰੀ ਜਿਤ ਪੰਚ ਦੋਖ ਤੇ ਰਹਤ ॥ ਨਾਨਕ ਕੋਟਿ ਮਧੇ ਕੋ ਐਸਾ ਅਪਰਸ ॥

Indree jit panch dokh tay rehat. Nanak kot madhay ko
aisa apras.

इंद्री जित पंच दोख ते रहत ॥ नानक कोटि मधे को ऐसा अपरस ॥

He has control over his sensory organs and is safe from
five evils (lust, anger, greed, attachment, and ego),
Nanak says only one out of millions can be such
a pure untouched person.

M5/274/3

Open to New Learning

ਬ੍ਰਹਮ ਗਿਆਨੀ ਕਾ ਭੋਜਨੁ ਗਿਆਨ ॥ ਨਾਨਕ ਬ੍ਰਹਮ ਗਿਆਨੀ ਕਾ ਬ੍ਰਹਮ ਧਿਆਨੁ ॥

Braham giani ka bhojan gyaan, Nanak braham giani ka Braham dhiyaan.

ब्रहम गिआनी का भोजनु गिआन ॥ नानक ब्रहम गिआनी का ब्रहम धिआनु ॥

Knowledge is the food for the enlightened one, he meditates on the Lord, says Nanak.

M5/273/2

From the above comparisons, it is evident that there is great similarity between Steve Taylor's attributes of enlightened people and those in SGGS. It is amazing how, centuries ago, authors of SGGS knew about enlightenment psychology that conforms to present thinking.

Let us now look into some other characteristics of enlightened people. They are spiritually so advanced, that they have been equated with God.

Guru Arjan Dev says *braham giani* is himself God:

ਬ੍ਰਹਮ ਗਿਆਨੀ ਕਉ ਖੋਜਹਿ ਮਹੇਸੁਰ ॥ ਨਾਨਕ ਬ੍ਰਹਮ ਗਿਆਨੀ ਆਪਿ ਪਰਮੇਸੁਰ ॥

Braham giani ko khojeh Mahesar, braham giani aap Parmaysur.

ब्रहम गिआनी कउ खोजहि महेसुर ॥ नानक ब्रहम गिआनी आपि परमेसुर ॥

Even Shiva searches for *braham giani*. Nanak says *braham giani* is himself God.

M5/273/12

Saadh, another name for enlightened person, is also equated with God by Guru Arjan Dev:

ਸਾਧ ਕੀ ਸੋਭਾ ਸਾਧ ਬਨਿ ਆਈ॥ਨਾਨਕ ਸਾਧ ਪ੍ਰਭ ਭੇਦੁ ਨ ਭਾਈ॥

Saadh ki sobha Saadh bun aayee, Nanak saadh Prabh bhed
na bhaayee.

साध की सोभा साध बनि आई॥ नानक साध प्रभ भेदु न भाई॥

The glory of *saadh* is his alone, O Nanak, there is no
difference between *saadh* and God.

M5/272/9

Guru Teg Bahadur defines *mukt*:

ਉਸਤਤਿ ਨਿੰਦਿਆ ਨਾਹਿ ਜਿਹਿ ਕੰਚਨ ਲੋਹ ਸਮਾਨਿ॥
ਕਹੁ ਨਾਨਕ ਸੁਨਿ ਰੇ ਮਨਾ ਮੁਕਤਿ ਤਾਹਿ ਤੈ ਜਾਨਿ॥

Ustat nindeya nahee jih kanchan loh samaan.
Kahu Nanak sunn ray mana mukt taahay tai jaan.

उसतति निंदिआ नाहि जिहि कंचन लोह समानि॥
कहु नानक सुनि रे मना मुकति ताहि तै जानि॥

He who is not affected by praise or denigration, for whom gold
and iron have the same value.
Listen O my mind, says Nanak, know him to be liberated.

M9/1427/5

Another quotation by Guru Teg Bahadur on liberated
person:

ਜਿਹਿ ਪ੍ਰਾਨੀ ਹਉਮੈ ਤਜੀ ਕਰਤਾ ਰਾਮੁ ਪਛਾਨਿ॥
ਕਹੁ ਨਾਨਕ ਵਹੁ ਮੁਕਤਿ ਨਰੁ ਇਹ ਮਨ ਸਾਚੀ ਮਾਨੁ॥

Jih praani haumai taji karta Ram pachhaan.
Kaho Nanak veh mukt nar, eh munn saachee maan.

> जिहि प्रानी हउमै तजी करता रामु पछानि ॥
> कहु नानक वहु मुकति नरु इह मन साची मानु ॥
>
> He who sheds his ego and recognizes the Lord;
> Says Nanak, he is a liberated being; accept this to be true.
>
> M9/1427/10

How does one progress towards attainment? As per SGGS there are five *khands* (stages) of spiritual growth as given by Guru Nanak from Page 7 line 11 to Page 8 line 7. These are summarized below:

> *Dharam Khand (Realm of righteous action). Realization that good deeds bring good results.*
>
> *Gian Khand (Realm of knowledge). Gaining knowledge about God and his vast creation.*
>
> *Saram Khand (Realm of spiritual endeavour). Purification of thought.*
>
> *Karam Khand (Realm of grace). God showers His grace on the seeker.*
>
> *Sach Khand (Realm of Truth). Attainment of godhood; merger with God.*

Most people on spiritual path would normally follow the above course. However, with sincere effort, guru's help, and most importantly, God's grace, the process can be shortened and all sins of present and past lives can be cleared in the present life itself. More on this in chapter titled 'Karam'.

Enlightenment is the final destiny for every soul, whether it happens now or hundreds of rebirths later. It is never too late to start the journey; the earlier the better. We must not waste this precious life on trivial pursuits. The fact that you are reading this book shows you are aware of the need to tread the spiritual path. Though we are all on the spiritual journey, most of us are not consciously aware of it, and therefore not pursuing it seriously.

Unlike in our material world, spiritual advancement is not a team effort, we must travel alone. Of course, company and advice of gurus and other holy people is necessary. What does one have to do? Worship and meditate on God, have honest and truthful dealings, listen to holy people and read spiritual literature. Inculcate qualities of an enlightened person and live by them. Share and care. Do this from the heart with full sincerity. When your desire for God is strong enough, you will find Him. It is your job to become a serious seeker, and it is God's job to shower His grace on you. Do not focus your attention on grace coming to you, instead focus on your worship - do not have any expectations.

"Enlightenment is when a wave realizes it is the ocean."

Thich Nhat Hanh (b. 1926)
Vietnamese Monk

CHAPTER 5

DEATH

Everything that is born or created in time must come to perish some day. This applies to everything, even the universe, because it was created at a point in time. The only One that is beyond time is God. He has always been there and will continue to be there forever.

Since we humans are all born at a point in time we must also die one day. Life spans of individuals may vary but the end is inevitable. Also, we do not determine the time of our birth, nor do we determine the time of departure. God does that. Unfortunately, we consider death to be long time away, so we don't bother to prepare for this event, which could actually happen any time - even this moment, without a warning.

Commenting on the reality of death Guru Nanak says:

ਸਰਫੈ ਸਰਫੈ ਸਦਾ ਸਦਾ ਏਵੈ ਗਾਈ ਵਿਹਾਇ ॥
ਨਾਨਕ ਕਿਸ ਨੋ ਆਖੀਐ ਵਿਣੁ ਪੁਛਿਆ ਹੀ ਲੈ ਜਾਇ ॥

Sarfai sarfai sadaa sadaa evai gayee vihaaye.
Nanak kis no aakhiyai vin puchheya hee lai jaaye.

सरफै सरफै सदा सदा एवै गई विहाइ ॥
नानक किस नो आखीऐ विणु पुछिआ ही लै जाइ ॥

> Bit by bit, all the time, life passes away.
> Nanak says, who do we complain to? He takes us away without asking us.
>
> M1/1412/16

Here are some more verses that tell us of the inevitability and unpredictability of death.

Guru Nanak again:

> ਆਵਤੁ ਕਿਨੈ ਨ ਰਾਖਿਆ ਜਾਵਤੁ ਕਿਉ ਰਾਖਿਆ ਜਾਇ॥
> ਜਿਸ ਤੇ ਹੋਆ ਸੋਈ ਪਰੁ ਜਾਨੈ ਜਾਂ ਉਸ ਹੀ ਮਾਹਿ ਸਮਾਇ॥
>
> Aavat kinai na raakheya jaavat kiu raakheya jaaye.
> Jis tay hoa soee par jaanai ja us hi maahay samaaye.
>
> आवतु किनै न राखिआ जावतु किउ राखिआ जाइ॥
> जिस ते होआ सोई परु जाणै जां उस ही माहि समाइ॥
>
> No one can stop our coming (being born), how could anyone stop us from going (dying)?
> The One who created us alone fully knows, we all go and merge in Him.
>
> M1/1329/10

Guru Angad Dev:

> ਜੇਹਾ ਚੀਰੀ ਲਿਖਿਆ ਤੇਹਾ ਹੁਕਮੁ ਕਮਾਹਿ॥ ਘਲੇ ਆਵਹਿ ਨਾਨਕਾ ਸਦੇ ਉਠੀ ਜਾਹਿ॥
>
> Jeha chiri likheya teha hukam kamaahay, ghallay aaveh Nanaka sadday uthi jaahay.
>
> जेहा चीरी लिखिआ तेहा हुकमु कमाहि॥ घले आवहि नानका सदे उठी जाहि॥

As it is ordained by Him, so His order comes to pass.

Says Nanak, we arrive (in this world) when He sends us, and depart when He beckons.

M2/1239/9

Guru Teg Bahadur:

ਜੋ ਉਪਜਿਓ ਸੋ ਬਿਨਸਿ ਹੈ ਪਰੋ ਆਜੁ ਕੈ ਕਾਲਿ॥

ਨਾਨਕ ਹਰਿ ਗੁਨ ਗਾਇ ਲੇ ਛਾਡਿ ਸਗਲ ਜੰਜਾਲ॥

Jo upjeo so binas hai paro aaj kai kaal.

Nanak Har gunh gaaye lay chhaad sagal janjaal.

जो उपजिओ सो बिनसि है परो आजु कै कालि॥

नानक हरि गुन गाइ ले छाडि सगल जंजाल॥

Whatever is created shall perish, today or tomorrow.

Nanak says, sing of Lord's virtues, and leave all entanglements (of *maya*).

M9/1429/4

Guru Nanak says, have no worries about death and no expectations from life:

ਮਰਨੈ ਕੀ ਚਿੰਤਾ ਨਹੀ ਜੀਵਣ ਕੀ ਨਹੀ ਆਸ॥

ਤੂ ਸਰਬ ਜੀਆ ਪ੍ਰਤਿਪਾਲਹੀ ਲੇਖੈ ਸਾਸ ਗਿਰਾਸ॥

Marnay ki chinta nahi jeevan ki nahi aas.

Tu sarab jia pritpaal-hi lekhay saas giraas.

मरणै की चिंता नही जीवण की नही आस॥

तू सरब जीआ प्रतिपालही लेखै सास गिरास॥

There is no worry of dying, and no expectation of living.
You look after all souls, and You keep account of every
breath we take and every morsel we eat.

M1/20/18

Those who are spiritually aware do not fear death. What is
there to fear? Death is only a stepping stone in the journey of our
soul towards salvation, towards becoming one with God. It is just
the end of one chapter which leads to the beginning of another.
If you have fulfilled your karmic debts you will not come back
into this physical world. If not, you get another chance to do that.

One should also understand that with death we get rid of
all our bodily pains, aches, ailments, and all other problems
associated with physical world, like worries, anxieties, desires,
mental pressures and so on. If we take rebirth the problems
start again.

Enlightened people like Bhagat Kabir not only accepted
death, but looked forward to it. This is what he says:

ਕਬੀਰ ਜਿਸੁ ਮਰਨੇ ਤੇ ਜਗੁ ਡਰੈ ਮੇਰੇ ਮਨਿ ਆਨੰਦੁ ॥
ਮਰਨੇ ਹੀ ਤੇ ਪਾਈਐ ਪੂਰਨੁ ਪਰਮਾਨੰਦੁ ॥

Kabir jis marnay tay jug darai meray munn anand.
Marnay hee tay paeeyai pooran parmanand.

कबीर जिसु मरने ते जगु डरै मेरे मनि आनंदु ॥
मरने ही ते पाईऐ पूरनु परमानंदु ॥

Kabir says, death which the world is afraid of, creates
peace in my mind.
Only in death can one find ultimate bliss.

Kabir/1365/12

This ultimate bliss after death doesn't come to everyone, but only to people like Bhagat Kabir, who awaken during their stay on earth. If everyone was to have blissfulness after death, there would be no point in living a difficult life on earth – it would be better to die.

How much time are we assured of before death takes us away? Very little, as little as the duration of one breath - that's all. Guru Nanak says:

ਹਮ ਆਦਮੀ ਹਾਂ ਇਕ ਦਮੀ ਮੁਹਲਤਿ ਮੁਹਤੁ ਨ ਜਾਣਾ ॥
ਨਾਨਕੁ ਬਿਨਵੈ ਤਿਸੈ ਸਰੇਵਹੁ ਜਾ ਕੇ ਜੀਅ ਪਰਾਣਾ ॥

Hum aadmi haan ik dami muhlat muhat na jaana.
Nanak binvai tisai sarevoh ja kay jia praana.

हम आदमी हां इक दमी मुहलति मुहतु न जाणा ॥
नानकु बिनवै तिसै सरेवहु जा के जीअ पराणा ॥

We humans are assured of life for duration of one breath
only, we do not know how long we'll live and when we'll die.
Nanak pleads us to worship the One who has given us our
soul and our life.

M1/660/11

If you were told you have only one day left before you die, how will you spend that day? I am sure you will do nothing wrong, and will do all the good things you have been thinking of doing. Perhaps better part of your time will be spent in worship and prayer. Why don't you do it now? You are not assured of even one minute, let alone a day.

Nanak reminds us here of *maya*, the illusion God has created which makes us forget death:

ਅਮਲੁ ਗਲੋਲਾ ਕੂੜ ਕਾ ਦਿਤਾ ਦੇਵਣਹਾਰਿ ॥

ਮਤੀ ਮਰਣੁ ਵਿਸਾਰਿਆ ਖੁਸੀ ਕੀਤੀ ਦਿਨ ਚਾਰਿ ॥

ਸਚੁ ਮਿਲਿਆ ਤਿਨ ਸੋਫੀਆ ਰਾਖਣ ਕਉ ਦਰਵਾਰੁ ॥

Amal galola koorh ka ditta devanhaar.

Matti maran visaareya khusi keeti din chaar.

Sach mileya tin sofia rakhan kao darvaar.

अमलु गलोला कूड़ का दिता देवणहारि॥

मती मरणु विसारिआ खुसी कीती दिन चारि॥

सचु मिलिआ तिन सोफीआ राखण कउ दरवारु॥

The Giver has given intoxicating drug of falsehood (*maya*).
Our mind forgets death, and we have fun for few days.
Those who are sober find the truth, and they get a place in
Lord's court.

M1/15/17

Death is one of the most common fears people have. Most of us are, perhaps, not scared of death per se, but it is the process of dying that worries us. The process could vary from just not getting up one morning from a peaceful sleep, to a very prolonged illness for periods lasting months and, even years, which cause immense emotional, physical and financial hardships, both to the patient and his close ones. Pray for a quick and peaceful departure, whenever it happens. If still God gives you pain and suffering, accept it as His will - it has a divine purpose, unknown to you.

Death could also be painful for those who are over-attached to their material wealth and can't see it go; as also those who have not lived an honest life and are scared of the judgment at the God's court.

What can one do to make our death easy? Follow this advice of Guru Amar Das:

ਕਿਆ ਜਾਣਾ ਕਿਵ ਮਰਹਗੇ ਕੈਸਾ ਮਰਣਾ ਹੋਇ॥
ਜੇ ਕਰਿ ਸਾਹਿਬੁ ਮਨਹੁ ਨ ਵੀਸਰੈ ਤਾ ਸਹਿਲਾ ਮਰਣਾ ਹੋਇ॥

Kia jaana kiv marhegay kaisa marna hoye.
Jay kar Sahib manho na veesrai ta sahila marna hoye.

किआ जाणा किव मरहगे कैसा मरणा होइ॥
जे करि साहिबु मनहु न वीसरै ता सहिला मरणा होइ॥

I don't know how I will die, what will death be like?
If your mind does not forget the Lord, then death will be easy.

M3/555/4

Guru Arjan Dev also advises us to prepare for life after death:

ਕਰਉ ਬੇਨੰਤੀ ਸੁਣਹੁ ਮੇਰੇ ਮੀਤਾ ਸੰਤ ਟਹਲ ਕੀ ਬੇਲਾ॥
ਈਹਾ ਖਾਟਿ ਚਲਹੁ ਹਰਿ ਲਾਹਾ ਆਗੈ ਬਸਨੁ ਸੁਹੇਲਾ॥

Karou benanti sunho meray meeta sant tehal kee bela;
Eeha khaat chalho Har laahaa aagai basan suhela.

करउ बेनंती सुणहु मेरे मीता संत टहल की बेला॥
ईहा खाटि चलहु हरि लाहा आगै बसनु सुहेला॥

O friends please listen to me, this is the time to serve
the saints.
Earn profit/goodwill by serving the Lord, your life hereafter
will be easy.

M5/13/14 & M5/205/14

Guru Nanak tells us to conquer death while we are still alive:

ਅੰਤਰ ਕੀ ਗਤਿ ਜਾਣੀਐ ਗੁਰ ਮਿਲੀਐ ਸੰਕ ਉਤਾਰਿ ॥
ਮੁਇਆ ਜਿਤੁ ਘਰਿ ਜਾਈਐ ਤਿਤੁ ਜੀਵਦਿਆ ਮਰੁ ਮਾਰਿ ॥
ਅਨਹਦ ਸਬਦਿ ਸੁਹਾਵਣੇ ਪਾਈਐ ਗੁਰ ਵੀਚਾਰਿ ॥

Antar ki gat jaaniyai gur miliyai sunk utaar.
Moeya jit ghar jaa-eeyai tit jeevdeya mar maar.
Anhad sabad suhavanay paayeeyai gur vichaar.

अंतर की गति जाणीऐ गुर मिलीऐ संक उतारि॥
मुइआ जितु घरि जाईऐ तितु जीवदिआ मरु मारि॥
अनहद सबदि सुहावणे पाईऐ गुर वीचारि॥

Know your inner state, meet the Guru to get rid of your doubts.
To reach your true home after death, you must conquer death while still alive.
The pleasing un-struck sound is obtained/heard by contemplating on the Guru.

M1/21/1

Bhagat Ravidas describes the stage after death:

ਬੇਗਮ ਪੁਰਾ ਸਹਰ ਕੋ ਨਾਉ ॥ ਦੂਖੁ ਅੰਦੋਹੁ ਨਹੀ ਤਿਹਿ ਠਾਉ ॥
ਨਾਂ ਤਸਵੀਸ ਖਿਰਾਜੁ ਨ ਮਾਲੁ ॥ ਖਉਫੁ ਨ ਖਤਾ ਨ ਤਰਸੁ ਜਵਾਲੁ ॥
ਅਬ ਮੋਹਿ ਖੂਬ ਵਤਨ ਗਹ ਪਾਈ ॥ ਊਹਾਂ ਖੈਰਿ ਸਦਾ ਮੇਰੇ ਭਾਈ ॥

Begum pura sahar ko nao, dukh andoh nahi tih thaao.
Na tasvees khiraaj na maal, khauf na khata na taras javaal.
Ab mohay khoob vatan geh paayee, oohan khair sadaa meray bhaayee.

बेगम पुरा सहर को नाउ॥ दूखु अंदोहु नही तिहि ठाउ॥
नां तसवीस खिराजु न मालु॥ खउफु न खता न तरसु जवालु
अब मोहि खूब वतन गह पाई॥ ऊहां खैरि सदा मेरे भाई॥

Sorrow-less place, is the name of the town, there is no pain or
anxiety there.
There are no troubles and no taxes on goods, there is no
fear, blemish or downfall.
Now I have found this most excellent place, O brother, there
is always peace and wellbeing there.

Ravidas/345/12

Guru Amar Das describes that stage thus:

ਤਿਥੈ ਉਂਘ ਨ ਭੁਖ ਹੈ ਹਰਿ ਅੰਮ੍ਰਿਤ ਨਾਮੁ ਸੁਖ ਵਾਸੁ॥
ਨਾਨਕ ਦੁਖ ਸੁਖ ਵਿਆਪਤ ਨਹੀ ਜਿਥੈ ਆਤਮ ਰਾਮ ਪ੍ਰਗਾਸੁ॥

Tithai oongh na bhukh hai Har amrit naam sukh vaas.
Nanak dukh sukh viapat nahi jithai aatam Ram pragaas.

तिथै ऊंघ न भुख है हरि अम्रित नामु सुख वासु॥
नानक दुखु सुखु विआपत नही जिथै आतम राम प्रगासु॥

There is no sleep or hunger there, they dwell in peace in the
pure Name of the Lord.
Nanak says, pain and pleasure do not exist there, and Lord's
soul enlightens.

M3/1414/11

Life after death will be trouble-free only for those who
worship God and live a righteous life. If you live a sinful life
here don't expect a blissful life hereafter. You will face plenty of
troubles and will be reincarnated in difficult environments. It

seems the following couplet was written by Urdu poet, Sheikh Ibrahim Zauq, keeping in mind the plight of such people, *"Ab Toh Ghabhrah Ke Yih Kahtein Hain Ke Mar Jaayengay. Mar Kay Bhi Chayen Na Paya To Kidhar Jaayengay?"* (Now when I shudder with fear, I seek solace in death. But if I don't find peace even after death, where will I go?)

Process of death will be easier for those who know and understand death. This understanding helps you drop the burden of ego and you live a more meaningful life. There is nothing more certain than death, yet people live as if it will never come to them. The arrival of death should be a cause for celebration, because, after living a purposeful life you are now moving closer to your Maker. Not welcoming death is an indication that you haven't lived a good life. Live life well and have faith in God, the thought of death will not trouble you.

Here is a story that will help you cope with the reality of death:

A sick man turned to his doctor as he was preparing to leave the examination room and said, "Doctor, I am afraid to die. Tell me what lies on the other side."

Very quietly, the doctor said, "I don't know".

"You don't know? You're a religious man, and you don't know what's on the other side?"

The doctor was holding the handle of the door - from the other side came a sound of scratching and whining, and as he opened the door, a dog sprang into the room, and he leaped on to the doctor with an eager show of gladness.

Turning to the patient, the doctor said, "Did you notice my dog? He's never been in this room before. He didn't know what to expect inside. He knew nothing except that his master was here, and when the door opened, he sprang in without fear. I know little of what is on the other side of death, but I do know one thing, my Master is there and that is enough!"

You will meet your Master on the other side of life. Go well prepared for the meeting. Time to prepare is now.

"As a well spent day brings happy sleep, so life well used brings happy death."

Leonardo da Vinci (1452-1519)
Italian Artist & Engineer

CHAPTER 6

REINCARNATION

What happens to us after death? Is it the end of the story? Do we go to some place and remain there ever after? Do we come back to this world in a new life? These are questions that have intrigued mankind since ancient times. Most religions have addressed these questions and have definitive views. Interestingly, there is a commonality in belief of religions born in the same geographical regions. Of the eight major religions of the world four were born in India and four in the area of present-day middle-east. Those born in India are Hinduism, Buddhism, Jainism and Sikhism while Judaism, Christianity, Islam and Zoroastrianism took birth in the middle-east region.

All religions of Indian origin believe in rebirth and those of the middle-east do not. With sufficient evidence, and new scientific studies, on people remembering their past lives, even the non-believers in rebirth are beginning to review their beliefs. There have been numerous cases where people have vividly remembered their past lives and their recollections have been properly recorded; which have been confirmed to be true. Scientists like Dr Brian Weiss, MD, Dr Michael Newton, PhD, and Dr Gary E Schwartz, PhD, have done remarkable research on past life, including past life regression, which confirms that their subjects indeed had had previous lives, which they were able to recall accurately.

The phenomenon of reincarnation continues to happen. In recent times there has been a case in Australia, where a boy named Billy Campbell, born in 2015 is believed to be reincarnation of Princess Diana. As a two-year old he saw a photograph of the Princess and told his parents that he used to be that Princess earlier. In 2019 his father David Campbell, a TV presenter, gave details of many things the boy remembered of his previous birth which make it difficult for anyone to deny this reincarnation.

While Indians have always believed in rebirth, the idea is not new even to the western or the middle-eastern world. There are references to such belief in their religions.

Reincarnation was part of the Christian doctrine till 553 AD, when it was dropped on orders of Roman Emperor, Justinian at the Fifth Ecumenical Council at Constantinople (now Istanbul). The empire at the time was divided in two parts with Western Empire headquartered at Rome and the Eastern at Constantinople. Though the decision against reincarnation was taken after voting by bishops from both empires, only two bishops from the Western Empire attended. There was threat to the lives of those who would vote in favour of reincarnation because two of the bishops who had earlier believed in the theory had been murdered. Emperor Justinian told the Church to say that people had only one life; thereafter they permanently went to heaven or hell, depending upon the kind of life they lived. It is believed that all copies of the Bible were confiscated in both the empires, destroyed and rewritten, with all references to reincarnation omitted. Why was this done? The Emperor and the majority of bishops believed that if people had the option of redeeming their lives/souls in future reincarnations they would not live this life with full devotion to the Church. Belief in rebirth would encourage people to communicate directly with God, who controlled reincarnation, thus bypassing the Church and reducing its power and influence.

Similarly there are reasons to believe that early followers of Islam, Judaism and Zoroastrianism had among them sects that believed in rebirth, and many descendants of these sects still exist. For various reasons this doctrine remained the domain of esoteric groups - in Christianity we have the Gnostics, in Islam the sects like *Ismaili*, *Alawis*, and various Sufi groups, and in Judaism the *Kabbalists*. Even in the holy books of the mainstream religions there are pointers to rebirth. For example Quran says, "How can you disbelieve in Allah, when you were lifeless and He brought you to life; then He will cause you to die, then He will bring you (back) to life, and then to Him you will be returned." (2:28). In the Bible there is a passage in John 9:2 where the disciples ask Jesus, "Rabbi, who sinned, this man or his parents, that he was born blind?". If a man is born blind for his sins these sins could have been committed only in a previous life. (Jewish priest is known as Rabbi and Jesus was a Jew.)

The ancient Greek philosopher figures like Socrates, Pythagoras, and Plato also believed in reincarnation. At the end of his life Socrates said, "I am confident that there truly is such a thing as living again, and that the living spring from the dead."

In India the doctrine of reincarnation has been exoteric, i.e. open to all. In SGGS it has been stated frequently and clearly. Here are some verses on rebirth.

Guru Nanak:

ਜੁੜਿ ਜੁੜਿ ਵਿਛੁੜੇ ਵਿਛੁੜਿ ਜੁੜੇ ॥ ਜੀਵਿ ਜੀਵਿ ਮੁਏ ਮੁਏ ਜੀਵੇ ॥
ਕੇਤਿਆ ਕੇ ਬਾਪ ਕੇਤਿਆ ਕੇ ਬੇਟੇ ਕੇਤੇ ਗੁਰ ਚੇਲੇ ਹੂਏ ॥

Jur jur vichhuray vichhur juray; jeev jeev mooye
mooye jeevai.
Keteya kay baap keteya kay betay ketay gur chelay hooye.

ਜੁੜਿ ਜੁੜਿ ਵਿਛੁੜੇ ਵਿਛੁੜਿ ਜੁੜੇ॥ ਜੀਵਿ ਜੀਵਿ ਮੁਏ ਮੁਏ ਜੀਵੇ॥
ਕੇਤਿਆ ਕੇ ਬਾਪ ਕੇਤਿਆ ਕੇ ਬੇਟੇ ਕੇਤੇ ਗੁਰ ਚੇਲੇ ਹੂਏ॥

Body and soul separate and meet again; this birth and death
happens repeatedly.
(Over many lives) one became fathers of many, sons of
many, gurus of many, and disciples of many.

M1/1238/12

Bhagat Kabir says:

ਐਸੇ ਘਰ ਹਮ ਬਹੁਤੁ ਬਸਾਏ॥ ਜਬ ਹਮ ਰਾਮ ਗਰਭ ਹੋਇ ਆਏ॥

Aisay ghar hum bahut basaaye, jab hum Ram garbh hoye aaye.

ऐसे घर हम बहुतु बसाए॥ जब हम राम गरभ होइ आए॥

I established such homes many times, before I came into the
womb this time, O Lord.

Kabir/326/1

Bhagat Kabir again:

ਧਾਵਤ ਜੋਨਿ ਜਨਮ ਭੂਮਿ ਥਾਕੇ ਅਬ ਦੁਖ ਕਰਿ ਹਮ ਹਾਰਿਓ ਰੇ॥
ਕਹਿ ਕਬੀਰ ਗੁਰ ਮਿਲਤ ਮਹਾ ਰਸੁ ਪ੍ਰੇਮ ਭਗਤਿ ਨਿਸਤਾਰਿਓ ਰੇ॥

Dhaavat jone janam bhram thaakay ab dukh kar hum
haareyo ray.
Kehat Kabir gur milat maha ras prem bhagat nistaareyo ray.

धावत जोनि जनम भ्रमि थाके अब दुख करि हम हारिओ रे॥
कहि कबीर गुर मिलत महा रसु प्रेम भगति निसतारिओ रे॥

I have been wandering in doubt and confusion over many lives, now because of the sufferings I am so defeated.

Says Bhagat Kabir, meeting with the Guru, I have obtained supreme joy, my love and devotion have saved me.

Kabir/335/17

Guru Amar Das:

ਇਤਨੇ ਜਨਮ ਭੂਲਿ ਪਰੇ ਸੇ ਜਾ ਪਾਇਆ ਤਾ ਭੂਲੇ ਨਾਹੀ॥
ਜਾ ਕਾ ਕਾਰਨੁ ਸੋਈ ਪਰੁ ਜਾਣੈ ਜੇ ਗੁਰ ਕੈ ਸਬਦਿ ਸਮਾਹੀ॥

Itnay janam bhool paray say ja paaya ta bhoolay naahi.
Ja ka kaaraj soyee par jaanay jay gur kai sabad samaahi.

इतने जनम भूलि परे से जा पाइआ ता भूले नाही॥
जा का कारजु सोई परु जाणै जे गुर कै सबदि समाही॥

Due to ignorance people live in forgetfulness (of God) over many lives, when they find Him, they no longer wander.

Only those immersed in Guru's Word can know that it is all His doing.

M3/162/9

Guru Arjan Dev's prayer seeking God to end reincarnation:

ਅਨਿਕ ਜਨਮ ਬਹੁ ਜੋਨੀ ਭ੍ਰਮਿਆ ਬਹੁਰਿ ਬਹੁਰਿ ਦੁਖ ਪਾਇਆ॥
ਤੁਮਰੀ ਕ੍ਰਿਪਾ ਤੇ ਮਾਨੁਖ ਦੇਹ ਪਾਈ ਹੈ ਦੇਹੁ ਦਰਸੁ ਹਰਿ ਰਾਇਆ॥

Anik janam bahu joni bhrameya bahur bahur dukh paaya.
Tumri kripa tay manukh deh paayee hai dehu daras Har Raaya.

ਅਨਿਕ ਜਨਮ ਬਹੁ ਜੋਨੀ ਭ੍ਰਮਿਆ ਬਹੁਰਿ ਬਹੁਰਿ ਦੁਖੁ ਪਾਇਆ ॥
ਤੁਮਰੀ ਕ੍ਰਿਪਾ ਤੇ ਮਾਨੁਖ ਦੇਹ ਪਾਈ ਹੈ ਦੇਹੁ ਦਰਸੁ ਹਰਿ ਰਾਇਆ ॥

Wandering over many different reincarnations, I endured
great pain.
By Your grace I have now obtained this human body, allow
me to have Your vision O Lord.

M5/207/9

Having vision of God means meeting God, attaining
salvation, which is the ultimate aim. It can only happen when
you are born as a human being.

Bhagat Ravidas also yearns for God's vision:

ਬਹੁਤ ਜਨਮ ਬਿਛੁਰੇ ਥੇ ਮਾਧਉ ਇਹੁ ਜਨਮੁ ਤੁਮ੍ਹਾਰੇ ਲੇਖੇ ॥
ਕਹਿ ਰਵਿਦਾਸ ਆਸ ਲਗਿ ਜੀਵਉ ਚਿਰ ਭਇਓ ਦਰਸਨੁ ਦੇਖੇ ॥

Bahut janam bichhuray thay Madho, eh janam
tumhaaray lekhay;
Keh Ravidas aas lug jeevau chir bhaeo darsan dekhay.

बहुत जनम बिछुरे थे माधउ इहु जनमु तुम्हारे लेखे ॥
कहि रविदास आस लगि जीवउ चिर भइओ दरसनु देखे ॥

For many incarnations I have been separated from You O
Lord, I dedicate this life to You.
Says Ravidas, I live in great expectation, it's been so long
since I saw You.

Ravidas/694/8

As per the ancient Indian thought we are born as a soul
detached from God to have an experience of duality, while
living in this material world. We continue to be born again

and again till we have all positive and negative experiences and have cleared our karmic debts.

There are two schools of thought on whether, after being born as human beings, we can slip back to lower forms or not. Some believe there is no going back to lower forms, the progress is only upward, or God-ward. As per SGGS, if we have not lived a good honest life we may slip back into lower forms. There is also a view that any going back is only temporary for leaning specific lessons; by and large the journey is upward.

This is what Guru Arjan Dev says:

ਸੰਤਨ ਕੈ ਦੂਖਨਿ ਸਰਪ ਜੋਨਿ ਪਾਇ ॥
ਸੰਤ ਕੈ ਦੂਖਨਿ ਤ੍ਰਿਗਦ ਜੋਨਿ ਕਿਰਮਾਇ ॥

Santan kai dookhan sarp jone paaye.
Sant kai dookhan trigad jone kirmaaye.

संतन कै दूखनि सरप जोनि पाइ ॥
संत कै दूखनि त्रिगद जोनि किरमाइ ॥

He who causes pain to the holy people will reincarnate as a snake.
He who causes pain to the holy will reincarnate as a crawling worm.

M5/279/17

Bhagat Trilochan also writes on this issue:

ਅੰਤਿ ਕਾਲਿ ਜੋ ਲਛਮੀ ਸਿਮਰੈ ਐਸੀ ਚਿੰਤਾ ਮਹਿ ਜੇ ਮਰੈ ॥
ਸਰਪ ਜੋਨਿ ਵਲਿ ਵਲਿ ਅਉਤਰੈ ॥

Unt kaal jo lachhmi simrai aisee chinta meh jay marai.
Sarp jone val val aotarai.

अंति कालि जो लछमी सिमरै ऐसी चिंता महि जे मरै॥
सरप जोनि वलि वलि अउतरै॥

At the last moment, he who worships wealth, and dies with
such thinking,
shall reincarnate again and again as a serpent.

Trilochan/526/5

Bhagat Trilochan then continues to say that even at the
last moment, if one thinks only of women he will be reborn as
a prostitute, if one thinks of his children he will be reborn as
a pig, and if one thinks of mansions/homes he will be reborn
as an evil spirit.

He finally tells us what to think in the dying moments:

ਅੰਤਿ ਕਾਲਿ ਨਾਰਾਇਣੁ ਸਿਮਰੈ ਐਸੀ ਚਿੰਤਾ ਮਹਿ ਜੇ ਮਰੈ॥
ਬਦਤਿ ਤਿਲੋਚਨੁ ਤੇ ਨਰ ਮੁਕਤਾ ਪੀਤੰਬਰੁ ਵਾ ਕੇ ਰਿਦੈ ਬਸੈ॥

Unt kaal Narayan simrai aisee chinta meh jay marai.
Badat Tilochan tay nar mukta Pitamber va kay ridhai bassai.

अंति कालि नाराइणु सिमरै ऐसी चिंता महि जे मरै॥
बदति तिलोचनु ते नर मुकता पीतम्बरु वा के रिदै बसै॥

At the last moment, one who worships the Lord, and dies in
such thinking;
Says Trilochan, such person shall be liberated, the Lord shall
reside in his heart.

Trilochan/526/10

Some very unfortunate people don't pray or think of God
even in their dying moments. There is a story of a shop owner,
a father of three sons, who is about to breathe his last. He asks

his wife where his elder son is. She says don't worry he is right here, and tells him this is the moment to pray. Then he asks about the middle son. Wife tells him he is also here and again asks him to pray. He then asks about his youngest son. His wife tells him that the youngest son is also next to him and begs him to think of God and pray. The man's last words were, "You good for nothing fools who is looking after the shop?"

If you haven't prayed while you were living in the world, at least pray when you are leaving the world.

"The soul comes from without into the human body, as into a temporary abode, and it goes out of it anew... it passes into other habitations, for the soul is immortal."

Ralph Waldo Emerson (1803-1882)
American Philosopher

CHAPTER 7

GURU

ੴ

Guru is a Sanskrit word, which as per *Advaya Taraka Upanishad*, is a combination of two syllables *gu* and *ru*. *Gu* means darkness and *ru* means destroyer, hence guru means the one who destroys or dispels darkness. This is also the meaning ascribed to guru in SGGS.

A true guru is a God-realized man or a woman, who has followers/disciples. Every enlightened person may or may not have followers, but a guru must have. The task of a guru is to make the disciple follow the spiritual path to enlightenment, and remains with him, to guide & supervise him, till the achievement of his goal. There is a very strong bond between the two based on a mutual commitment and respect. In the west guru is considered more or less like a teacher. Some use this word to define a specialist in a particular field, like management guru or fitness guru and so on.

In the ancient Indian tradition there were six grades of teachers as under:

1. *Adhyapak*: Gives information.
2. *Upadhya*: Imparts knowledge with information.
3. *Acharya*: Imparts skill.
4. *Pandit*: Gives deep insight.

5. *Dhrishta*: Has visionary view on a subject.

6. *Guru*: Leads from darkness to light.

Guru is at the top of the ladder. He is no ordinary teacher or expert, he is much more. To give you an idea here are a few differences between an ordinary teacher and the guru:

A teacher has many students, guru has few disciples.

Teacher is not selected by his students, guru and disciple find and accept each other.

Teacher imparts knowledge, guru imparts spiritual wisdom.

Teacher takes responsibility for his students, guru makes the disciples responsible.

Teacher leads a student to success, guru leads the disciple to liberation.

Teacher has limited association with students, guru has lifetime association with disciples.

Teacher boosts student's ego, guru annihilates disciple's ego.

Teacher broadens his student's mental horizon, guru awakens disciple's consciousness.

Teacher is concerned with mind of the student, guru is concerned with the soul of the disciple.

Teacher need not be spiritually awakened - guru is.

A guru is not judged by the number of followers he has, but by number of those he leads to enlightenment.

Let us now focus on guru's greatness as described in SGGS. Guidance of a guru is of immense value for those in pursuit of enlightenment. Guru Nanak says there is no awakening without the guru:

ਭਾਈ ਰੇ ਗੁਰ ਬਿਨੁ ਗਿਆਨੁ ਨ ਹੋਇ॥

Bhaayee ray gur bin giyaan na hoye.

भाई रे गुर बिनु गिआनु न होइ॥

O brother, without the guru, there is no awakening.

M1/59/7

Guru Angad Dev says, without the guru there is total darkness:

ਜੇ ਸਉ ਚੰਦਾ ਉਗਵਹਿ ਸੂਰਜ ਚੜਹਿ ਹਜਾਰ॥
ਏਤੇ ਚਾਨਣ ਹੋਦਿਆਂ ਗੁਰ ਬਿਨੁ ਘੋਰ ਅੰਧਾਰ॥

Jay sau chanda oogveh suraj chareh hazaar.
Aitay chaanan hondeyan gur bin ghor andhaar.

जे सउ चंदा उगवहि सूरज चड़हि हजार॥
एते चानण होदिआं गुर बिनु घोर अंधार॥

If a hundred moons came up, and a thousand suns arose;
Despite such immense light, without the guru there is utter darkness.

M2/463/1

Guru Ram Das also says that there is darkness without guru, as also there is no salvation without him:

ਗੁਰ ਬਿਨੁ ਘੋਰੁ ਅੰਧਾਰੁ ਗੁਰੂ ਬਿਨੁ ਸਮਝ ਨ ਆਵੈ॥
ਗੁਰ ਬਿਨੁ ਸੁਰਤਿ ਨ ਸਿਧਿ ਗੁਰੂ ਬਿਨੁ ਮੁਕਤਿ ਨ ਪਾਵੈ॥

Gur bin ghor andhaar guru bin samajh na aavai.
Gur bin surat na sidh guru bin mukt na paavai.

गुर बिनु घोरु अंधारु गुरू बिनु समझ न आवै॥
गुर बिनु सुरति न सिधि गुरू बिनु मुकति न पावै॥

Without the guru there is utter darkness, without the guru
there is no clear understanding.
Without the guru, there is no awareness, nor achievement;
without the guru there is no salvation.

M4/1399/16

Guru holds a highly revered and coveted position in the
Indian tradition, and he is often equated with God. This is
what Guru Ram Das says:

ਗੁਰ ਗੋਵਿੰਦੁ ਗੋਵਿੰਦੁ ਗੁਰੂ ਹੈ ਨਾਨਕ ਭੇਦੁ ਨ ਭਾਈ॥

Gur Govind Govind guru hai, Nanak bheyd na bhaayee.

गुर गोविंदु गोविंदु गुरू है नानक भेदु न भाई॥

The guru is God, and God is guru, Nanak says,
O brother there is no difference.

M4/442/18

Guru Arjan Dev also equates guru with God:

ਨਾਨਕ ਸੋਧੇ ਸਿੰਮ੍ਰਿਤਿ ਬੇਦ॥ ਪਾਰਬ੍ਰਹਮ ਗੁਰ ਨਾਹੀ ਭੇਦ॥

Nanak sodhay simrit beyd; parbrahm gur naahi bheyd.

नानक सोधे सिम्रिति बेद॥ पारब्रहम गुर नाही भेद॥

Nanak has studied the *Simritees* and the Vedas.
There is no difference between God and the guru.

M5/1142/8

This is a couplet by Bhagat Kabir (not in SGGS), on God and guru being equal. He puts himself in a dilemma about choosing between God and guru and then finds an interesting way out. He says:

"Guru Govind Dou Khaday Kaku Laagoon Paaye?"
[Guru and God are both standing in front of me, whose feet should I touch (show respect to) first?]

He doesn't know what to do; it is a tricky situation. The guru gives him an indication to go to God first. He hesitates, then goes to guru and touches his feet first saying:

"Balihari Guru Aapanay Jin Govind Diyo Bataaye."
(I submit myself unto my guru, because he is the one who made me realize God.)

Bhagat Kabir defines guru thus:

> ਕਹੁ ਕਬੀਰ ਮੈ ਸੋ ਗੁਰੁ ਪਾਇਆ ਜਾ ਕਾ ਨਾਉ ਬਿਬੇਕ ॥
>
> Kaho Kabir mai so gur paayaa ja ka nao bibek.
>
> कहु कबीर मै सो गुरु पाइआ जा का नाउ बिबेकु ॥
>
> **Says Kabir, I have found the guru, whose name is awareness.**
>
> **Kabir/793/11**

Guru Arjan Dev speaks of the necessity of worshipping a guru for attaining salvation:

> ਗੁਰ ਕੇ ਚਰਨ ਰਿਦੈ ਲੈ ਧਾਰਉ ॥ ਗੁਰੁ ਪਾਰਬ੍ਰਹਮੁ ਸਦਾ ਨਮਸਕਾਰਉ ॥
> ਮਤ ਕੋ ਭਰਮਿ ਭੁਲੈ ਸੰਸਾਰਿ ॥ ਗੁਰ ਬਿਨੁ ਕੋਇ ਨ ਉਤਰਸਿ ਪਾਰਿ ॥
>
> Gur kay charan ridai lai dhaarao, gur Parbraham sadaa namaskaarao.
> Matt ko bharam bhulai sansaar, gur bin koye na utras paar.

ਗੁਰ ਕੇ ਚਰਨ ਰਿਦੈ ਲੈ ਧਾਰਉ॥ ਗੁਰੁ ਪਾਰਬ੍ਰਹਮੁ ਸਦਾ ਨਮਸਕਾਰਉ॥
ਮਤ ਕੋ ਭਰਮਿ ਭੁਲੈ ਸੰਸਾਰਿ॥ ਗੁਰ ਬਿਨੁ ਕੋਇ ਨ ਉਤਰਸਿ ਪਾਰਿ॥

Let guru's feet touch your heart, always bow before guru, the God.
Let there be no doubt, without the guru, no one can cross
over (attain salvation).

M5/864/2

Guru Amar Das says you can't even worship without the guru's guidance:

ਭਾਈ ਰੇ ਗੁਰ ਬਿਨੁ ਭਗਤਿ ਨ ਹੋਇ॥ ਬਿਨੁ ਗੁਰ ਭਗਤਿ ਨ ਪਾਈਐ ਜੇ ਲੋਚੈ ਸਭੁ ਕੋਇ॥

Bhaayee ray gur bin bhagat na hoye, bin gur bhagat na
paayeeyai jay lochai sabh koye.

भाई रे गुर बिनु भगति न होइ॥ बिनु गुर भगति न पाईऐ जे लोचै सभु कोइ॥

O brother, there can be no worship without the guru.
Without the guru, worship is not possible, even though
everyone may want it.

M3/31/17

Guru Ram Das on devotion to guru:

ਹਮ ਮਲਿ ਮਲਿ ਧੋਵਹ ਪਾਵ ਗੁਰੂ ਕੇ ਜੋ ਹਰਿ ਹਰਿ ਕਥਾ ਸੁਨਾਵੈ॥

Hum mal mal dhoveh paav guru kay jo Har Har katha sunavai.

हम मलि मलि धोवह पाव गुरू के जो हरि हरि कथा सुनावै॥

I rub and wash guru's feet, who tells us the story of the Lord.

M4/172/15

Guru Arjan Dev again highlights the need for a guru to attain liberation:

ਕੋਟਿ ਜਤਨਾ ਕਰਿ ਰਹੇ ਗੁਰ ਬਿਨੁ ਤਰਿਓ ਨ ਕੋਇ॥

Kot jatnaa kar rahay gur bin tareyo na koye.

कोटि जतना करि रहे गुर बिनु तरिओ न कोइ॥

Trying a million things, people have grown weary, but without the guru, none has swum across.

M5/51/4

Without the guru the inner filth of ego is not cleansed and one loses the game of life, says Guru Arjan Dev:

ਕਿਰਿਆਚਾਰ ਕਰਹਿ ਖਟੁ ਕਰਮਾ ਇਤੁ ਰਾਤੇ ਸੰਸਾਰੀ॥
ਅੰਤਰਿ ਮੈਲੁ ਨ ਉਤਰੈ ਹਉਮੈ ਬਿਨੁ ਗੁਰ ਬਾਜੀ ਹਾਰੀ॥

Kiriachaar kareh khutt karma it raatay sansaaree.
Antar mael na utrai haumai bin gur baaji haaree.

किरिआचार करहि खटु करमा इतु राते संसारी॥
अंतरि मैलु न उतरै हउमै बिनु गुर बाजी हारी॥

People perform rituals and religious rites, the world is engrossed in these things.
Without the guru they are not cleansed of the filth of their ego, they lose the game of life.

M5/495/10

Guru Arjan Dev now advises us to leave aside our cleverness and follow the guru:

ਮਨ ਮੇਰੇ ਕਰਤੇ ਨੋ ਸਾਲਾਹਿ॥ ਸਭੇ ਛਡਿ ਸਿਆਣਪਾ ਗੁਰ ਕੀ ਪੈਰੀ ਪਾਹਿ॥

Munn meray kartay no salaahay, sabhay chhad sianpa gur ki pairee paahay.

मन मेरे करते नो सालाहि॥ सभे छडि सिआणपा गुर की पैरी पाहि॥

O my mind, praise the Creator. Leave aside all your cleverness, and be at the feet of the guru.

M5/43/17

As we have seen, it is not possible to rise spiritually without the help of a guru. But where do we find a true guru? It is a difficult search because, for one true guru, there are thousands of fakes out to fleece you. The number of followers a guru has is no criteria for his genuineness. We have seen in the recent past how the biggest crowd pulling gurus and *babas* turned out to be the worst criminals. Gullible people easily fall prey to the sweet talk and some tricks here and there by these fakes. We don't give much to the tricks shown by roadside magicians, but same trick shown by a so-called guru becomes a miracle. A true guru does not need large crowds to sustain his ego – he has already overcome that.

This is not a new problem, it's been there since olden times. Jesus told his disciples, "Beware of false prophets, which come to you in sheep's clothing, but inwardly they are ravening wolves," (Matthew 7:15). I know of a case in recent times where the so-called guru took full advantage of his disciple, ill treated him, took all his money and then left him in the lurch.

In present times it is indeed difficult to find a true guru. Guru Gobind Singh, the 10th Guru, resolved these problems when he ordained all Sikhs to accept SGGS as their guru. He told the seekers to search for God in the *gurbani* of SGGS. Therefore, you need not have a living guru, just read and follow the advice given in SGGS - all your needs of a spiritual guru will be met.

In Sikhism, the most commonly used word for God is 'Waheguru', which means wondrous guru, or wondrous destroyer of darkness. Interestingly, this name for God has not been used in SGGS by any of the Sikh Gurus. It only figures in Bhatt *bani*, on pages 1402-1404; and also in *Vaars* of Bhai Gurdas (not part of SGGS). However, the Sikh salutation, *"Waheguru Ji Ka Khalsa, Waheguru Ji Ki Fateh"* was given by Guru Gobind Singh.

"I have never said that there is no need for a guru. All depends on what you call guru. He need not be in human form."

Ramana Maharshi (1879-1950)
Indian Sage

CHAPTER 8

MAYA

Is our universe and everything we see around us real, or is it false and just an illusion (*maya*)? The answer is both. It all depends on our perception - how we look at it. If we see it from the physicality point of view the universe is real. Everything around us, the sun, stars, earth, jungles, mountains, lakes, oceans, all are as real as you and me. Similarly, learning, earning, relatives, friends, teachers, homes, schools, temples - everything is real. How can we deny this?

But then so is everything very real in our dream world. The dreams are so real that our body reacts as if the dream events were actually happening to us. If there is a threat situation our body actually starts shaking & sweating, and our heartbeat goes up as it does in real life. Responding to a threat in the dream we also make sounds and noises which even wake up the person sleeping close by. During the dream we experience all sorts of real-life emotions such as fear, joy, anxiety, happiness, sadness and so on. But when we wake up it's all gone. It was just a dream.

If our life is seen in a similar way, it is only a dream, but a dream that lasts somewhat longer - a lifetime. However, when seen in the context of our soul's journey of thousands of lives, one life's journey may not seem all that long.

After we die, we wake up in a different world which is not in the material plane but a spiritual one. The physicality is gone. It will be experienced again after we are reborn – which is the beginning of another life-time, another dream. We continue this cycle of birth and death till salvation.

When we see the world from a physical point of view it is real, but seen from spiritual angle it is all false, untrue, illusion, *maya*. In SGGS our gurus see life mainly from spiritual viewpoint hence they believe physical life to be a false dream.

Guru Arjan Dev says this creation is all false:

ਸੰਤ ਸਜਨ ਸੁਨਹੁ ਸਭਿ ਮੀਤਾ ਝੂਠਾ ਏਹੁ ਪਸਾਰਾ॥
ਮੇਰੀ ਮੇਰੀ ਕਰਿ ਕਰਿ ਡੂਬੇ ਖਪਿ ਖਪਿ ਮੁਏ ਗਵਾਰਾ॥
ਗੁਰ ਮਿਲਿ ਨਾਨਕ ਨਾਮੁ ਧਿਆਇਆ ਸਾਚਿ ਨਾਮਿ ਨਿਸਤਾਰਾ॥

Sant sajjan sunoh sabh meeta, jhootha ehu psaara.
Meri meri kar kar doobay khap khap mooye gwaara.
Gur mil Nanak naam dhiaaya saach naam nistaara.

संत सजन सुनहु सभि मीता झूठा एहु पसारा॥
मेरी मेरी करि करि डूबे खपि खपि मुए गवारा॥
गुर मिलि नानक नामु धिआइआ साचि नामि निसतारा॥

O saints, gentlemen, and all friends, listen; this creation is all false.
Trying to own everything people drown, foolish people just struggle and die.
Meet the Guru, Nanak says, meditate on Lord's name; with the help of the True Name you will sail through.

M5/380/3

The idea of sailing through (*nistaara*) is frequently mentioned in SGGS, because our life is compared to a scary ocean.

Crossing that dreaded ocean means having lived in such a way that it leads to salvation.

Guru Teg Bahadur also speaks of the false world:

ਜਗ ਰਚਨਾ ਸਭ ਝੂਠ ਹੈ ਜਾਨਿ ਲੇਹੁ ਰੇ ਮੀਤ॥
ਕਹਿ ਨਾਨਕ ਥਿਰੁ ਨਾ ਰਹੈ ਜਿਉ ਬਾਲੂ ਕੀ ਭੀਤਿ॥

Jug rachna sabh jhooth hai jaan lehu ray meet.
Keh Nanak thir na rahay jiu baaloo ki bheet.

जग रचना सभ झूठ है जानि लेहु रे मीत॥
कहि नानक थिरु ना रहै जिउ बालू की भीति॥

The creation is all false, know this, my friend.
Says Nanak, it shall not endure, it is like a wall of sand.

ਰਾਮੁ ਗਇਓ ਰਾਵਨੁ ਗਇਓ ਜਾ ਕਉ ਬਹੁ ਪਰਵਾਰੁ॥
ਕਹੁ ਨਾਨਕ ਥਿਰੁ ਕਛੁ ਨਹੀ ਸੁਪਨੇ ਜਿਉ ਸੰਸਾਰੁ॥

Ram gaeyo Ravan gaeyo ja kau bahu parvaar.
Kahu Nanak thir kachhu nahi supnay jiu sansaar.

रामु गइओ रावनु गइओ जा कउ बहु परवारु॥
कहु नानक थिरु कछु नही सुपने जिउ संसारु॥

Ram has gone, so has Ravan, even though they had large (great) families.
Nanak says, nothing is permanent, the world is like a dream.

M9/1429/2

Believing this world to be real, we get entangled in it so badly that we forget it is an illusion, and we drift away from true purpose of life, which is to advance spiritually.

Here is another verse by Guru Arjan Dev on dreamlike world:

> ਚੰਚਲੁ ਸੁਪਨੈ ਹੀ ਉਰਝਾਇਓ ॥
> ਇਤਨੀ ਨ ਬੂਝੈ ਕਬਹੁ ਚਲਨਾ ਬਿਕਲ ਭਇਓ ਸੰਗਿ ਮਾਇਓ ॥
>
> Chanchal supnai hee urjhaayeo.
> Itni na bhoojay kab-hoo chalna bikal bhayeo sung maayeo.
>
> चंचलु सुपनै ही उरझाइओ ॥
> इतनी न बूझै कबहू चलना बिकल भइओ संगि माइओ ॥
>
> The fickle dream has entangled man.
> He doesn't understand that he may die any moment, he has
> gone crazy with *maya*.
>
> M5/531/5

The more we get attached to *maya* the lesser is the chance of our reaching God's kingdom. The wealth we accumulate becomes a hindrance to our salvation. Jesus Christ said, "Again I tell you, it is easier for a camel to go through the eye of a needle than for a rich man to enter the kingdom of God." (Matthew 19:24). If you are in pursuit of material success you are going further away from God. Of course, we do need some material things to sustain ourselves in this physical world, but the lesser we can manage with, the better.

Would it be wise for us to get emotionally attached to things we seem to possess in our dreams? Certainly not, because those things are mere illusions. They cannot accompany us, they disappear the moment we wake up.

Guru Nanak also tells us that *maya* of this world will not accompany us:

> ਬਾਬਾ ਮਾਇਆ ਸਾਥਿ ਨ ਹੋਇ ॥ ਇਨਿ ਮਾਇਆ ਜਗੁ ਮੋਹਿਆ ਵਿਰਲਾ ਬੂਝੈ ਕੋਇ ॥
>
> Baba, maya saath na hoye; in maya jug moheya virla
> bhoojai koye.

बाबा माइआ साथि न होइ॥ इनि माइआ जगु मोहिआ विरला बूझै कोइ॥

O sir, *maya* does not accompany us.
This *maya* has bewitched the world, but very few realize this.

M1/595/11

Guru Nanak was a guest of a rich man for few days. Before leaving he gave his host a small sewing needle and told him to keep it till they met again. The rich man was happy and he told his wife about it. She was furious. She said you know Guru Nanak is an old man, he could die anytime, if he does how will you return the needle, and we'll be indebted for life. You cannot take the needle to heaven and return it there. The man realized his mistake, ran after Guru Nanak, caught up a few days later, and begged him to accept the needle back. Guru Nanak said you now realize that you cannot take away even a small needle with you, so why accumulate so much wealth. The man came back home and sold all his valuables and spent the money for benefit of the poor, keeping the bare minimum for himself.

Though the world is only an illusion, it creates an extremely powerful influence on us. We want to possess everything there is in the material world. *Maya* puts us on a chase that is really endless. This was aptly stated by American writer Elbert Hubbard when he said, "Life is just one damn thing after another." We are never satisfied with *maya*. We just forget that it is all false, all temporary.

Bhagat Kabir says the power of *maya* is so strong that it cheated even the gods:

ਸਰਪਨੀ ਤੇ ਉਪਰਿ ਨਹੀ ਬਲੀਆ ॥
ਜਿਨਿ ਬ੍ਰਹਮਾ ਬਿਸਨੁ ਮਹਾਦੇਉ ਛਲੀਆ ॥

> Sarpani tay ooper nahi baliya.
> Jin Brahma, Bisan, Mahadeo chhaliya.
>
> सरपनी ते ऊपरि नही बलीआ॥
> जिनि ब्रह्मा बिसनु महादेउ छलीआ॥
>
> **Nothing is more powerful than the serpent (*maya*);**
> **Which deceived even Brahma, Vishnu and Mahadev.**
>
> Kabir/480/16

Guru Teg Bahadur again tells us that none of the manifestations of *maya* will accompany us:

> ਧਨੁ ਦਾਰਾ ਸੰਪਤਿ ਸਗਲ ਜਿਨਿ ਅਪੁਨੀ ਕਰਿ ਮਾਨਿ॥
> ਇਨ ਮੈ ਕਛੁ ਸੰਗੀ ਨਹੀ ਨਾਨਕ ਸਾਚੀ ਜਾਨਿ॥
>
> Dhan daara sampat sagal jin apni kar maan.
> In mein kachhu sangee nahi Nanak saachi jaan.
>
> धनु दारा स्मपति सगल जिनि अपुनी करि मानि॥
> इन मै कछु संगी नही नानक साची जानि॥
>
> **Money, wife, wealth - all these things you claim as your own;**
> **None of these shall accompany you, says Nanak, know this**
> **to be true.**
>
> M9/1426/15

Another aspect of *maya* is that anything that is born or created in time will die in time. Some insects have a life span of few hours, human beings last several decades and the universe lasts billions of years. But in the end they all must perish. Only God remains, because God is the only Truth, He is not false, He is not an illusion. He is not born in time. As mentioned in the first chapter, He is *Akaal Moorat* - Timeless, *Ajuni* – beyond the cycle of death and rebirth, *Saibhang* – was not created by anyone, He created Himself.

When we die nothing material (*maya*) will accompany us. Only the imprint of our good and bad deeds will remain with our souls.

Here Guru Teg Bahadur says life is like a bubble:

ਜੈਸੇ ਜਲ ਤੇ ਬੁਦਬੁਦਾ ਉਪਜੈ ਬਿਨਸੈ ਨੀਤ ॥
ਜਗ ਰਚਨਾ ਤੈਸੇ ਰਚੀ ਕਹੁ ਨਾਨਕ ਸੁਨਿ ਮੀਤ ॥

Jaisay jal tay budbuda upjai binsai neet.
Jug rachna taisay rachi kahu Nanak sunn meet.

जैसे जल ते बुदबुदा उपजै बिनसै नीत ॥
जग रचना तैसे रची कहु नानक सुनि मीत ॥

Like bubbles in the water well up and disappear regularly.
Listen O friend, says Nanak, the universe is created like that.
M9/1427/16

Guru Teg Bahadur further clarifies how *maya's* strong influence has made man forget God:

ਕਾਮ ਕ੍ਰੋਧ ਮੋਹ ਬਸਿ ਪ੍ਰਾਨੀ ਹਰਿ ਮੂਰਤਿ ਬਿਸਰਾਈ ॥
ਝੂਠਾ ਤਨੁ ਸਾਚਾ ਕਰਿ ਮਾਨਿਓ ਜਿਉ ਸੁਪਨਾ ਰੈਨਾਈ ॥

Kaam krodh moh bus praani Har murat bisraayee.
Jhootha tann saachaa kar maneyo jiu supna rainaayee.

काम क्रोध मोह बसि प्रानी हरि मूरति बिसराई ॥
झूठा तनु साचा करि मानिओ जिउ सुपना रैनाई ॥

Lust, anger and attachment have so overpowered the man that he has forgotten the Lord's image/vision. He believes the false body to be true, but it is like a dream of the night.

ਜੋ ਦੀਸੈ ਸੋ ਸਗਲ ਬਿਨਾਸੈ ਜਿਉ ਬਾਦਰ ਕੀ ਛਾਈ ॥
ਜਨ ਨਾਨਕ ਜਗੁ ਜਾਨਿਓ ਮਿਥਿਆ ਰਹਿਓ ਰਾਮ ਸਰਨਾਈ ॥

Jo deesai so sagal binaasai jiu baadar ki chhaayee.
Jan Nanak jug janeyo mithiya reheyo Ram sarnaayee.

जो दीसै सो सगल बिनासै जिउ बादर की छाई ॥
जन नानक जगु जानिओ मिथिआ रहिओ राम सरनाई ॥

Whatever is seen, shall all perish, like the shadow of a cloud.
Says Nanak, one who knows the world to be false, dwells in Lord's refuge.

M9/219/6

Bhagat Kabir says one must always dwell on God's name as nothing else is permanent:

ਕਿਆ ਮਾਂਗਉ ਕਿਛੁ ਥਿਰੁ ਨਾਹੀ ॥ ਰਾਮ ਨਾਮ ਰਖੁ ਮਨ ਮਾਹੀ ॥

Kya maangao kichhu thir naahee, Ram naam rakh munn maahee.

किआ मांगउ किछु थिरु नाही ॥ राम नाम रखु मन माही ॥

What should I ask for? Nothing is permanent.
Just keep Lord's Name in the mind.

Kabir/692/9

In the verse below Guru Amar Das says that *maya* is a constant source of pain, yet we continue to pursue it:

ਹਮ ਕੀਆ ਹਮ ਕਰਹਗੇ ਹਮ ਮੂਰਖ ਗਾਵਾਰ ॥
ਕਰਨੈ ਵਾਲਾ ਵਿਸਰਿਆ ਦੂਜੈ ਭਾਇ ਪਿਆਰੁ ॥

Hum keeya hum karhagay hum moorakh gaawaar.
Karnai wala visreya doojai bhai piyaar.

हम कीआ हम करहगे हम मूरख गावार ॥
करणै वाला विसरिआ दूजै भाइ पिआरु ॥

I have done it, and I will do it again - I am a stupid rustic.
I have forgotten the Creator, I am in love of duality (*maya*).

ਮਾਇਆ ਜੇਵਡ ਦੁਖੁ ਨਹੀ ਸਭਿ ਭਵਿ ਥਕੇ ਸੰਸਾਰੁ ॥
ਗੁਰਮਤੀ ਸੁਖੁ ਪਾਈਐ ਸਚੁ ਨਾਮੁ ਉਰ ਧਾਰਿ ॥

Maya jevad dukh nahi sabh bhav thakay sansaar.
Gurmati sukh paayeeyai such naam ur dhaar.

माइआ जेवडु दुखु नही सभि भवि थके संसारु ॥
गुरमती सुखु पाईऐ सचु नामु उर धारि ॥

There is no pain greater than that of *maya*, it drives everyone to wander the world till exhaustion.
Find happiness from guru's teachings, with True Name enshrined in the heart.

M3/39/11

Guru Teg Bahadur tells us that pursuit of *maya* is so captivating that it makes us forget everything else:

ਪ੍ਰਾਨੀ ਕਛੁ ਨ ਚੇਤਈ ਮਦਿ ਮਾਇਆ ਕੈ ਅੰਧੁ ॥
ਕਹੁ ਨਾਨਕ ਬਿਨੁ ਹਰਿ ਭਜਨ ਪਰਤ ਤਾਹਿ ਜਮ ਫੰਧ ॥

Praani kachhu na chetayee madh maya kai andh.
Kahu Nanak bin Har bhajan parat taahay jum phand.

ਪ੍ਰਾਨੀ ਕਛੂ ਨ ਚੇਤਈ ਮਦਿ ਮਾਇਆ ਕੈ ਅੰਧੁ॥
ਕਹੁ ਨਾਨਕ ਬਿਨੁ ਹਰਿ ਭਜਨ ਪਰਤ ਤਾਹਿ ਜਮ ਫੰਧ॥

Man does not think of anything else, he is so blinded by the
intoxicating *maya*.
Says Nanak, because of not singing Lord's praises, he is
caught by the noose of death.

M9/1427/16

The 13th century Persian poet, Rumi rightly said, "The more awake one is to the material world, the more one is asleep to the spirit."

Guru Nanak now tells us how everyone is so entrapped by *maya* that no one seems to be interested in God:

ਸੁਤ ਕੰਚਨ ਸਿਉ ਹੇਤੁ ਵਧਾਇਆ॥ ਸਭੁ ਕਿਛੁ ਅਪਨਾ ਇਕੁ ਰਾਮੁ ਪਰਾਇਆ॥

Sut kanchan siu heyt vadhaayaa, sabh kichhu apna ik Ram
praayaa.

सुत कंचन सिउ हेतु वधाइआ॥ सभु किछु अपना इकु रामु पराइआ॥

Love for his progeny and for gold (wealth) keeps increasing.
He sees everything as his own, except the Lord, which he
thinks belongs to someone else.

M1/1342/14

One day a man asked God, "What's the difference in your love and my love?" God smiled and replied, "A bird in the sky is my love and a bird in the cage is your love". We yearn for control and ownership of everything - which gives us nothing but pain.

In this chapter I have given few quotations on *maya*, but SGGS is full of references to it, and about the need to overpower its terrible influences.

There are two major hurdles in our way to spiritual development. One is *maya* and the other ego. We look at ego in the next chapter.

"Do not be misled by what you see around you, or be influenced by what you see. You live in a world which is a playground of illusion, full of false paths, false values and false ideals. But you are not part of that world."

Sai Baba (1838-1918)
Indian Saint

CHAPTER 9

EGO

ੴ

Ego is often referred to as 'The Problem of Life.' It is the barrier between our individual souls and the Supreme Soul from which we stand separated. As per ancient Indian belief we have been seduced by ego into a state of ignorance and illusion, and therefore we need to break this barrier. "Ego is the biggest enemy of humans," says Rig Veda. SGGS is full of references to ego, and the need to get rid of it. The word used for ego in SGGS is *haumai*, a combination of *hau* (meaning 'I') and *mai* (meaning 'am'). It implies conceit, an exaggerated opinion about oneself, and excessive pride. For success in material world some pride is required, and may be even desirable. However, for those on spiritual path ego is the biggest hindrance.

Even small ego is bad because it has the habit of bloating and taking complete hold of you. The higher you climb in life the bigger the ego. For some people this ego becomes so large that it makes them challenge even God. Brahma, the Hindu creator god could not meet the Supreme God just because he was unable to shed his big ego. That is the power of ego you have to fight.

Truth is, where ego is, God is not, and where God is, ego automatically disappears. The two cannot co-exist, as Guru Amar Das says:

ਹਉਮੈ ਨਾਵੈ ਨਾਲਿ ਵਿਰੋਧੁ ਹੈ ਦੁਇ ਨ ਵਸਹਿ ਇਕ ਠਾਇ॥

Haumai naavai naal virodh hai doye na vaseh ikk thaaye.

हउमै नावै नालि विरोधु है दुइ न वसहि इक ठाइ॥

Ego is opposed to God, the two cannot live in one place together.

M3/560/12

Bhagat Ravidas addresses God here on shedding of his ego:

ਜਬ ਹਮ ਹੋਤੇ ਤਬ ਤੂ ਨਾਹੀ ਅਬ ਤੂਹੀ ਮੈ ਨਾਹੀ॥

Jabb hum hotay tabb tu naahi abb tuhi mai naahi.

जब हम होते तब तू नाही अब तूही मै नाही॥

When I (ego) existed You did not, now it is only You, I'm no longer there.

Ravidas/657/17

Bhagat Kabir has similar views:

ਜਬ ਹਮ ਹੋਤੇ ਤਬ ਤੁਮ ਨਾਹੀ ਅਬ ਤੁਮ ਹਹੁ ਹਮ ਨਾਹੀ॥
ਅਬ ਹਮ ਤੁਮ ਏਕ ਭਏ ਹਹਿ ਏਕੈ ਦੇਖਤ ਮਨੁ ਪਤੀਆਹੀ॥

Jabb hum hotay tabb tum naahi abb tum hahu hum naahi.
Abb hum tum ek bhaye heh ekkai dekhat mun patiaahi.

जब हम होते तब तुम नाही अब तुम हहु हम नाही॥
अब हम तुम एक भए हहि एकै देखत मनु पतीआही॥

When I existed You did not. Now it is only You, I am no longer there.
Now You and I are one, seeing this my mind is at rest.

Kabir/339/7

What Bhagats Ravidas and Kabir are saying is, either it is me (my ego) or You (God). Both cannot be there together. Ego is indeed a very strong devil that you have to conquer.

In the verse below Guru Nanak explains how ego controls us at every stage of life, in everything we do. This happens because we are totally detached from God and take a very selfish view all the time. Only when we understand this separation and eliminate it, can we hope to seek entrance into God's domain:

ਹਉ ਵਿਚਿ ਆਇਆ ਹਉ ਵਿਚਿ ਗਇਆ ॥ ਹਉ ਵਿਚਿ ਜੰਮਿਆ ਹਉ ਵਿਚਿ ਮੁਆ ॥

Hau vich aaya hau vich gaiya, hau vich jameya hau vich mua.

हउ विचि आइआ हउ विचि गइआ॥ हउ विचि जमिआ हउ विचि मुआ॥

In ego one arrives, in ego one departs, in ego one is born, in ego one dies.

ਹਉ ਵਿਚਿ ਦਿਤਾ ਹਉ ਵਿਚਿ ਲਇਆ ॥ ਹਉ ਵਿਚਿ ਖਟਿਆ ਹਉ ਵਿਚਿ ਗਇਆ ॥

Hau vich ditta hau vich laiya, hau vich khatteya hau vich gaiya.

हउ विचि दिता हउ विचि लइआ॥ हउ विचि खटिआ हउ विचि गइआ॥

In ego one gives, and in ego one takes, in ego one earns, and in ego one loses.

M1/466/10

This verse continues as translated below:

"In ego one is truthful or false, in ego one reflects on virtue and sin, in ego one takes form in heaven or hell.

In ego one laughs, in ego one cries, in ego one collects dirt, in ego one washes clean, in ego one loses social caste and class.

In ego one is foolish, in ego one is wise. One does not understand the significance of salvation and liberation.

In ego one loves *maya*, and in ego one is kept in darkness (by *maya*), in ego life comes into being.

Only when one understands ego, the entrance to Lord's kingdom is known; without spiritual wisdom, one keeps babbling and getting upset."

Guru Angad Dev further explains the nature of ego and how it gets us stuck in the cycle of death and rebirth:

ਹਉਮੈ ਏਹਾ ਜਾਤਿ ਹੈ ਹਉਮੈ ਕਰਮ ਕਮਾਹਿ॥
ਹਉਮੈ ਏਈ ਬੰਧਨਾ ਫਿਰਿ ਫਿਰਿ ਜੋਨੀ ਪਾਹਿ॥

Haumai eha jaat hai haumai karam kamaahay.
Haumai eyee bandhana phir phir joni paahay.

हउमै एहा जाति है हउमै करम कमाहि॥
हउमै एई बंधना फिरि फिरि जोनी पाहि॥

This is the nature of ego, people perform their actions in ego.
This is the bondage of ego which makes us take birth again and again.

M2/466/16

As long as one is controlled by ego there is no hope. Guru Arjan Dev puts it simply:

ਜਬ ਲਗੁ ਮੇਰੀ ਮੇਰੀ ਕਰੈ॥ ਤਬ ਲਗੁ ਕਾਜੁ ਏਕੁ ਨਹੀ ਸਰੈ॥
ਜਬ ਮੇਰੀ ਮੇਰੀ ਮਿਟਿ ਜਾਇ॥ ਤਬ ਪ੍ਰਭ ਕਾਜੁ ਸਵਾਰਹਿ ਆਇ॥

Jabb lagg meri meri karai, tabb lagg kaaj ek nahi sarai.
Jabb meri meri mit jaaye, tabb Prabh kaaj swaareh aaye.

जब लगु मेरी मेरी करै॥ तब लगु काजु एकु नही सरै॥
जब मेरी मेरी मिटि जाइ॥ तब प्रभ काजु सवारहि आइ॥

As long as you keep saying, 'mine mine', not even a single task is accomplished.
When 'mine mine' is obliterated, God comes and resolves all affairs.

M5/1160/19

Another verse by Guru Arjan Dev where he advises us to eliminate ego:

ਸਗਲ ਸਿਆਨਪ ਛਾਡਿ ॥ ਕਰਿ ਸੇਵਾ ਸੇਵਕ ਸਾਜਿ ॥
ਅਪਨਾ ਆਪੁ ਸਗਲ ਮਿਟਾਇ ॥ ਮਨ ਚਿੰਦੇ ਸੋਈ ਫਲ ਪਾਇ ॥

Sagal syanap chhaad, kar sewa sewak saaj.
Apna aap sagal mitaaye, munn chinday seyee phal paaye.

सगल सिआनप छाडि ॥ करि सेवा सेवक साजि ॥
अपना आपु सगल मिटाइ ॥ मन चिंदे सेई फल पाइ ॥

Leave aside all your cleverness, serve (the Lord) and become
a true servant.
Erase all your self-identity (ego), you will then receive the
fruits of your mind's desires.

M5/895/3

Now Bhagat Kabir tells us that ego gives tremendous pain in this life and, because of it, we shall suffer worst pain in afterlife:

ਕਰੈ ਗੁਮਾਨੁ ਚੁਭਹਿ ਤਿਸੁ ਸੂਲਾ ਕੋ ਕਾਢਨ ਕਉ ਨਾਹੀ ॥
ਅਜੈ ਸੁ ਚੋਭ ਕਉ ਬਿਲਲ ਬਿਲਾਤੇ ਨਰਕੇ ਘੋਰ ਪਚਾਹੀ ॥

Karai gumaan chubeh tis soola ko kaadan kau naahi.
Ajai su chobh kau bilal bil-laatay narkay ghor pachaahi.

करै गुमानु चुभहि तिसु सूला को काढन कउ नाही ॥
अजै सु चोभ कउ बिलल बिलाते नरके घोर पचाही ॥

One who is proud of himself is stuck with thorns, and there is
no one to pull them out.
Now, he cries bitterly, in hell he will suffer worst pain.

Kabir/969/15

Ego strikes very cunningly and surreptitiously. Often when people begin to gain some level of spiritual understanding ego takes over. Instead of being humble they become egoistic because of their knowledge. Most of the so called god-men and religious preachers fall in this category. If there is truly a saintly person, in all likelihood, he is hidden from the public eye and is busy somewhere with his devotion to God. He does not need the public glare to satisfy his ego – he doesn't have one. Buddha, it is believed, had the lowest ego. If someone asked him about God he always kept quiet. What could he tell about the Almighty who was beyond description? His silence often made people think he did not believe in God. Truth about God's knowledge is, "He who knows tells not, he who tells knows not." Those who make so much noise about knowing God hardly know Him. Those who know Him hardly speak. However, there are some enlightened people who have been ordained by God to spread His word who are in public view as writers and speakers; but they are few and far between.

The grip ego has on our lives, gives rise to our ever increasing desire for attachment and ownership of material things. The earlier we stop being over dependent on such things the better.

Here Guru Nanak tells us that egoistic people cannot attain God and therefore cannot be happy:

ਹਠੁ ਅਹੰਕਾਰੁ ਕਰੈ ਨਹੀ ਪਾਵੈ ॥ ਪਾਠ ਪੜੈ ਲੇ ਲੋਕ ਸੁਣਾਵੈ ॥
ਤੀਰਥਿ ਭਰਮਸਿ ਬਿਆਧਿ ਨ ਜਾਵੈ ॥ ਨਾਮ ਬਿਨਾ ਕੈਸੇ ਸੁਖੁ ਪਾਵੈ ॥੪॥

Huth ahankaar karai nahi paavai; paath parai lay lok sunaavai.
Teerath bharmas biyaadh na jaavai; naam bina kaisay sukh paavai.

हठु अहंकारु करै नही पावै ॥ पाठ पड़ै ले लोक सुणावै ॥
तीरथि भरमसि बिआधि न जावै ॥ नाम बिना कैसे सुखु पावै ॥

> Stubborn and egoistic people do not attain (Him); they read
> out holy scripts for others.
>
> They wander around on pilgrimages, but their disease is not
> removed. How can they have happiness without the
> True Name?
>
> M1/905/19

Guru Nanak further tells us that you cannot find God with
egoistic deeds and that shedding of ego is a pre-requisite for
finding the Truth and for attaining high spiritual status:

> ਹਉਮੈ ਕਰਤ ਭੇਖੀ ਨਹੀ ਜਾਨਿਆ ॥ ਗੁਰਮੁਖਿ ਭਗਤਿ ਵਿਰਲੇ ਮਨੁ ਮਾਨਿਆ ॥
> ਹਉ ਹਉ ਕਰਤ ਨਹੀ ਸਚੁ ਪਾਈਐ ॥ ਹਉਮੈ ਜਾਇ ਪਰਮ ਪਦੁ ਪਾਈਐ ॥
>
> Haumai karat bhekhi nahi jaaneya; gurmukh bhagat virlay
> munn maanaya.
> Hau hau karat nahee such paayee-ai; haumai jaaye param
> padd payee-ai.
>
> हउमै करत भेखी नही जानिआ ॥ गुरमुखि भगति विरले मनु मानिआ ॥
> हउ हउ करत नही सचु पाईऐ ॥ हउमै जाइ परम पदु पाईऐ ॥
>
> God is not known by egoistic deeds; rare are the God-
> oriented worshippers who control their minds.
> You cannot attain Truth by repeated indulgence in ego; only
> when ego departs the high spiritual position is attained.
>
> ਹਉਮੈ ਕਰਿ ਰਾਜੇ ਬਹੁ ਧਾਵਹਿ ॥ ਹਉਮੈ ਖਪਹਿ ਜਨਮਿ ਮਰਿ ਆਵਹਿ ॥
> ਹਉਮੈ ਨਿਵਰੈ ਗੁਰ ਸਬਦੁ ਵੀਚਾਰੈ ॥ ਚੰਚਲ ਮਤਿ ਤਿਆਗੈ ਪੰਚ ਸੰਘਾਰੈ ॥
>
> Haumai kar raajay boh dhaaveh; haumai khapeh janam
> mar aaveh.
> Haumai nivrai gur sabad vichaarai; chanchal mutt tiaagai
> panch sanghaarai.

हउमै करि राजे बहु धावहि॥ हउमै खपहि जनमि मरि आवहि॥
हउमै निवरै गुर सबदु वीचारै॥ चंचल मति तिआगै पंच संघारै॥

Because of ego kings want to rule over others; the ego
exhausts them and they die, to be born again.
Ego is overcome by contemplating on Guru's word; then the
fickle mind is subdued and the five senses are brought
under control.

M1/226/14

Baba Bulle Shah (1680-1757), the famous Punjabi Sufi poet,
shares above views of Guru Nanak on the need to demolish
the ego. He says, *"Bulle Shah Gull Taeeyon Mukdee, Jadon Mai
Nu Dilon Gawaeeyai."* (The issue - of attainment - is settled
only when you let go of the ego from within your heart.)

Guru Amar Das says, serve the True Lord and kill the ego
within, to attain happiness:

ਸਤਿਗੁਰੁ ਸੇਵੇ ਸੋ ਸੁਖੁ ਪਾਏ ਜਿਨ ਹਉਮੈ ਵਿਚਹੁ ਮਾਰੀ॥
ਨਾਨਕ ਪੜਣਾ ਗੁਨਣਾ ਇਕੁ ਨਾਉ ਹੈ ਬੂਝੈ ਕੋ ਬੀਚਾਰੀ॥

Satgur sevay so sukh paaye jin haumai vichoh maaree.
Nanak parhnaa gun-na ik Nao hai bhoojhai ko bichaaree.

सतिगुरु सेवे सो सुखु पाए जिन हउमै विचहु मारी॥
नानक पड़णा गुनणा इकु नाउ है बूझै को बीचारी॥

Those who serve the True Guru, kill the ego from within,
attain happiness.
Nank says, there is only One Name to be studied and
contemplated; only few understand and reflect upon it.

M3/1246/16

Finally, a bit of advice from Guru Teg Bahadur for the saintly:

ਸਾਧੋ ਮਨ ਕਾ ਮਾਨੁ ਤਿਆਗਉ ॥
ਕਾਮੁ ਕ੍ਰੋਧੁ ਸੰਗਤਿ ਦੁਰਜਨ ਕੀ ਤਾ ਤੇ ਅਹਿਨਿਸਿ ਭਾਗਉ ॥

Saadho munn ka maan teyaagou.
Kaam karodh sangat durjan ki ta tay ahnis bhaagou.

साधो मन का मानु तिआगउ ॥
कामु क्रोधु संगति दुरजन की ता ते अहिनिसि भागउ ॥

O saintly people, shed the ego of your mind.
Day and night, run away from lust, anger and bad company.

M9/219/1

It should now be clear how ego is preventing us from walking the spiritual path. Even in our day to day worldly affairs ego is a great hindrance because it does not allow us to develop healthy relationships. It is too demanding and makes us too selfish. Good relationships are built by sharing and caring.

"The ego is only an illusion, but a very influential one. Letting the ego illusion become your identity can prevent you from knowing your true self."

Dr Wayne W Dyer (1940-2015)
American Motivational Expert

CHAPTER 10

ONENESS

ੴ

Let me start with this couplet from an old song on Guru Nanak written by Charan Singh Safri, which brings out the essence of Oneness:

> *"Nanak Deeyan Gujhiaan Ramzaan Nu Be-Samajh Zamaana Kee Jaanay.*
> *Jin Sabh Jug Apna Samajh Leya, Apna Tay Begaana Kee Jaanay"*
> (What can the ignorant world know of Nanak's hidden indications?
> For him, who has embraced the whole world, there is no separation between self and the other.)

In the first chapter titled 'God' we saw Guru Nanak's view on *Ekoankaar*, where he said, not only is there One God, but there is Oneness and inter-connectedness of His entire creation. Let us explore this further, and look at some verses in SGGS which touch upon the concept of Oneness.

As pointed out earlier, ego is a problem in almost every aspect of our life. It is a problem here too. Ego creates and sustains on our individuality and just cannot tolerate any idea that challenges it. Accepting Oneness and being part of the whole amounts to dropping of the ego, which it will not accept and will give every reason why we should not give up our distinctiveness. Only when we understand and accept this position of the ego, can we start fighting it. When we are successful in neutralizing our ego we are awakened, we have embraced Oneness.

Guru Ram Das says, we are all made from the same source:

ਏਕੋ ਪਵਣੁ ਮਾਟੀ ਸਭ ਏਕਾ ਸਭ ਏਕਾ ਜੋਤਿ ਸਬਾਈਆ ॥

Eko pavan maati sabh eka sabh eka jyot sabaayiaa.

एको पवणु माटी सभ एका सभ एका जोति सबाईआ ॥

Everyone breathes same air, is made of same clay and has the same divine light.

M4/96/9

We don't see the same light because we are blinded.

In the following verse Guru Arjan Dev tells us that God permeates everything, therefore, we are all connected with everything there is:

ਜਪਿ ਏਕ ਪ੍ਰਭੁ ਅਨੇਕ ਰਵਿਆ ਸਰਬ ਮੰਡਲਿ ਛਾਇਆ ॥
ਬ੍ਰਹਮੋ ਪਸਾਰਾ ਬ੍ਰਹਮੁ ਪਸਰਿਆ ਸਭੁ ਬ੍ਰਹਮੁ ਦ੍ਰਿਸਟੀ ਆਇਆ ॥

Japp ek Prabhoo anek raveya sarab mandal chhaaya.
Brhamay pasaara Brahm pasareya sabh Brahm dristi aaya.

जपि एक प्रभू अनेक रविआ सरब मंडलि छाइआ ॥
ब्रहमो पसारा ब्रहमु पसरिआ सभु ब्रहमु द्रिसटी आइआ ॥

Worship the One Lord, which pervades everything in the entire universe.
God created the universe and He permeates through it; everywhere you look, you see God.

M5/782/18

If God is in everything, then we are all parts of the same Oneness. There is no difference between you, me, and anybody/anything else.

Bhagat Namdev has similar views:

ਸਭੁ ਗੋਬਿੰਦੁ ਹੈ ਸਭੁ ਗੋਬਿੰਦ ਹੈ ਗੋਬਿੰਦ ਬਿਨੁ ਨਹੀ ਕੋਈ ॥
ਸੂਤੁ ਏਕੁ ਮਣਿ ਸਤ ਸਹੰਸ ਜੈਸੇ ਓਤਿ ਪੋਤਿ ਪ੍ਰਭੁ ਸੋਈ ॥

Sabh Gobind hai sabh Gobind hai, Gobind bin nahi koyee.
Soot ek munn sat sahans jaisay oat poat Prabh soyee.

सभु गोबिंदु है सभु गोबिंदु है गोबिंद बिनु नही कोई ॥
सूतु एकु मणि सत सहंस जैसे ओति पोति प्रभु सोई ॥

Everything is God, everything is God, there is nothing without God.
As a thread holds hundreds and thousands of beads, similarly God is woven into everything in the creation.

Namdev/485/3

Bhagat Kabir says all men and women are created in God's image, and all gurus and saints are common to all (because we are all One):

ਏਤੇ ਅਉਰਤ ਮਰਦਾ ਸਾਜੇ ਏ ਸਭ ਰੂਪ ਤੁਮ੍ਹਾਰੇ ॥
ਕਬੀਰੁ ਪੂੰਗਰਾ ਰਾਮ ਅਲਹ ਕਾ ਸਭ ਗੁਰ ਪੀਰ ਹਮਾਰੇ ॥

Etay aurat mardaa saajay e sabh roop tumhaaray,
Kabir poongra Ram Allah ka sabh gur peer hamaaray.

एते अउरत मरदा साजे ए सभ रूप तुम्हारे ॥
कबीरु पूंगरा राम अलह का सभ गुर पीर हमारे ॥

You have created so many women and men, they are all in your image;
I am a child of Ram and Allah, says Kabir, and all gurus & saints are mine.

Kabir/1349/16

Once again Guru Arjan Dev says God is in everything, in the material world as well as the spiritual:

ਦਸੇ ਦਿਸਾ ਰਵਿਆ ਪ੍ਰਭੁ ਏਕੁ ॥ ਧਰਨਿ ਅਕਾਸ ਸਭ ਮਹਿ ਪ੍ਰਭ ਪੇਖੁ ॥

ਜਲ ਥਲ ਬਨ ਪਰਬਤ ਪਾਤਾਲ ॥ ਪਰਮੇਸੁਰ ਤਹ ਬਸਹਿ ਦਇਆਲ ॥

ਸੂਖਮ ਅਸਥੂਲ ਸਗਲ ਭਗਵਾਨ ॥ ਨਾਨਕ ਗੁਰਮੁਖਿ ਬ੍ਰਹਮੁ ਪਛਾਨ ॥

Dassay disa raveya Prabh ek, dharan aakaas sabh meh
Prabh pekh.
Jal thal bun parbat paataal, Parmesvar teh baseh dayaal.
Sookham asthool sagal Bhagwaan, Nanak gurmukh
Brham pachhaan.

दसे दिसा रविआ प्रभु एकु ॥ धरनि अकास सभ महि प्रभ पेखु ॥

जल थल बन परबत पाताल ॥ परमेस्वर तह बसहि दइआल ॥

सूखम असथूल सगल भगवान ॥ नानक गुरमुखि ब्रहमु पछान ॥

The One Lord pervades in all directions, you can see Him in
everything on earth and in the sky.
In the manifest and the un-manifest, Lord is everywhere, says
Nanak, the God-oriented people recognize the Creator.

M5/299/16

As long as we are in the grip of our ego, we think of ourselves as separate from other people. Because of this separation, we are unnecessarily haunted by those 'others' who are more successful than us. Most of us operate from a scarcity syndrome; believing there are limited resources in the world and only few can have them - so the 'others' would snatch them from us. As long as there are these 'others', we cannot be at peace, because we feel they want to succeed at our cost and are always looking for opportunities to win by defeating us. We torture ourselves mentally all the time, thinking about these 'others' - who have a higher job position, more money, bigger house, better car, smarter wife, intelligent children, and what not? They are our enemy and competitors who give us hell all the time. French Philosopher, Jean-Paul Sartre aptly summed it up when he said, "Hell is other people".

The only way to tackle these 'others' is to make them our own - embrace Oneness. With this shift in thinking the others become our 'own.' Now their success is our success and their defeat our defeat. There is no enemy now, no competitor. We are all part of Oneness.

Once you begin to believe in Oneness of the creation, your outlook towards life changes dramatically. Now everyone and everything, including you, is part of the whole. That being so, how can you think of harming anyone, how can you not think of helping anyone who's in need. As Rumi, the Persian poet says, "After all you are just another me and I'm just another you". Two things emerge from this changed outlook. One, your relationships take a new turn and become strong and authentic. You feel everyone is part of your family, you can even say that everyone is part of you. Two, you develop an attitude of helping people; community service becomes a sacred duty. The one who was troubling you as the other is now your very own.

To begin with it is a little difficult to grasp this concept of Oneness, because we have been so brain-washed to believe in our individuality of I, me, and mine, that we cannot accept a position of we, us, and ours. We work so hard for our individual achievements, how can we share them? It becomes easier to embrace Oneness when we contemplate on the spiritual side of our being. Our soul, which is our true-self, is a part of the Supreme Soul of God. That is our connectedness with God and everything else. The Source of all creation is the same. How can there be differences amongst us? This realization and acceptance comes as we awaken.

Let us now see some verses of SGGS, which reflect this shift in thinking from 'otherness' to Oneness. Speaking in the spirit of this Oneness Guru Arjan Dev says:

ਨਾ ਕੋ ਮੇਰਾ ਦੁਸਮਨੁ ਰਹਿਆ ਨਾ ਹਮ ਕਿਸ ਕੇ ਬੈਰਾਈ ॥
ਬ੍ਰਹਮੁ ਪਸਾਰੁ ਪਸਾਰਿਓ ਭੀਤਰਿ ਸਤਿਗੁਰ ਤੇ ਸੋਝੀ ਪਾਈ ॥

Na ko meyra dusman reheyaa na hum kis kay bairaayee.
Brahm pasaar pasaareyo bheetar Satgur sojhi paayee.

ना को मेरा दुसमनु रहिआ ना हम किस के बैराई ॥
ब्रहमु पसारु पसारिओ भीतरि सतिगुर ते सोझी पाई ॥

No one is my enemy anymore, and I am not anyone's
enemy either;
God who created His expanse is within all,
my True Guru explained this to me.

M5/671/7

Guru Arjan Dev again, on how our perception changes
when we meet holy people, who awaken us:

ਬਿਸਰਿ ਗਈ ਸਭ ਤਾਤਿ ਪਰਾਈ ॥ ਜਬ ਤੇ ਸਾਧਸੰਗਤਿ ਮੋਹਿ ਪਾਈ ॥
ਨਾ ਕੋ ਬੈਰੀ ਨਹੀ ਬਿਗਾਨਾ ਸਗਲ ਸੰਗਿ ਹਮ ਕਉ ਬਨਿ ਆਈ ॥

Bisar gayee sabh taat praayee, jabb tay saadhsangat
mohay paayee.
Na ko bairee nahi begaana sagal sung hum kao bun aayee.

बिसरि गई सभ ताति पराई ॥ जब ते साधसंगति मोहि पाई ॥
ना को बैरी नही बिगाना सगल संगि हम कउ बनि आई ॥

My jealousy of others has totally disappeared, ever since
I found company of the holy.
No one is my enemy, no one is a stranger to me, I have
friendship with all.

M5/1299/13

Guru Arjan Dev once again on improved relationships with all, and end of separateness:

> ਸਭੁ ਕੋ ਮੀਤੁ ਹਮ ਆਪਨ ਕੀਨਾ ਹਮ ਸਭਨਾ ਕੇ ਸਾਜਨ ॥
> ਦੂਰਿ ਪਰਾਇਓ ਮਨ ਕਾ ਬਿਰਹਾ ਤਾ ਮੇਲੁ ਕੀਓ ਮੇਰੈ ਰਾਜਨ ॥
>
> Sabh ko meet hum aapan keena hum sabhna kay saajan.
> Door praayeo munn ka birha ta mail keeyo meyrai raajan.
>
> सभु को मीतु हम आपन कीना हम सभना के साजन॥
> दूरि पराइओ मन का बिरहा ता मेलु कीओ मेरै राजन॥
>
> **I have made friends with all, I am everyone's friend.**
> **The sense of separation has departed from my mind, and**
> **I am united with my Lord.**
>
> M5/671/8

SGGS tells us not only to wish others well but also help them in every possible way. Towards this end, as we will see later, the spirit and attitude of community service is highly encouraged – by serving others we are indeed serving God. We all belong to Him because we are born from the same Supreme source, there is no difference, we are One. So when we are good to others we ourselves rise spiritually. From this feeling of Oneness emerges the Sikh prayer, *"Nanak Naam Chardhi Kala, Teray Bhaanay Sarbat Da Bhalaa."* (Nanak says, by God's grace we are in ever-rising high spirits, by His wish may the whole world prosper.)

For better understanding Oneness, feel it from within your heart, not from your mind. Heart is the unifying force while the mind is more trained to see divisiveness.

"If you feel oneness even for a fraction of a second, you will feel that your human life is totally transformed and immortalized. Pray to the Supreme to grant you conscious, constant and inseparable oneness with Him. Then the question of separativity will automatically be solved."

Sri Chinmoy (1931-2007)
Indian Spiritual Guru

CHAPTER 11

ACCEPTANCE

ੴ

In the course of our lives we come across problems, difficulties, hardships and other trying conditions. These could be related to health, relationships, finance or other spheres of life. When these conditions are severe and sudden, the normal reaction is to deny them, saying this can't happen to me. We do not easily accept anything bad happening to us. Also, we tend to make others responsible for our miseries, and do not take the blame ourselves. We even question God why He is doing this to us.

The only way to deal with a problem is to first accept that we indeed have a problem and that at some level we ourselves are responsible for it. Only then can we hope to deal with it effectively.

Acceptance is one of the recurring themes of SGGS, which helps us live a happy and contented life, whatever the challenges. What does it mean? What do we have to accept? We must first accept ownership of the situation; and the fact that, though not clearly visible, we are ourselves responsible for it. We then accept that it is all God's will, His command, His order, His wish. Punjabi words for God's will/command are *hukam* or *raza*. Acceptance is also referred to as *bhaana mann-na* which means gracefully accepting whatever happens to us – good or bad. We should also understand that God doesn't give us difficult times without reason.

Our ego may tell us that we have everything under our control but truly we have nothing. We can only attempt to resolve the problem to the best of our ability. The outcome is all God's will.

Guru Nanak says:

> ਹੁਕਮੇ ਆਵੈ ਹੁਕਮੇ ਜਾਇ॥ ਆਗੈ ਪਾਛੈ ਹੁਕਮਿ ਸਮਾਇ॥
>
> Hukmay aavai hukmay jaaye, aagai paachhai hukam samaaye.
>
> हुकमे आवै हुकमे जाइ॥ आगै पाछै हुकमि समाइ॥
>
> **We are born as per His order, and we depart as per His order.**
> **As in the past, so in the future, His will shall prevail.**
>
> M1/151/11

We neither have control over the timing and conditions of our birth, nor of death, but we want to have full control on the course of life in between. We must accept that this course of our life is also going as per God's plan for us.

These difficult times are given to us by God for the purpose of our spiritual growth. We should be thankful to Him for giving us these learning experiences and to accept them as His *hukam*. Thank Him for our miseries? Yes indeed. We'll see more of this in chapter on 'Suffering'.

Guru Nanak says we can progress spiritually by accepting God's will:

> ਕਿਵ ਸਚਿਆਰਾ ਹੋਈਐ ਕਿਵ ਕੂੜੈ ਤੁਟੈ ਪਾਲਿ॥
> ਹੁਕਮਿ ਰਜਾਈ ਚਲਣਾ ਨਾਨਕ ਲਿਖਿਆ ਨਾਲਿ॥
>
> Kiv sachiaara hoeeyai kiv kooreh tuttai paal.
> Hukam rajaayee chalna Nanak likheya naal.

ਕਿਵ ਸਚਿਆਰਾ ਹੋਈਐ ਕਿਵ ਕੂੜੈ ਤੁਟੈ ਪਾਲਿ ॥
ਹੁਕਮਿ ਰਜਾਈ ਚਲਣਾ ਨਾਨਕ ਲਿਖਿਆ ਨਾਲਿ ॥

How can we become true (enlightened)? And how can the veil
of falsehood be broken down?
By living in accordance with God's will.

M1/1/6

Acceptance does not mean that we resign to our fate and do
nothing to improve our troubled situation. We must do our best,
with best of intentions, and then accept whatever comes our way
as God's wish. That is the central teaching of Bhagwat Gita too.
For any result, our effort is the first requirement, the outcome
depends on God's will. If God wants something to come our way
no one can stop it, and if He doesn't, nobody can give it.

God's will runs over the entire universe and He cares
for every living being. Whatever pleases God is good for us.

Guru Nanak says:

ਜੀਅ ਜੰਤ ਸਭਿ ਸਰਣਿ ਤੁਮਾਰੀ ਸਰਬ ਚਿੰਤ ਤੁਧੁ ਪਾਸੇ ॥
ਜੋ ਤੁਧੁ ਭਾਵੈ ਸੋਈ ਚੰਗਾ ਇਕ ਨਾਨਕ ਕੀ ਅਰਦਾਸੇ ॥

Jia jantt sabh saran tumhaari sarab chint tudh paasay.
Jo tudh bhaavai soyee changa ik Nanak ki ardaasay.

जीअ जंत सभि सरणि तुम्हारी सरब चिंत तुधु पासे ॥
जो तुधु भावै सोई चंगा इक नानक की अरदासे ॥

All living beings are under Your refuge, You take care of all
their worries.
Whatever pleases You is good for me, this alone is
Nanak's prayer.

M1/795/13

We normally like to take credit for everything good that happens to us and blame others, including God, for our misfortunes. Whether it is good or bad, the acceptance of God's will must be complete, without condition.

As Bhagat Kabir says:

ਬੰਦੇ ਬੰਦਗੀ ਇਕਤੀਆਰ॥ ਸਾਹਿਬੁ ਰੋਸੁ ਧਰਉ ਕਿ ਪਿਆਰੁ॥

Banday bandagi iktiyaar, Sahib ros dharao kay peyaar.

बंदे बंदगी इकतीआर॥ साहिबु रोसु धरउ कि पिआरु॥

O man, accede to Lord's worship.
Whether the Lord gives you His dislike or His love.
Kabir/338/15

Guru Arjan Dev expresses same feelings in this verse:

ਜੋ ਜੋ ਕਰੈ ਸੋਈ ਮਾਨਿ ਲੇਹੁ॥ ਬਿਨੁ ਮਾਨੇ ਰਲਿ ਹੋਵਹਿ ਖੇਹ॥
ਤਿਸ ਕਾ ਭਾਣਾ ਲਾਗੈ ਮੀਠਾ॥ ਗੁਰ ਪ੍ਰਸਾਦਿ ਵਿਰਲੇ ਮਨਿ ਵੂਠਾ॥

Jo jo karai soyee maan leh; bin maanay ral hoveh kheh.
Tis ka bhaana laagai meetha; gur prasaad virlay munn vootha.

जो जो करै सोई मानि लेहु॥ बिनु माने रलि होवहि खेह॥
तिस का भाणा लागै मीठा॥ गुर प्रसादि विरले मनि बूठा

Accept whatever the Lord does; if you don't, you shall mingle with the dust.
His command feels pleasant; by Guru's grace, He dwells in the mind of the chosen ones.
M5/896/3

Once you begin to accept and enjoy everything that happens to you as God's gift, you are well on your way towards godhood.

Guru Nanak writes:

ਜਿਨਾ ਭਾਣੇ ਕਾ ਰਸੁ ਆਇਆ॥ ਤਿਨ ਵਿਚਹੁ ਭਰਮੁ ਚੁਕਾਇਆ॥
ਨਾਨਕ ਸਤਿਗੁਰੁ ਐਸਾ ਜਾਣੀਐ ਜੋ ਸਭਸੈ ਲਏ ਮਿਲਾਇ ਜੀਉ॥

Jina bhaanay ka ras aayaa, tin vichoh bharam chukaayaa.
Nanak Satgur aisa janeeyai jo sabhsai laiye milaaye jio.

जिना भाणे का रसु आइआ॥ तिन विचहु भरमु चुकाइआ॥
नानक सतिगुरु ऐसा जाणीऐ जो सभसै लए मिलाइ जीउ॥

**Those who begin to relish God's command, all their doubts
are removed from within.
O Nanak, know True Guru to be such, who unites all
(with the Lord).**

M1/72/7

Complete acceptance of His will also helps obliterate ego which, as we saw, is the major stumbling block in our spiritual progress. Bhagat Kabir tells us here that by accepting His command one enters the realm of godhood:

ਜੋ ਕਿਛੁ ਹੋਆ ਸੁ ਤੇਰਾ ਭਾਣਾ॥ ਜੋ ਇਵ ਬੂਝੈ ਸੁ ਸਹਜਿ ਸਮਾਣਾ॥

Jo kichhu hoaa su tera bhaana, jo iv bhoojai su sehaj
smaanaa.

जो किछु होआ सु तेरा भाणा॥ जो इव बूझै सु सहजि समाणा॥

**Whatever happens is according to Your will.
Whoever understands this, naturally/peacefully merges into
godhood.**

Kabir/1349/10

Do not run away from God when you are going through troubled times. There is no place to escape. This is the time to come closer to Him and strengthen your love, faith and trust in Him. Learn to have patience, with the understanding that there will certainly be relief when the time is right and leave that to God to decide. His timing is always perfect. Do your best under the circumstances and pray to God to give you the strength to cope with difficult times. Communicate with Him from the purity of your heart, leaving aside the cleverness of your head.

Guru Amar Das further emphasizes wisdom of acceptance:

ਭਾਣਾ ਮੰਨੇ ਸੋ ਸੁਖੁ ਪਾਏ ਭਾਣੇ ਵਿਚਿ ਸੁਖੁ ਪਾਇਦਾ॥

Bhaana mannay so sukh paaye bhaanay vich sukh paayeda.

भाणा मंने सो सुखु पाए भाणे विचि सुखु पाइदा॥

He who accepts God's will, finds happiness; happiness is to be found in accepting God's will.

M3/1063/18

Guru Amar Das then cautions us against not accepting God's will:

ਭਾਣਾ ਨ ਮੰਨੇ ਬਹੁਤੁ ਦੁਖੁ ਪਾਈ॥
ਭਰਮੇ ਭੂਲਾ ਆਵੈ ਜਾਏ ਘਰੁ ਮਹਲੁ ਨ ਕਬਹੂ ਪਾਇਦਾ॥

Bhaana na mannay bahut dukh paayee.
Bharmay bhoola aavai jaaye, ghar mehal na kab-hoo paayeda.

भाणा न मंने बहुतु दुखु पाई॥
भरमे भूला आवै जाए घरु महलु न कबहू पाइदा॥

If you do not accept God's will you suffer immense pain.
Lost in confusion people keep coming and going (rebirths), they never find God's abode.

M3/1064/3

Guru Nanak on acceptance with gratefulness:

> ਕੁਦਰਤਿ ਕਵਣ ਕਹਾ ਵੀਚਾਰੁ ॥ ਵਾਰਿਆ ਨ ਜਾਵਾ ਏਕ ਵਾਰ ॥
> ਜੋ ਤੁਧੁ ਭਾਵੈ ਸਾਈ ਭਲੀ ਕਾਰ ॥ ਤੂ ਸਦਾ ਸਲਾਮਤਿ ਨਿਰੰਕਾਰ ॥
>
> Kudrat kavan kaha vichaar, vareya na java ek vaar.
> Jo tudh bhaavai saayee bhali kaar, tu sadaa slamat Nirankaar.
>
> कुदरति कवण कहा वीचारु ॥ वारिआ न जावा एक वार ॥
> जो तुधु भावै साई भली कार ॥ तू सदा सलामति निरंकार ॥
>
> What power do I have to contemplate the whole
> creation;
> sacrifice of my life is not good enough (I'm too small);
> Whatever suits You is best for me, O Formless One, you are
> ever unharmed/complete.
>
> M1/4/2

Guru Ram Das's words below will also help you accept
God's will:

> ਆਪੇ ਹਰਿ ਇਕ ਰੰਗੁ ਹੈ ਆਪੇ ਬਹੁ ਰੰਗੀ ॥ ਜੋ ਤਿਸੁ ਭਾਵੈ ਨਾਨਕਾ ਸਾਈ ਗਲ ਚੰਗੀ ॥
>
> Aappay Har ik rung hai aappay boh rungee, jo tis bhaavai
> Nanaka saayee gull changee.
>
> आपे हरि इक रंगु है आपे बहु रंगी ॥ जो तिसु भावै नानका साई गल चंगी ॥
>
> God is both, formless One, at spiritual level, as well as in
> many forms in the physical plane (He manifests
> in everything).
> Whatever pleases You my Lord, says Nanak, that alone is
> good for me.
>
> M4/726/13

When faced with difficult problems and situations, accept them, don't deny, and then make this small prayer of acceptance, "Whatever pleases You O Lord is best for me." You will immediately feel better.

Even psychologists now believe that accepting our problems greatly helps in coping with them, and they have a treatment called, Accepting and Commitment Therapy (ACT), where patients are motivated to first accept their ailments and then to make commitment for overcoming them.

Resistance to an issue is harmful and is never the way out from an uncomfortable situation. Carl Jung, the Swiss Psychiatrist said, "What you resist, persists." Though this is how the quote became popular, what he actually said was, "What you resist doesn't only persist but it grows and gets worst." Non-acceptance is not only unwise but dangerous too. Lao Tzu, the Chinese philosopher said, "Life is a series of natural and spontaneous changes. Don't resist them; that only creates sorrow. Let reality be reality. Let things flow naturally forward in whatever way they like."

Acceptance must be complete, unconditional and pure. Do not sully it with questioning, doubt, complaint, bargaining or hesitation. Simply accept your problems as God's wish.

Here is a poem about a man's helplessness, and acceptance of his inability, to unfold a rosebud:

> *It is only a tiny rosebud,*
>
> *A flower of God's design;*
>
> *But I cannot unfold the petals,*
>
> *With these clumsy hands of mine.*
>
> *The secret of unfolding flowers,*
>
> *Is not known to such as I;*
>
> *God opens this flower so easily,*

But in my hands they die.

If I cannot unfold a rosebud,

This flower of God's design;

Then how can I have the wisdom,

To unfold this life of mine?

So I'll trust in God for leading,

Each moment of my day;

I will look to God for guidance,

In each step of the way.

The path that lies before me,

Only my Lord knows;

I'll trust God to unfold the moments,

Just as He unfolds the rose.

(Many claimants, real author unknown)

"No amount of self-improvement can make up for any lack of self-acceptance."

Robert Holden, PhD (b. 1965)
British Expert on Psychology & Spirituality

CHAPTER 12

SURRENDER

ੴ

The word 'surrender' has a very negative connotation. It implies weakness, giving up, humiliation, defeat etc. Only losers surrender, winners and achievers don't. In spirituality however, surrender has a totally different, almost opposite meaning. We don't surrender to any person, group or organization, but to the will of God. It requires full faith and trust in God, as also, great amount of patience. This surrender is from a position of strength, not weakness. Imagine the possibilities when you invoke God to show you the way. To be able to fully trust God is a major step forward in our spiritual journey. This is spiritual surrender – a step beyond acceptance. Acceptance helps you deal with life's problems and difficulties whereas surrender leads you to godhood. Acceptance has more of a psychological construct while surrender has a spiritual one.

In pursuit of God-realization we should be prepared to sacrifice anything and everything. In the verse below Guru Nanak seeks complete surrender:

ਜਉ ਤਉ ਪ੍ਰੇਮ ਖੇਲਣ ਕਾ ਚਾਉ ॥ ਸਿਰੁ ਧਰਿ ਤਲੀ ਗਲੀ ਮੇਰੀ ਆਉ ॥
ਇਤੁ ਮਾਰਗਿ ਪੈਰੁ ਧਰੀਜੈ ॥ ਸਿਰੁ ਦੀਜੈ ਕਾਣਿ ਨ ਕੀਜੈ ॥

Jao tao prem khelan ka chaao, sirr dhar tali gali meri aao.
It maarag payer dhareejai, sirr deejai kaan na keejai.

जउ तउ प्रेम खेलण का चाउ॥ सिरु धरि तली गली मेरी आउ॥
इतु मारगि पैरु धरीजै॥ सिरु दीजै काणि न कीजै॥

If you are keen to play the game of love (of God),
Step onto my path with your head on your palm.
When you step onto this path,
(Be prepared to) give even your head, without wavering.

M1/1412/2

Going to someone with your head on your palm is a metaphor for being prepared to sacrifice everything, even your life – complete surrender.

Many people wrongly attribute the above verse to Guru Gobind Singh. It is actually by Guru Nanak Dev and appears at Page 1412 of SGGS. Guru Gobind's *bani* is not part of SGGS. He is likely to have quoted these words of Guru Nanak in his speeches while seeking volunteers to join *Khalsa Panth*.

Guru Arjan Dev also speaks of complete surrender when he says:

ਪਹਿਲਾ ਮਰਣੁ ਕਬੂਲਿ ਜੀਵਣ ਕੀ ਛਡਿ ਆਸ॥
ਹੋਹੁ ਸਭਨਾ ਕੀ ਰੇਣੁਕਾ ਤਉ ਆਉ ਹਮਾਰੈ ਪਾਸਿ॥

Pehla maran kabool jeevan ki chhad aas.
Hoh sabhna ki renuka tao aao hamaaray paas.

पहिला मरणु कबूलि जीवण की छडि आस॥
होहु सभना की रेणुका तउ आउ हमारै पासि॥

First, accept death, and give up all hope of life.
Become the dust of everyone's feet, and then you may
come to Me.

M5/1102/10

Becoming dust of everyone's feet means total humility and submission.

In the following verse Guru Arjan Dev encourages those on path of spirituality to surrender and asks them not to waver:

ਤੂ ਕਾਹੇ ਡੋਲਹਿ ਪ੍ਰਾਣੀਆ ਤੁਧੁ ਰਾਖੈਗਾ ਸਿਰਜਣਹਾਰੁ ॥
ਜਿਨਿ ਪੈਦਾਇਸਿ ਤੂ ਕੀਆ ਸੋਈ ਦੇਇ ਆਧਾਰੁ ॥

Tu kaahay doleh praaniya tudh raakhaiga Sirjanhaar.
Jin paidaayis tu keeya soyee dei aadhaar.

ਤੂ ਕਾਹੇ ਡੋਲਹਿ ਪ੍ਰਾਣੀਆ ਤੁਧੁ ਰਾਖੈਗਾ ਸਿਰਜਣਹਾਰੁ ॥
ਜਿਨਿ ਪੈਦਾਇਸਿ ਤੂ ਕੀਆ ਸੋਈ ਦੇਇ ਆਧਾਰੁ ॥

O mortal being, why waver (on surrender)? The Creator will protect you.
He who gave you life, will also give you sustenance.

M5/724/6

Guru Arjan Dev again says there is nothing to worry when God is with you:

ਜਾ ਤੂ ਮੇਰੈ ਵਲਿ ਹੈ ਤਾ ਕਿਆ ਮੁਹਛੰਦਾ ॥
ਤੁਧੁ ਸਭੁ ਕਿਛੁ ਮੈਨੋ ਸਉਪਿਆ ਜਾ ਤੇਰਾ ਬੰਦਾ ॥

Ja tu merai val hai ta kiya muh-chhanda;
Tudh sabh kichhu maino saupeya ja tera banda.

ਜਾ ਤੂ ਮੇਰੈ ਵਲਿ ਹੈ ਤਾ ਕਿਆ ਮੁਹਛੰਦਾ ॥
ਤੁਧੁ ਸਭੁ ਕਿਛੁ ਮੈਨੋ ਸਉਪਿਆ ਜਾ ਤੇਰਾ ਬੰਦਾ ॥

When You are on my side, I don't have to depend on anyone else.
You gave me everything when You made me Your own.

M5/1096/15

There are two major obstacles that prevent us from surrendering. First is our own doubt and wavering. We do not have full faith and belief that God will take care of us when we surrender to His will. Complete surrender happens when we leave all our worries to Him and do not doubt that He will help us; whenever required, and in a manner He considers best. The truth is, we may think we have surrendered, but soon, when confronted with a difficult situation, we again start worrying about all kinds of things - most of them imaginary and unlikely to come about. Our mind is overindulgent in worries. The second obstacle is the ego. It just cannot allow us to believe that we have lost control over our life-situation, and that we need outside help. Spiritual surrender implies demolition of ego. Surrender, therefore is not as easy as it may sound. Getting rid of worries, as also ego, are no mean achievements.

Bhagat Kabir tells us to be prepared for anything, and that will help us surrender:

ਸੁਰਗ ਬਾਸੁ ਨ ਬਾਛੀਐ ਡਰੀਐ ਨ ਨਰਕਿ ਨਿਵਾਸੁ ॥
ਹੋਨਾ ਹੈ ਸੋ ਹੋਈ ਹੈ ਮਨਹਿ ਨ ਕੀਜੈ ਆਸ ॥

Surag baas na baachheeyai dareeyai na nark nivaas.
Hona hai so hoyee hai maneh na keejai aas.

सुरग बासु न बाछीऐ डरीऐ न नरकि निवासु ॥
होना है सो होई है मनहि न कीजै आस ॥

Do not seek a place in heaven, do not be afraid of living in hell.
Whatever will be will be, do not have any expectations.

Kabir/337/10

Here Sheikh Farid expresses his disenchantment with material life. He is so disgusted with it that he is prepared to give up his life. You require this kind of urge and devotion before you can completely surrender to God's will:

ਫਰੀਦਾ ਬਾਰਿ ਪਰਾਇਐ ਬੈਸਣਾ ਸਾਂਈ ਮੁਝੈ ਨ ਦੇਹਿ॥
ਜੇ ਤੁ ਏਵੈ ਰਖਸੀ ਜੀਉ ਸਰੀਰਹੁ ਲੇਹਿ॥

Farida baar praayeeyai baisna Saeen mujhai na deh.
Jay tu evai rakhsee jio sareeroh leh.

फरीदा बारि पराइऐ बैसणा सांई मुझै न देहि॥
जे तू एवै रखसी जीउ सरीरहु लेहि॥

Says Farid, O Lord, do not make me sit at another's door (life of materialism).
If this is how you will keep me (dependent on materialism), then You rather take away my body and my soul.

Farid/1380/1

Guru Amar Das's prayer of surrender:

ਹਰਿ ਜੀਉ ਸਦਾ ਤੇਰੀ ਸਰਣਾਈ॥
ਜਿਉ ਭਾਵੈ ਤਿਉ ਰਾਖੁ ਮੇਰੇ ਸੁਆਮੀ ਏਹ ਤੇਰੀ ਵਡਿਆਈ॥

Har jio sadaa teri sarnaayee,
Jiu bhaavai tiu raakhoh meray Suamee, eh teri vadeyaayee.

हरि जीउ सदा तेरी सरणाई॥
जिउ भावै तिउ राखहु मेरे सुआमी एह तेरी वडिआई॥

O Lord, I am forever under your shelter.
Keep me as You wish, my Lord, this is all your greatness.

M3/1333/18

Guru Ram Das prays to the Husband Lord for surrender:

ਅਬ ਹਮ ਚਲੀ ਠਾਕੁਰ ਪਹਿ ਹਾਰਿ॥

ਜਬ ਹਮ ਸਰਣਿ ਪ੍ਰਭੂ ਕੀ ਆਈ ਰਾਖੁ ਪ੍ਰਭੁ ਭਾਵੈ ਮਾਰਿ॥

Abb humm chalee Thakur peh haar;

Jabb humm saran Prabh ki aayee raakh Prabh bhaavai maar.

अब हम चली ठाकुर पहि हारि॥

जब हम सरणि प्रभू की आई राखु प्रभू भावै मारि॥

Now having been finally defeated I am going to my
Husband Lord.

When I have come under Your shelter, O Lord, it doesn't
matter, whether You let me live or kill me.

M4/527/15

In the verse below Bhagat Kabir speaks of the spiritual journey which must be undertaken alone, individually, because if there are others with you they may pull you back. They may discourage you and put doubts in your mind. You must surrender and burn the bridges behind you when you undertake this journey:

ਕਬੀਰ ਸਾਧੂ ਕਉ ਮਿਲਨੇ ਜਾਈਐ ਸਾਥਿ ਨ ਲੀਜੈ ਕੋਇ॥

ਪਾਛੈ ਪਾਉ ਨ ਦੀਜੀਐ ਆਗੈ ਹੋਇ ਸੁ ਹੋਇ॥

Kabir saadhu kau milnay jayeeyai saath na leejai koye.

Paachhay paao na deejeeyai aagay hoye so hoye.

कबीर साधू कउ मिलने जाईऐ साथि न लीजै कोइ॥

पाछै पाउ न दीजीऐ आगै होइ सु होइ॥

Kabir, when you go to meet a holy man (for spiritual learning),
do not have anyone else accompany you.

Do not step back, whatever happens let it happen.

Kabir/1370/12

Guru Ram Das again speaks of ultimate surrender:

> ਜੋ ਸੁਖੁ ਦੇਹਿ ਤ ਤੁਝਹਿ ਅਰਾਧੀ ਦੁਖਿ ਭੀ ਤੁਝੈ ਧਿਆਈ ॥
>
> ਜੇ ਭੁਖ ਦੇਹਿ ਤ ਇਤ ਹੀ ਰਾਜਾ ਦੁਖ ਵਿਚਿ ਸੂਖ ਮਨਾਈ ॥
>
> ਤਨੁ ਮਨੁ ਕਾਟਿ ਕਾਟਿ ਸਭੁ ਅਰਪੀ ਵਿਚਿ ਅਗਨੀ ਆਪੁ ਜਲਾਈ ॥
>
> Jay sukh deh ta tujheh araadhee dukh bhi tujhai dhiaayee.
>
> Jay bhukh deh ta it hi raaja dukh vich sookh manaayee.
>
> Tann mann kaat kaat sabh arpi vich agni aap jalaayee.
>
> जे सुखु देहि त तुझहि अराधी दुखि भी तुझै धिआई ॥
>
> जे भुख देहि त इत ही राजा दुख विचि सूख मनाई ॥
>
> तनु मनु काटि काटि सभु अरपी विचि अगनी आपु जलाई ॥
>
> (O Lord), whether You give me pleasure or pain, I will still worship You.
>
> If You keep me hungry, I will feel fulfilled, in pain I will feel pleasure.
>
> (If needed) I will cut my body and mind into pieces and offer it, by burning it in fire myself.
>
> M4/757/11

Guru Ram Das, as a humble devotee, yet again pleads for complete surrender:

> ਪਖਾ ਫੇਰੀ ਪਾਣੀ ਢੋਵਾ ਜੋ ਦੇਵਹਿ ਸੋ ਖਾਈ ॥
>
> ਨਾਨਕੁ ਗਰੀਬੁ ਢਹਿ ਪਇਆ ਦੁਆਰੈ ਹਰਿ ਮੇਲਿ ਲੈਹੁ ਵਡਿਆਈ ॥
>
> Pakha pheri paani dhova jo deveh so khaayee.
>
> Nanak gareeb dheh paiya duarai Har mail laihu vadeaayee.
>
> पखा फेरी पाणी ढोवा जो देवहि सो खाई ॥
>
> नानकु गरीबु ढहि पइआ दुआरै हरि मेलि लैहु वडिआई ॥

I will fan (Your believers), will fetch water for them, whatever You give I shall eat.
Nanak says, this poor me has dropped at Your door, it will be Your magnanimity if You accept me.

M4/757/13

Before the advent of electric fans, huge cloth fans were manually swung over the gathering to make them feel comfortable in hot season. This, along with offering cold water, was done as community service.

Like acceptance, surrender to God's will, does not mean passivity. You don't just surrender and sit back doing nothing; hoping God will resolve all your problems. In fact your effort should double and become more focused. God will help you do that. When you truly put your faith in God, He is pleased. When that happens you're blessed, because now He will move heaven and earth to help you. What more can you ask for? Word of caution; have no expectations.

"Surrender is not a weakness, it is a strength. It takes tremendous strength to surrender life to the supreme - to the cosmic unfolding."

Mooji (b. 1954)
Jamaican Spiritual Teacher

CHAPTER 13

WORSHIP

ੴ

The word 'worship' means to love, revere, respect or admire someone, or something, with deep devotion. You could have such feelings for your parents, teachers, seniors or others close to you. Many people worship entities like demigods/goddesses, stones, trees, idols etc.

Here we are concerned only with worship of God, because that's what is needed for our spiritual development. Worship is the most important thing you could do to attain your life's purpose. It is the true worship that helps you connect with God and will finally get you to be one with Him. Sincere worship is also one of the ways of mitigating your sins of the past.

What is God's worship? It is to express your deepest feelings for God in any way you feel appropriate. Some of the things you could do are:

Singing or chanting God's praises.

Contemplating/meditating on God.

Expressing love and devotion to God.

Thanking God for everything you have.

Being in awe of God and His creation.

Talking to God.

Seeing God in everything/everywhere.

Seeking God and His blessings.

You also worship God when you do the following:

Clean and honest living.

Helping people in need.

Inculcating qualities like love, compassion, empathy, respect, humility, gratitude and so on.

Using your special talents for benefit of the society.

Working for any other noble cause.

Words used in SGGS for worship include, *pooja, simran, simar, bhagti, bhajan, kirtan, jupp, araadhna, chintan, dhayaana, ardaas* and so on. What exactly you do is not so important. It is the ever-increasing urge to connect with God and the sincerity of effort that makes the difference. If food is offered to a man who is dying of hunger he will not be bothered about any technicalities of eating. He'll just lap it up any way. Similarly a person who is utterly hungry for God's love will worship Him any way he finds appropriate. He will not need to ask which particular technique or procedure he should follow. He will find the way. Guru Nanak arrived by singing God's praises with full intensity and devotion. In the chapters that follow we will look at different forms of worship that include prayer, remembrance, *seva, kirtan* and gratitude.

There is no single path of worship. You will not be wrong if you follow any of the many paths that you feel appropriate and are comfortable with. Dalai Lama said, "People take different roads seeking fulfillment and happiness. Just because they are not on your road does not mean they are lost." The important thing is that during worship your mind should be fully in it. There is no point in reading scriptures, going on pilgrimages, listening to spiritual discourses, or singing *gurbani,* if your mind is not in it.

Let us see some verses on worship in SGGS. Here Guru Nanak implores you to worship only the One Lord:

ਜਪਹੁ ਤ ਏਕੋ ਨਾਮਾ॥ ਅਵਰਿ ਨਿਰਾਫਲ ਕਾਮਾ॥

Jap-ho te eko naama; avar nirafal kaama.

जपहु त एको नामा॥ अवरि निराफल कामा॥

Chant only One Name. All other effort is useless.

M1/728/5

In the verse below Guru Nanak prays to God to give him the urge to sing His praises:

ਇਕ ਨਾਨਕ ਕੀ ਅਰਦਾਸਿ ਜੇ ਤੁਧੁ ਭਾਵਸੀ॥
ਮੈ ਦੀਜੈ ਨਾਮ ਨਿਵਾਸੁ ਹਰਿ ਗੁਣ ਗਾਵਸੀ॥

Ik Nanak ki ardaas jay tudh bhaavsee.
Mai deejai naam nivaas Har gunh gaavsee.

इक नानक की अरदासि जे तुधु भावसी॥
मै दीजै नाम निवासु हरि गुण गावसी॥

Nanak makes this plea, if it pleases You.
Let Your Name reside in me, so that I sing of Your virtues.

M1/752/6

Guru Nanak again prays for singing Lord's praises:

ਮੈ ਦੀਜੈ ਨਾਮ ਨਿਵਾਸੁ ਅੰਤਰਿ ਸਾਂਤਿ ਹੋਇ॥
ਗੁਣ ਗਾਵੈ ਨਾਨਕ ਦਾਸੁ ਸਤਿਗੁਰੁ ਮਤਿ ਦੇਇ॥

Mai deejai naam nivaas antar saant hoye.
Gunh gaavai Nanak daas Satgur matt deye.

मै दीजै नाम निवासु अंतरि सांति होइ॥
गुण गावै नानक दासु सतिगुरु मति देइ॥

> O Lord, let Your Name reside in me so that I find inner peace.
> May Nanak the servant, sing of Your virtues, O True Guru,
> give me this wisdom.
>
> M1/753/3

Notice how, all the verses by Guru Nanak quoted above, pertain to singing God's praises. That's the form of worship he chose.

Guru Amar Das tells us that, with actions such as repeated reading of religious texts without devotion, observing silence for prolonged periods without serious contemplation, and adorning different types of clothing and appearances, one cannot attain salvation. Only true worship will help:

> ਪੜਿ ਪੜਿ ਪੰਡਿਤ ਮੋਨੀ ਥਾਕੇ ਭੇਖੀ ਮੁਕਤਿ ਨ ਪਾਈ ॥
> ਨਾਨਕ ਬਿਨੁ ਭਗਤੀ ਜਗੁ ਬਉਰਾਨਾ ਸਚੈ ਸਬਦਿ ਮਿਲਾਈ ॥
>
> Parh parh pandit moni thhakay bheykhi mukt na payee.
> Nanak bin bhagti jug bauraana sachai sabad milaayee.
>
> पड़ि पड़ि पंडित मोनी थाके भेखी मुकति न पाई ॥
> नानक बिनु भगती जगु बउराना सचै सबदि मिलाई ॥
>
> The pandits with repeated readings, the silent yogis, and
> those adopting different appearances have grown weary, they
> have not attained liberation.
> O Nanak, without worship, the world is getting mad, only True
> Word enables meeting (with the Lord).
>
> M3/440/3

Bhagat Kabir emphasizes that we should focus on love of God only, other things do not matter:

ਕਬੀਰ ਪ੍ਰੀਤਿ ਇਕ ਸਿਉ ਕੀਏ ਆਨ ਦੁਬਿਧਾ ਜਾਇ॥
ਭਾਵੈ ਲਾਂਬੇ ਕੇਸ ਕਰੁ ਭਾਵੈ ਘਰਰਿ ਮੁਡਾਇ॥

Kabir preet ik siu keeye aan dubhida jaaye.
Bhaavai laambay kes kar bhaavai gharar mudaaye.

कबीर प्रीति इक सिउ कीए आन दुबिधा जाइ॥
भावै लांबे केस करु भावै घररि मुडाइ॥

Kabir says, when you love the One Lord all doubts disappear.
It doesn't matter then whether you keep long hair or shave
off your head.

Kabir/1365/15

Some people see a contradiction in Bhagat Kabir's statement that it does not matter whether you keep long hair or not, with Guru Gobind Singh's edict to *Khalsa Panth* for growing long hair. The two pertain to totally different time-frames, for different audiences, with different intent. Bhagat Kabir is addressing those fake believers who adopt different appearances, more to show off, than any spiritual achievement. Guru Gobind Singh's edict comes in 1699, a full 181 years after Bhagat Kabir's death in 1518, and is specifically addressed to the *Khalsa*, to give them a distinct identity.

Guru Ram Das says chanting with single mindedness leads to shedding of the ego:

ਜਿਨ ਜਪਿਆ ਇਕ ਮਨਿ ਇਕ ਚਿਤਿ ਤਿਨ ਲਥਾ ਹਉਮੈ ਭਾਰੁ॥
Jin japeya ik munn ik chit tin latha haumai bhaar.
जिन जपिआ इक मनि इक चिति तिन लथा हउमै भारु॥

Those who worship Him with single mindedness and focused attention get rid of the burden of their ego.

M4/302/9

Guru Amar Das also stresses the point of focused attention:

ਸਤਿਗੁਰ ਕੀ ਸੇਵਾ ਸਫਲੁ ਹੈ ਜੇ ਕੋ ਕਰੇ ਚਿਤੁ ਲਾਇ ॥

Satgur ki seva safal hai jay ko karay chit laaye.

सतिगुर की सेवा सफलु है जे को करे चितु लाइ॥

Worship of the True Guru is fruitful, if one does it with full attention/devotion.

M3/644/15

Focused attention on God during your worship is of utmost importance. This is what Guru Gobind Singh says in *Dasam Granth*, *"Aik Chit Jih Ik Chhin Dhiyaaeo, Kaal Phas Kay Beech Na Aaeo."* (He who meditates with single minded attention even for a moment, death has no hold over him.)

A good example of single minded worship lies in the ancient story of a young boy Bhagat Prahlad, which is mentioned in SGGS several times. Bhagat Prahlad was son of King Harnakhas and a sincere devotee of Lord Vishnu. His father was granted special powers that, he believed, made him immortal. His ego took hold of him and he thought he was superior to even God. He ordered his entire kingdom to worship only him, no one else. All followed but his son Prahlad refused - he would only worship the Lord. The king went mad that his own son disobeyed him. He made several attempts to have him killed, but nothing worked. He finally asked his sister Holika, who had a boon of protection against fire, to sit on a pyre with young Prahlad in her lap. This, he thought, was the surest way of killing him. Before the pyre was lit, Prahlad went into deep devotional meditation. As a result, the fire could not harm him, while Holika, despite her boon, was burnt to death. With the Lord on the side of Bhagat Prahlad, his father's boon of immortality was also compromised and he was killed. Prahlad became the King and gave his people a benevolent rule for many years. He is now revered as a saint.

The festival of *Holi* is observed in the memory of this event - as victory of worship over ego-led brutality. That is how sincere and deep devotion protects those who single mindedly worship the Lord.

This is what Guru Ram Das says about Harnakhas and Bhagat Prahlad:

ਹਰਿ ਜੁਗੁ ਜੁਗੁ ਭਗਤ ਉਪਾਇਆ ਪੈਜ ਰਖਦਾ ਆਇਆ ਰਾਮ ਰਾਜੇ॥
ਹਰਣਾਖਸੁ ਦੁਸਟੁ ਹਰਿ ਮਾਰਿਆ ਪ੍ਰਹਲਾਦੁ ਤਰਾਇਆ॥

Har jug jug bhagat upaaya paij rakhda aaya Raam Raajay.
Harnakhas dust Har maareya Prahlad taraaya.

हरि जुगु जुगु भगत उपाइआ पैज रखदा आइआ राम राजे॥
हरणाखसु दुसटु हरि मारिआ प्रहलादु तराइआ॥

In every age the Lord produces sincere worshippers and maintains their dignity;
He killed the tyrant Harnakhas and saved Prahlad.

M4/451/12

Complete story of Bhagat Prahlad is given by Guru Amar Das at page 1133/1 and by Bhagat Namdev at page 1165/5.

Bhagat Kabir reminds us of the need to take up worship as early as possible:

ਅਬ ਨ ਭਜਸਿ ਭਜਸਿ ਕਬ ਭਾਈ॥ ਆਵੈ ਅੰਤੁ ਨ ਭਜਿਆ ਜਾਈ॥
ਜੋ ਕਿਛੁ ਕਰਹਿ ਸੋਈ ਅਬ ਸਾਰੁ॥ ਫਿਰਿ ਪਛੁਤਾਹੁ ਨ ਪਾਵਹੁ ਪਾਰੁ॥

Abb na bhajas bhajas kabb bhaayee; aavai unt na bhajeya jaayee.
Jo kichhu kareh soee abb saar; phir pachhutaaho na paavoh paar.

अब न भजसि भजसि कब भाई॥ आवै अंतु न भजिआ जाई॥
जो किछु करहि सोई अब सारु॥ फिरि पछुताहु न पावहु पारु॥

If you do not sing His praises now, when will you do it, O
brother? When the end comes, you will not be able to do that.
Whatever you ought to do, now is the right time. Otherwise
you shall regret, and you shall not be able to get across
(this fiery ocean of life).

Kabir/1159/10

We should follow Bhagat Kabir's above advice on starting
worship earliest, for two reasons. One, we don't know when we
may die. The end could come right now, and we may have to
depart without having earned God's love and grace. Two, old
age is not the best time for worship because we have too many
health problems, both physical and mental. Serious worship
demands absolute fitness of body, mind and soul. Aches and
pains of old age do not permit deep and focused worship. Those
who believe that worship is to be left for old age, need to have
a relook. Guru Har Krishan and Guru Gobind Singh, both
devout worshippers, took over *Guruship* at age five and nine
respectively. Bhagat Prahlad is another example of a young
worshipper. Though desirable, this doesn't mean young age
is the only time to start God worship. If you missed the boat
earlier, it is never too late – start now.

Guru Arjan Dev speaks of uselessness of life without worship:

बिठु सिमरन दिठु रैठि ब्रिथा बिहाइ॥ मेघ बिठा जिउ खेती जाइ॥
Bin simran din rayan birtha bihaaye, megh bina jiu
kheti jaaye.
बिनु सिमरन दिनु रैनि ब्रिथा बिहाइ॥ मेघ बिना जिउ खेती जाइ॥

> Without God's worship day and night pass in vain.
> Like the crop that is lost if it doesn't rain.
>
> M5/269/5

Life indeed goes waste if you don't appreciate and worship the Beloved Lord. Bulleh Shah says, *"Jinhan Qadar Na Keeti Yaar Di Hath Khaali Oh Malday Vekhay."* (Those who did not appreciate/worship the worthiness of their Beloved Lord, I have seen them go empty handed.) Notice, he is calling God his Yaar (beloved), typical Sufi style. We will see more of this in the chapter on 'Relationship with God'.

Some people worship entities other than God with the belief that they will help them reach God. Why take this indirect approach when a direct connection is available? Your true identity, or your true-self, is your soul, and that is in connection with God. Empower your true-self by worshipping God, the true Giver. Of course, all guidance you need is available in SGGS.

For most people God worship is an important but not an urgent issue. Do not delay, start now and make it a daily commitment. He doesn't like it if you remember Him only when you need Him.

"God can be experienced only in the heart that creates the atmosphere of praise and worship and adoration."

AW Tozer (1897-1963)
American Spiritual Mentor

CHAPTER 14

PRAYER

A prayer is the words we use to communicate with God. The prayer can be a formal one like we do at a religious congregation, or an informal and personal one which we do in our own way, at time and place of own liking.

If you truly wish to gain spiritually you must make your own direct connection with God through prayer. As they say God has no grand children. We are all connected to Him directly and He listens to us and takes care of us. However, guidance of a guru or other spiritually awakened guides can be of immense value.

There are many verses in SGGS on praying. Let us see some of them. In this Guru Nanak makes a prayer of offering himself to God:

ਨਾਨਕੁ ਏਕ ਕਹੈ ਅਰਦਾਸਿ ॥ ਜੀਉ ਪਿੰਡੁ ਸਭੁ ਤੇਰੈ ਪਾਸਿ ॥

Nanak ek kahai ardaas, jio pind sabh terai paas.

नानकु एक कहै अरदासि॥ जीउ पिंडु सभु तेरै पासि॥

Nanak says this one prayer.
My soul, body, and everything else are all offered to You.

M1/354/11

In the last chapter we saw Guru Nanak saying that we should chant only One Name. In the verse below, he emphasizes that we must also pray to only One Supreme God. He says:

> ਹਰਿ ਇਕੋ ਦਾਤਾ ਸੇਵੀਐ ਹਰਿ ਇਕੁ ਧਿਆਈਐ ॥
> ਹਰਿ ਇਕੋ ਦਾਤਾ ਮੰਗੀਐ ਮਨ ਚਿੰਦਿਆ ਪਾਈਐ ॥
>
> Har ikko daata seveeyai Har ikk dhiayeeyai.
> Har ikko daata mangeeyai munn chindeya paayeeyai.
>
> हरि इको दाता सेवीऐ हरि इकु धिआईऐ ॥
> हरि इको दाता मंगीऐ मन चिंदिआ पाईऐ ॥
>
> Serve only the One Giver and meditate on that One Lord.
> Seek only from the One Giver, and receive your
> mind's desire.
>
> M1/590/3

This mind's desire should pertain to our spiritual needs and for strengthening of our faith in God. But we mostly seek things of the physical world that include wealth, fame, power, and everything else that goes with it. We assume these things will bring happiness, but they don't. Such a chase takes us away from God and ultimately ends in disaster. God is not so much interested in our material success. He will give these things if He feels we need them; not because we pray for them.

We often pray for the wellbeing of our parents, siblings, spouses, children, friends, and so on. That is indeed good for enrichment of our soul. The more we pray for others the more we benefit. That's the law of giving and receiving; the more we give out something the more we receive. It also reaffirms our belief in Oneness of creation - praying for others means praying for a part of us. If you come across someone suffering from any kind of pain, do pray for him, whether or not you know him personally. Even when you are going through a bad patch yourself, do not forget to pray for others.

Choose wisely what you seek, and pray to God directly. Guru Arjan Dev cautions us about praying for false material gifts:

ਝੂਠਾ ਮੰਗਣੁ ਜੇ ਕੋਈ ਮਾਗੈ ॥ ਤਿਸ ਕਉ ਮਰਤੇ ਘੜੀ ਨ ਲਾਗੈ ॥

Jhootha mangan jay koyee maagai, tis kau martay ghari na laagai.

झूठा मंगणु जे कोई मागै ॥ तिस कउ मरते घड़ी न लागै ॥

He who seeks false/undesirable things, doesn't take long to die.

M5/109/1

The death here obviously doesn't mean physical death, but a moral one. By pursuing falsehood we hurt our souls.

A simple prayer by Guru Angad Dev on seeking only that which pleases the Lord:

ਤੂੰ ਸਚਾ ਦਾਤਾਰੁ ਨਿਤ ਦੇਵਹਿ ਚੜਹਿ ਸਵਾਇਆ ॥
ਨਾਨਕੁ ਮੰਗੈ ਦਾਨੁ ਜੋ ਤੁਧੁ ਭਾਇਆ ॥

Toon sacha daataar nit deveh chareh savaaya, Nanak mangay daan jo tudh bhaaya.

तूं सचा दातारु नित देवहि चड़हि सवाइआ ॥ नानकु मंगै दानु जो तुधु भाइआ ॥

You are the True Giver, You give daily in an ever increasing measure. Nanak asks only for that which pleases You.

M2/150/12

Another piece of advice from Guru Angad Dev:

ਆਪੇ ਜਾਣੈ ਕਰੇ ਆਪਿ ਆਪੇ ਆਣੈ ਰਾਸਿ ॥
ਤਿਸੈ ਅਗੈ ਨਾਨਕਾ ਖਲਿਇ ਕੀਚੈ ਅਰਦਾਸਿ ॥

Aapay jaanay karay aap aapay aanai raas;
Tisai aagai Nanaka khalei keechai ardaas.

आपे जाणै करे आपि आपे आणै रासि ॥
तिसै अगै नानका खलिइ कीचै अरदासि ॥

He Himself knows (all beings), He creates them and,
Himself sees them through.
Says Nanak, stand before Him, and pray.

M2/1093/9

Guru Arjan Dev says pray to the Lord who gives happiness
and destroys fear:

ਸੁਖਦਾਤਾ ਭੈ ਭੰਜਨੋ ਤਿਸੁ ਆਗੈ ਕਰਿ ਅਰਦਾਸਿ ॥
ਮਿਹਰ ਕਰੇ ਜਿਸੁ ਮਿਹਰਵਾਨੁ ਤਾਂ ਕਾਰਜੁ ਆਵੈ ਰਾਸਿ ॥

Sukhdaata bhai bhanjano tis aagai kar ardaas.
Mehar karay jis meharbaan ta kaaraj aavai raas.

सुखदाता भै भंजनो तिसु आगै करि अरदासि ॥
मिहर करे जिसु मिहरवानु तां कारजु आवै रासि ॥

Pray to Him who is the giver of happiness and destroyer of fear.
On whosoever the benevolent Lord showers His grace, his
affairs are settled well.

M5/44/16

This prayer by Guru Arjan Dev is for seeking strength to
prevent wavering (on his belief in God):

ਡੰਡਉਤਿ ਬੰਦਨ ਅਨਿਕ ਬਾਰ ਸਰਬ ਕਲਾ ਸਮਰਥ ॥
ਡੋਲਨ ਤੇ ਰਾਖਹੁ ਪ੍ਰਭੂ ਨਾਨਕ ਦੇ ਕਰਿ ਹਥ ॥

Dandaut bandhan anik baar sarab kalaa samrath.
Dolan tay rakhoh Prabhu Nanak day kar hath.

डंडउति बंदन अनिक बार सरब कला समरथ ॥
डोलन ते राखहु प्रभू नानक दे करि हथ ॥

I bow down to thee, many times, O all-powerful,
all-capable Lord.
O God please save Nanak from wavering, by extending
Your helping hand.

M5/256/4

These following verses indicate that God will meet our
needs, even if we do not ask, because He knows what is best
for us. Guru Nanak says:

ਜੇ ਚੁਪੈ ਜੇ ਮੰਗਿਐ ਦਾਤਿ ਕਰੇ ਦਾਤਾਰੁ ॥

Jay chupai jay mangiyai daat karay dataar.

जे चुपै जे मंगिऐ दाति करे दातारु ॥

Whether we remain silent or we ask, the Giver bestows
His gifts.

M1/1242/9

Guru Amar Das makes a similar statement:

ਵਿਣੁ ਬੋਲਿਆ ਸਭੁ ਕਿਛੁ ਜਾਣਦਾ ਕਿਸੁ ਆਗੈ ਕੀਚੈ ਅਰਦਾਸਿ ॥
ਨਾਨਕ ਘਟਿ ਘਟਿ ਏਕੋ ਵਰਤਦਾ ਸਬਦਿ ਕਰੇ ਪਰਗਾਸ ॥

Vin boleya sabh kichhu jaan-da kis aagai keechai ardaas.
Nanak ghat ghat eko varatada sabad karay pargaas.

विणु बोलिआ सभु किछु जाणदा किसु आगै कीचै अरदासि॥
नानक घटि घटि एको वरतदा सबदि करे परगास॥

Without our saying, He knows everything about us,
who else do we pray to?
O Nanak, One Lord pervades every heart, the word
(of *gurbani*) brings enlightenment.

M3/1420/11

Guru Amar Das again says God knows everything about us:

ਇਕਿ ਗੁਰਮੁਖਿ ਆਪਿ ਮਿਲਾਇਆ ਬਖਸੇ ਭਗਤਿ ਭੰਡਾਰ॥
ਤੂ ਆਪੇ ਸਭੁ ਕਿਛੁ ਜਾਣਦਾ ਕਿਸੁ ਆਗੈ ਕਰੀ ਪੂਕਾਰ॥

Ik gurmukh aap milaaya baksay bhagat bhandaar.
Tu aapay sabh kischu jaan-da kis aagai kari pukaar.

इकि गुरमुखि आपि मिलाइआ बखसे भगति भंडार॥
तू आपे सभु किछु जाणदा किसु आगै करी पूकार॥

You unite some God-oriented people with Yourself and You
bless them with the treasures of worship.
You know everything Yourself, who else can I make a plea to?

M3/1258/14

It doesn't matter whether you give voice to your prayers, or do them silently, or just leave everything to God. The important thing is to maintain contact with God and to continuously build your faith in Him. On His own He will look after your needs. Remember, needs, not greed. There is always enough to satisfy everyone's needs, but never to satisfy everyone's greed.

That is about material needs and desires. As regards your spiritual needs, the more you pray for it the better.

Here is a verse by Guru Arjan Dev on how God provides sustenance to all living beings and why one should not worry:

ਜਨਨਿ ਪਿਤਾ ਲੋਕ ਸੁਤ ਬਨਿਤਾ ਕੋਇ ਨ ਕਿਸ ਕੀ ਧਰਿਆ ॥
ਸਿਰਿ ਸਿਰਿ ਰਿਜਕੁ ਸੰਬਾਹੇ ਠਾਕੁਰੁ ਕਾਹੇ ਮਨ ਭਉ ਕਰਿਆ ॥

Janan pita lok sut banita koye na kis ki dhareya.
Sirr sirr rijak sambhahay Thakur kaahay munn bhao kareya.

जननि पिता लोक सुत बनिता कोइ न किस की धरिआ ॥
सिरि सिरि रिजकु स्मबाहे ठाकुरु काहे मन भउ करिआ ॥

Mother, father, other people, son or wife; finally, no one is of any help.
But God provides sustenance to everyone, so why worry?

M5/10/11

In continuation of the above verse, here is an interesting observation by Guru Arjan Dev on migratory birds:

ਉਡੇ ਉਡਿ ਆਵੈ ਸੈ ਕੋਸਾ ਤਿਸੁ ਪਾਛੈ ਬਚਰੇ ਛਰਿਆ ॥
ਤਿਨ ਕਵਣੁ ਖਲਾਵੈ ਕਵਣੁ ਚੁਗਾਵੈ ਮਨ ਮਹਿ ਸਿਮਰਨੁ ਕਰਿਆ ॥

Ooday ood aavai sai kosa tis paachhai bachray chhareya.
Tin kavan khalaavai kavan chugaavai munn meh simran kareya.

ऊडे ऊडि आवै सै कोसा तिसु पाछै बचरे छरिआ ॥
तिन कवणु खलावै कवणु चुगावै मन महि सिमरनु करिआ ॥

They (ducks) come flying hundreds of miles, leaving their young ones behind.
Who will feed them and who will find food for them? They contemplate/pray in their minds.

M5/10/12

When winters get extremely cold in the Siberian region the ducks migrate to more pleasant climes of South Asia - to return only when the temperatures begin to rise again. However, their young ones, who cannot undertake this long journey, remain in Siberia. The parent birds are worried, who will look after them? They kind of pray for them. It's believed that because of this prayer the young ones are able to find food in cracks in rocks and elsewhere. The prayers are thoughts that travel and can influence a situation thousands of miles away.

I have come across even a more profound interpretation of the above verse which says the parent ducks, perhaps, actually transmit food to their off-springs through teleportation. This is difficult to believe, but who knows? Dr Mani Bhaumik, PhD, in his book, 'Code Name God' writes, "These experiments.... have been utilized to achieve a form of quantum teleportation once thought to belong to the realm of science fiction.... opening the possibility that in some future epoch we could reconstruct a physical mass, particle by particle..." In more recent times, China has shown some success in teleportation experiments.

Does prayer work? Yes! There have been many studies which prove that prayer does help. In these studies, groups of people were asked to collectively pray for one set of patients recovering in the hospital, while no one prayed for another set of patients with similar ailments. At the end of these studies, it was found that patients who were prayed for recovered remarkably better than those not prayed for. Prayer can create miracles. Collective prayer works even better.

There was a little girl who prayed for snow on her birthday, but the birthday happened to be in the month of July. Obviously being summer season it didn't snow. When asked if she was disappointed because God didn't answer her prayer, she replied, "He *did* answer me, He said *No*". This is the right attitude towards prayer. Seek what you think is best for you and for others, but leave it to God to determine what to give - and accept that happily.

Should one pray for material things? Prayer should mainly be to thank God for what you have received and to seek His wisdom. However, you may pray for material things, but keep these four things in mind. One, do not ask for anything that involves hurting, defeating or harming someone; even those who may have harmed you. Two, do not allow your prayers to be contaminated with negative thoughts and emotions like jealousy, revenge, hatred etc. Three, do not bargain with God by promising something you will do/give if your prayer is answered. He does not need anything from you and you are not His equal to bargain with Him. Four, be like the little girl – gracefully accept what you get.

The best thing you can pray for is God's love and benevolence for all.

"Prayer does not change God, but it changes him who prays."

Soren Kierkegaard (1813-1855)
Danish Philosopher

CHAPTER 15

RITUALS

ੴ

Ritual is a practice, procedure, ceremony, service, sacrifice etc. done on a specific occasion or at a regular interval. A daily reading of scriptures, a weekly *satsang*, a monthly visit to the temple, and a yearly pilgrimage, are all rituals. Similarly, bathing in holy waters, watching sunrise every day, offering water to the sun, keeping fasts, lighting lamps, and doing rain dances to please rain gods, are also forms of rituals. Some, not so desirable, are rituals involving killing of animals for offerings to please various deities and gods. On the extreme side, even human beings are sometimes offered as sacrifices. All societies across the world have rituals – some good, some not so good. Most rituals are not formally documented but passed down by word of mouth. With passage of time some old rituals are done away with and new ones are introduced.

Guru Nanak came on the scene when the society was heavily burdened with too many unwanted rituals. In the caste ridden society, *brahmins* had a strong grip on the people and made them indulge in all sorts of ceremonies and procedures, mainly to get benefits for themselves; as also to further strengthen their hold on the society. Guru Nanak strongly condemned rituals, which did not serve any useful purpose. We cannot say he was against rituals per se but he certainly put them in proper perspective. He was against bad exploitative rituals, not against good ones that promoted brotherhood of mankind.

Getting rid of meaningless and wasteful rituals that weighed heavy on ordinary people, was a major task Guru Nanak took upon himself. He has spoken extensively about it in SGGS.

Guru Nanak was born in a Hindu family. When he was a young boy, his parents arranged a ceremony for him to wear the *janeu* (sacred thread) as was the Hindu custom. The honourable pandit, was invited to do the needful, but Guru Nanak refused to wear the thread, and challenged the pandit thus:

ਦਇਆ ਕਪਾਹ ਸੰਤੋਖੁ ਸੂਤੁ ਜਤੁ ਗੰਢੀ ਸਤੁ ਵਟੁ ॥

ਏਹੁ ਜਨੇਊ ਜੀਅ ਕਾ ਹਈ ਤ ਪਾਡੇ ਘਤੁ ॥

Daya kpaah santokh soot jutt gandhee satt vatt.

Eh janeu jia ka hayee ta paaday ghatt.

दइआ कपाह संतोखु सूतु जतु गंढी सतु वटु ॥

एहु जनेऊ जीअ का हई त पाडे घतु ॥

Where compassion is the cotton, contentment the thread, modesty the knot and truth the twist. Such is the sacred thread of the soul, if you have it O pandit, put it on me.

ਨਾ ਏਹੁ ਤੁਟੈ ਨ ਮਲੁ ਲਗੈ ਨਾ ਏਹੁ ਜਲੈ ਨ ਜਾਇ ॥

ਧੰਨੁ ਸੁ ਮਾਣਸ ਨਾਨਕਾ ਜੋ ਗਲਿ ਚਲੈ ਪਾਇ ॥

Na eh tuttai na mal laggai na eh jalai na jaaye.

Dhan su manas Nanaka jo gal challay paaye.

ना एहु तुटै न मलु लगै ना एहु जलै न जाइ ॥

धंनु सु माणस नानका जो गलि चले पाइ ॥

(Such thread) does not break or get dirty, it cannot be burnt or lost.

Blessed are those, O Nanak, who wear such a thread around their neck.

ਚਉਕੜਿ ਮੁਲਿ ਅਣਾਇਆ ਬਹਿ ਚਉਕੈ ਪਾਇਆ ॥
ਸਿਖਾ ਕੰਨਿ ਚੜਾਈਆ ਗੁਰੁ ਬ੍ਰਾਹਮਣੁ ਥਿਆ ॥
ਓਹੁ ਮੁਆ ਓਹੁ ਝੜਿ ਪਇਆ ਵੇਤਗਾ ਗਇਆ ॥

Chaukar mool anaaeya beh chaukay paayeaa.
Sikha kann charaayea gur brahman thia.
Oh mua oh jhar payeyaa vetagga gaya.

चउकड़ि मुलि अणाइआ बहि चउकै पाइआ ॥
सिखा कंनि चड़ाईआ गुरु ब्राहमणु थिआ ॥
हु मुआ ओहु झड़ि पइआ वेतगा गइआ ॥

(The pandit) buys the thread for a small price, and sitting in
the enclosure, he puts it on the boy.
He whispers into boy's ears that he is now the boy's guru.
When the person dies, the thread falls away, and his poor
soul has to depart thread-less.

M1/471/2

Another comment by Guru Nanak on uselessness of the
sacred thread and the mark on forehead:

ਨਾਨਕ ਸਚੇ ਨਾਮ ਬਿਨੁ ਕਿਆ ਟਿਕਾ ਕਿਆ ਤਗੁ ॥
Nanak sachay naam bin kiya tikka kiya tagg.
नानक सचे नाम बिनु किआ टिका किआ तगु ॥

Says Nanak, without the True Name, what use is the mark on
the forehead or the thread?

M1/467/6

Guru Amar Das says there is a need for people to have right
state of mind which is much better than the ritual of physical
pilgrimage to sixty eight places:

ਇਹੁ ਮਨੁ ਕਾਸੀ ਸਭਿ ਤੀਰਥ ਸਿਮ੍ਰਿਤਿ ਸਤਿਗੁਰ ਦੀਆ ਬੁਝਾਇ ॥
ਅਠਸਠਿ ਤੀਰਥ ਤਿਸੁ ਸੰਗਿ ਰਹਹਿ ਜਿਨ ਹਰਿ ਹਿਰਦੈ ਰਹਿਆ ਸਮਾਇ ॥

Ih munn Kaasi sabh teerath simrit Satgur diya bhujaaye.
Athsath teerath tis sangh reheh jin Har hirdai
reheyaa samaaye.

इहु मनु कासी सभि तीरथ सिम्रिति सतिगुर दीआ बुझाइ ॥
अठसठि तीरथ तिसु संगि रहहि जिन हरि हिरदै रहिआ समाइ ॥

Benares (Kashi) and all other places of pilgrimage are within
this mind, the True Guru has explained.
Sixty-eight places of pilgrimage remain with those, in whose
heart the Lord pervades.

M3/491/17

The sixty-eight places of pilgrimage mentioned above, and
often referred to in SGGS, are the Hindu centres that include
4 *Dhams*, 12 *Jyotirlings* and 52 *Shakti Peeths*. SGGS does not
recommend these pilgrimages. It only highlights the need for
inner cleansing instead of physical bathing at these places.

Now Guru Nanak also decries things like pilgrimage, self-
imposed suffering, compassion and charity, which he believed
brought minimal benefit, if not done with love and humility.
He says:

ਤੀਰਥੁ ਤਪੁ ਦਇਆ ਦਤੁ ਦਾਨੁ ॥ ਜੇ ਕੋ ਪਾਵੈ ਤਿਲ ਕਾ ਮਾਨੁ ॥
ਸੁਣਿਆ ਮੰਨਿਆ ਮਨਿ ਕੀਤਾ ਭਾਉ ॥ ਅੰਤਰਗਤਿ ਤੀਰਥਿ ਮਲਿ ਨਾਉ ॥

Teerath tapp daya dutt daan, jay ko paavai til ka maan.
Suneya manneya munn keeta bhao, antargat teerath mal naao.

तीरथु तपु दइआ दतु दानु ॥ जे को पावै तिल का मानु ॥
सुणिआ मंनिआ मनि कीता भाउ ॥ अंतरगति तीरथि मलि नाउ ॥

> Pilgrimages, religious suffering, compassion or charity;
> These things, if at all, bring honour as miniscule as a
> sesame seed.
> By listening about God, believing in Him and keeping Him in
> the mind with love, one makes inner pilgrimage, and washes
> away dirt of the mind.
>
> M1/4/14

Guru Nanak says those who are satisfied with external bathing alone are not pure. Pure are those who have enshrined God's love in their minds:

> ਸੂਚੇ ਏਹਿ ਨ ਆਖੀਅਹਿ ਬਹਨਿ ਜਿ ਪਿੰਡਾ ਧੋਇ ॥
> ਸੂਚੇ ਸੇਈ ਨਾਨਕਾ ਜਿਨ ਮਨਿ ਵਸਿਆ ਸੋਇ ॥
>
> Soochay eh na aakhiyeh behen je pinda dhoye.
> Soochey seyee Nanaka jin munn vaseya soye.
>
> सूचे एहि न आखीअहि बहनि जि पिंडा धोइ ॥
> सूचे सेई नानका जिन मनि वसिआ सोइ ॥
>
> Don't call them pure, who feel satisfied merely by washing
> their bodies.
> Only those are pure, says Nanak, within whose minds the
> Lord resides.
>
> M1/472/9

Obviously he is not denouncing bathing here, but highlights the greater need for cleansing the mind and creating space for God to reside. Guru Nanak further emphasizes the uselessness of effort by people who are filthy and fake inside:

ਅੰਦਰਹੁ ਝੂਠੇ ਪੈਜ ਬਾਹਰਿ ਦੁਨੀਆ ਅੰਦਰਿ ਫੈਲੁ ॥
ਅਠਸਠਿ ਤੀਰਥ ਜੇ ਨਾਵਹਿ ਉਤਰੈ ਨਾਹੀ ਮੈਲੁ ॥

Androh jhoothay paij bahar duniya ander phayal.
Athsath tirath jay naaveh utrai naahi mayal.

अंदरहु झूठे पैज बाहरि दुनीआ अंदरि फैलु ॥
अठसठि तीरथ जे नावहि उतरै नाही मैलु ॥

There are those who are false within, but make honourable
appearance on the outside.
Even by bathing at the sixty-eight places of pilgrimage, their
mind's filth is not removed.

M1/473/15

Bhagat Kabir also strongly condemned meaningless rituals
and those who propagated them. Here he has something for
the fake ritualistic pandits:

ਗਜ ਸਾਢੇ ਤੈ ਤੈ ਧੋਤੀਆ ਤਿਹਰੇ ਪਾਇਨਿ ਤਗ ॥
ਗਲੀ ਜਿਨ੍ਹਾ ਜਪਮਾਲੀਆ ਲੋਟੇ ਹਥਿ ਨਿਬਗ ॥
ਓਇ ਹਰਿ ਕੇ ਸੰਤ ਨ ਆਖੀਅਹਿ ਬਾਨਾਰਸਿ ਕੇ ਠਗ ॥

Gaj saadhay tai tai dhotia tehray paayin tug.
Gali jinah japmaaliya lotay hath nibug.
Oye Har kay sant na aakhiyeh Banaras kay thug.

गज साढे तै तै धोतीआ तिहरे पाइनि तग ॥
गली जिन्हा जपमालीआ लोटे हथि निबग ॥
ओइ हरि के संत न आखीअहि बानारसि के ठग ॥

They wear three and a half yard long loin cloth, and triple-wound sacred threads.

They wear rosaries around their necks, and carry shining jugs in their hands.

They should not be called Saints of the Lord - they are the thugs of Benares.

Kabir/476/1

Bhagat Kabir again taunts the pandit:

ਹਮ ਘਰਿ ਸੂਤੁ ਤਨਹਿ ਨਿਤ ਤਾਨਾ ਕੰਠਿ ਜਨੇਊ ਤੁਮਾਰੇ ॥
ਤੁਮ ਤਉ ਬੇਦ ਪੜਹੁ ਗਾਇਤ੍ਰੀ ਗੋਬਿੰਦੁ ਰਿਦੈ ਹਮਾਰੇ ॥

Hum ghar soot taneh nit taana kanth janeu tumaaray.
Tum tao beyd paroh gayitri Gobind ridai hamaaray.

हम घरि सूतु तनहि नित ताना कंठि जनेऊ तुमारे॥
तुम्ह तउ बेद पड़हु गाइत्री गोबिंदु रिदै हमारे॥

I weave the thread in my house everyday, while you wear the sacred thread around your neck, (O pandit)
You read the Vedas and sacred hymns, while God resides in my heart.

Kabir/482/11

There is no substitute for true worship, emphasizes Bhagat Kabir:

ਕਬੀਰ ਗੰਗਾ ਤੀਰ ਜੁ ਘਰੁ ਕਰਹਿ ਪੀਵਹਿ ਨਿਰਮਲ ਨੀਰ ॥
ਬਿਨੁ ਹਰਿ ਭਗਤਿ ਨ ਮੁਕਤਿ ਹੋਇ ਇਉ ਕਹਿ ਰਮੇ ਕਬੀਰ ॥

Kabir Ganga teer ju ghar kareh peeveh nirmal neer.
Bin Har bhagat na mukat hoye iu keh ramay Kabir.

कबीर गंगा तीर जु घरु करहि पीवहि निरमल नीरु॥
बिनु हरि भगति न मुकति होइ इउ कहि रमे कबीर॥

Kabir says, even if people build their homes on the banks of
the holy river Ganges and drink its pure water.
Without worship of the Lord, even they are not liberated,
proclaims Kabir.

Kabir/1367/6

Bhagat Kabir has some advice for the followers of Islam too:

ਰੋਜਾ ਧਰੈ ਨਿਵਾਜ ਗੁਜਾਰੈ ਕਲਮਾ ਭਿਸਤਿ ਨ ਹੋਈ॥
ਸਤਰਿ ਕਾਬਾ ਘਟ ਹੀ ਭੀਤਰਿ ਜੇ ਕਰਿ ਜਾਨੈ ਕੋਈ॥

Roja dharai niwaaj gujaarai kalma bhist na hoyee.
Satar Kaba ghatt hee bheetar jay kar jaanai koyee.

रोजा धरै निवाज गुजारै कलमा भिसति न होई॥
सतरि काबा घट ही भीतरि जे करि जानै कोई॥

Fasting, praying, and reading the *Kalma*, shall not get you
the paradise.
The *Kaba* is hidden within your heart, if you only knew it.

Kabir/480/5

Finally, another beautiful verse by Guru Nanak for people
going on ritualistic pilgrimages but are dirty inside:

ਨਾਵਣ ਚਲੇ ਤੀਰਥੀ ਮਨਿ ਖੋਟੈ ਤਨਿ ਚੋਰ॥
ਇਕੁ ਭਾਉ ਲਥੀ ਨਾਤਿਆ ਦੁਇ ਭਾ ਚੜੀਅਸੁ ਹੋਰ॥
ਬਾਹਰਿ ਧੋਤੀ ਤੂਮੜੀ ਅੰਦਰਿ ਵਿਸੁ ਨਿਕੋਰ॥
ਸਾਧ ਭਲੇ ਅਣਨਾਤਿਆ ਚੋਰ ਸਿ ਚੋਰਾ ਚੋਰ॥

Naavan challay teerathi munn khotay tunn chor.

Ikk bhao lathee naateya doi bha charius hor.

Bahar dhoti toomari andar vis nikor.

Saadh bhalay un-nateya chor se chora chor.

नावण चले तीरथी मनि खोटै तनि चोर॥

इकु भाउ लथी नातिआ दुइ भा चड़ीअसु होर॥

बाहरि धोती तूमड़ी अंदरि विसु निकोर॥

साध भले अणनातिआ चोर सि चोरा चोर॥

Pilgrims go to bathe but their minds are evil and their bodies
are thieves/false.

While on one hand a part of their filth is removed by bathing,
on the other they accumulate twice as much.

Like a bitter melon, they are washed on the outside, but
inside they are filled with bitterness.

The holy people are blessed even without such bathing, while
thieves remain thieves (even after bathing).

M1/789/9

There are many more verses in the SGGS against irrelevant
rituals, and there is greater focus on mind purification.
However, many unnecessary rituals are still encouraged
by various religious institutions because they bring visitors
who make large offerings. One should only indulge in those
activities that either create a yearning for God, or in some
way help the needy. Everything else is a waste of time. With
our continued indulgence in purposeless rituals we are going
against the teachings of SGGS.

I recently saw a new ritual being created relating to the
Hukamnama. Hukamnama or the 'daily edict' is a verse picked
up at random from SGGS everyday in every *gurdwara* and
displayed on a board for people to read and follow. Nowadays

the *Hukamnama* from Golden Temple, Amritsar is passed down to Sikhs all over the world through numerous WhatsApp groups. This is a good ritual and is well appreciated. However, someone in the chain has added a new procedure, which asks readers to first cover their head and remove their shoes before opening the *Hukamnama* post. Does that make any sense? If that be so then we must cover our head and remove shoes before opening any device that contains content from SGGS. We should also do that before putting on a TV channel that has *gubani* content. Introduction of such rituals is best avoided.

I conclude the chapter with this beautiful poem by Tagore which clarifies what is a right ritual and what is not:

Go not to the temple to put flowers upon the feet of God. First fill your own house with the fragrance of love...

Go not to the temple to light candles before the altar of God. First remove the darkness of sin from your heart...

Go not to the temple to bow down your head in prayer. First learn to bow in humility before your fellowmen....

Go not to the temple to pray on bended knees. First bend down to lift someone who is down-trodden........

Go not to the temple to ask for forgiveness for your sins. First forgive from your heart those who have sinned against you.

Rabindranath Tagore (1861-1941)
Indian Poet, Nobel Laureate

CHAPTER 16

EQUALITY

Since time immemorial inequality amongst peoples has been the way of life, even though many societies found it undesirable. Total equality is a utopian dream which is almost impossible. The manner in which our society evolved there was no way it could practice equality. On one hand there were kings, emperors, presidents, ministers, princes, generals, business tycoons and other rich and powerful people; on the other there were the underprivileged and deprived sections of society. In between lay the vast majority of middle class. Though there have been changes and modifications in the socio-economic structures, no society or nation has been able to adequately bridge the gaps between various segments – in some cases the gaps have only widened. This has been the bane of India, and of many other nations.

In the world of relativity and materialism, some inequality is perhaps needed, where distinctions and comparisons become necessary. In such environment, some individuals are bound to do better than others. It is fine if they move ahead in life due to their hard work, dedication, devotion, leading ability and so on. What is not acceptable is when success or failure is determined by one's race, caste, religion, colour of the skin etc. - over which the individual has no control.

Guru Nanak (1469-1539) was born at a time when there was great social divide based on the prevailing caste system.

Those from lower castes were treated shabbily and denied even the basic human rights. They were not allowed to enter places of worship. Just touching them was considered to make a person unclean, which had to be cleansed with a body bath. They were not even allowed to draw water from the common village wells. Guru Nanak who belonged to a high *Bedi* clan was perturbed at the situation and strongly condemned the caste system.

He proclaimed:

ਸਭੁ ਕੋ ਉਚਾ ਆਖੀਐ ਨੀਚੁ ਨ ਦੀਸੈ ਕੋਇ ॥

Sabh ko oocha aakheeyai neech na deesai koye.

सभु को ऊचा आखीऐ नीचु न दीसै कोइ ॥

Call everyone exalted, I do not see any one who is lowly.

M1/62/12

Bhagat Kabir expresses the same views on equality in this famous couplet:

ਅਵਲਿ ਅਲਹ ਨੂਰੁ ਉਪਾਇਆ ਕੁਦਰਤਿ ਕੇ ਸਭ ਬੰਦੇ ॥
ਏਕ ਨੂਰ ਤੇ ਸਭੁ ਜਗੁ ਉਪਜਿਆ ਕਉਨ ਭਲੇ ਕੋ ਮੰਦੇ ॥

Awal Allah noor upaaya kudrat kay sabh banday.
Ek noor tay sabh jug upjeya kaun bhalay ko manday.

अवलि अलह नूरु उपाइआ कुदरति के सभ बंदे ॥
एक नूर ते सभु जगु उपजिआ कउन भले को मंदे ॥

The Primal God created the light, all mortal beings are His.
From that One light, the entire world was created, so who is good, and who is bad?

Kabir/1349/19

One of the basic teachings of SGGS is the equality of mankind. In the eyes of God all humans, whether man or woman, rich or poor, from high or low caste, are all equal. Remember, Guru Nanak preached this at a time when, inequality, even in the west, was the accepted norm. Women particularly suffered more, because they were considered as inferior human beings. Equality for women is not covered in this chapter. We shall see it in the next one titled, 'Status of Women'.

During Guru Nanak's times *brahmins* were considered as the highest class of society. They were solely responsible for all matters of spiritual and religious concern; not because of their knowledge and competence, but because they were born into *brahmin* families. They perpetuated this caste system because it suited them. It made them more influential, and brought many attendant benefits.

Bhagat Kabir was totally against inequality. He gave a new definition of a true *brahmin* when he said:

ਕਹੁ ਕਬੀਰ ਜੋ ਬ੍ਰਹਮੁ ਬੀਚਾਰੈ ॥ ਸੋ ਬ੍ਰਾਹਮਣੁ ਕਹੀਅਤੁ ਹੈ ਹਮਾਰੈ ॥

Kahu Kabir jo Brahm bichaarai, so brahman kahiyat hai hamaarai.

कहु कबीर जो ब्रहमु बीचारै ॥ सो ब्राहमणु कहीअतु है हमारै ॥

Says Kabir, only he who contemplates on God, is considered a *brahmin* by me.

Kabir/324/19

In matters of spirituality, people from modest backgrounds have achieved greater success compared to those burdened with material abundance and high social status. Despite their low castes, Bhagat Kabir (weaver), Bhagat Ravidas (shoe maker), Bhagat Namdev (tailor), Bhagat Sain (barber), and Bhagat Sadhna (butcher), all attained high spiritual position because of their deep devotion and sincere worship of God.

Their writings were chosen to form part of SGGS. They didn't care about high or low social background. In fact Bhagat Kabir spoke of his low caste with great pride when he said:

ਕਬੀਰ ਮੇਰੀ ਜਾਤਿ ਕਉ ਸਭੁ ਕੋ ਹਸਨੇਹਾਰੁ ॥
ਬਲਿਹਾਰੀ ਇਸ ਜਾਤਿ ਕਉ ਜਿਹ ਜਪਿਓ ਸਿਰਜਨਹਾਰੁ ॥

Kabir meri jaat kau sabh ko hasnayhaar.
Balihaaree is jaat kau jih japeyo Sirjanhaar.

कबीर मेरी जाति कउ सभु को हसनेहारु ॥
बलिहारी इस जाति कउ जिह जपिओ सिरजनहारु ॥

Kabir says, everyone laughs at my (low) caste.
I offer myself as sacrifice unto this caste, which makes me sing praises of the Creator.

Kabir/1364/12

Some more verses that condemn casteism and inequality.

Guru Nanak says:

ਜਾਣਹੁ ਜੋਤਿ ਨ ਪੂਛਹੁ ਜਾਤੀ ਆਗੈ ਜਾਤਿ ਨ ਹੇ ॥

Jaanoh jyot na poochhoh jaati aagai jaat na hay.

जाणहु जोति न पूछहु जाती आगै जाति न हे ॥

Recognize the Lord's light (within), and do not consider the caste; there is no caste in the life hereafter.

M1/349/13

Guru Amar Das cautions against ego born out of high caste:

ਜਾਤਿ ਕਾ ਗਰਬੁ ਨ ਕਰੀਅਹੁ ਕੋਈ ॥ ਬ੍ਰਹਮੁ ਬਿੰਦੇ ਸੋ ਬ੍ਰਾਹਮਣੁ ਹੋਈ ॥
ਜਾਤਿ ਕਾ ਗਰਬੁ ਨ ਕਰਿ ਮੂਰਖ ਗਵਾਰਾ ॥ ਇਸੁ ਗਰਬ ਤੇ ਚਲਹਿ ਬਹੁਤੁ ਵਿਕਾਰਾ ॥

Jaat ka garbh na karioh koyee, Brahm binday so
brahman hoyee.

Jaat ka garbh na kar murakh gwara, is garbh tay chalay
bahut vikaara.

जाति का गरबु न करीअहु कोई॥ ब्रहमु बिंदे सो ब्राहमणु होई॥

जाति का गरबु न करि मूरख गवारा॥ इसु गरब ते चलहि बहुतु विकारा॥

Let no one be proud of his caste, only he who learns about
God is a *brahmin*.

Do not be proud of your caste, you stupid rustic, too much evil
comes from this pride.

M3/1127/19

Guru Nanak says we all have the same divine light and
therefore all are born equal:

ਸਭ ਮਹਿ ਜੋਤਿ ਜੋਤਿ ਹੈ ਸੋਇ॥ ਤਿਸ ਕੈ ਚਾਨਣਿ ਸਭ ਮਹਿ ਚਾਨਣੁ ਹੋਇ॥

Sabh meh jyot jyot hai soye; tis kai chanan sabh meh
chanan hoye.

सभ महि जोति जोति है सोइ॥ तिस कै चानणि सभ महि चानणु होइ॥

The spark of divine light is in everyone, the same light;
That light shines and enlightens everyone.

M1/663/8

Guru Nanak again on divine light in all:

ਗੁਰਮੁਖਿ ਏਕ ਦ੍ਰਿਸਟਿ ਕਰਿ ਦੇਖਹੁ ਘਟਿ ਘਟਿ ਜੋਤਿ ਸਮੋਈ ਜੀਉ॥

Gurmukh ek drisht kar dekhoh ghat ghat jyot samoyee jiu.

गुरमुखि एक द्रिसटि करि देखहु घटि घटि जोति समोई जीउ॥

O *gurmukh,* see all from a common view point, and you will
find the spark of same divine light in all.

M1/599/2

High education and over intelligence, of which *brahmins*
were so proud of, are not necessary for spiritual growth;
in fact they often become a hindrance, as they boost one's
ego. In the following two verses Guru Arjan Dev speaks
of this:

ਜੋ ਪ੍ਰਾਣੀ ਗੋਵਿੰਦੁ ਧਿਆਵੈ ॥ ਪੜਿਆ ਅਣਪੜਿਆ ਪਰਮ ਗਤਿ ਪਾਵੈ ॥

Jo pranee Govind dhyaavai, pareya unpareya param gatt
paavai.

जो प्राणी गोर्विंदु धिआवै ॥ पड़िआ अणपड़िआ परम गति पावै ॥

He who meditates on the Lord,
Attains the highest spiritual status - educated or not.

M5/197/18

He says the same about intellect:

ਸਿਆਨਪ ਕਾਹੂ ਕਾਮਿ ਨ ਆਤ ॥ ਜੋ ਅਨਰੂਪਿਓ ਠਾਕੁਰਿ ਮੇਰੈ ਹੋਇ ਰਹੀ ਉਹ ਬਾਤ ॥

Sianap kahoo kaam na aat, jo anroopeyo Thakur meyrai hoye
rahee oh baat.

सिआनप काहू कामि न आत ॥ जो अनरूपिओ ठाकुरि मेरै होइ रही उह बात ॥

One's high intellect is of no use, whatever my Master has
planned, that alone comes to pass.

M5/496/10

Justice to the poor and weaker sections of the society has always been major area of concern for the awakened saints. Bhagat Kabir says anyone who fights for such people to the end is really brave:

ਸੂਰਾ ਸੋ ਪਹਿਚਾਨੀਐ ਜੁ ਲਰੈ ਦੀਨ ਕੇ ਹੇਤ॥
ਪੁਰਜਾ ਪੁਰਜਾ ਕਟਿ ਮਰੈ ਕਬਹੂ ਨ ਛਾਡੈ ਖੇਤੁ॥

Soora so pehchaniyai ju larai deen kay heyt; purja purja kut marai kabhoo na chhaadai kheyt.

सूरा सो पहिचानीऐ जु लरै दीन के हेत॥
पुरजा पुरजा कटि मरै कबहू न छाडै खेतु॥

Consider him to be brave who fights for the poor, and who would rather be cut into pieces than leave the battleground/struggle.

Kabir/1105/5

Some people mistakenly believe that the above couplet was a call by Guru Gobind Singh to fight for the religion. As you would notice, it is not Guru Gobind Singh's couplet but Bhagat Kabir's. Also, the call is to fight for the poor, not the religion. The meaning of *deen* here is the poor, the meek, the downtrodden – like *deen dayal* (kind to the poor) or *deen kay daatay* (giver to the poor). So the call is to fight for justice to the poor so as to give them equal opportunity in life.

Even though inequality amongst mankind is strongly condemned in SGGS, it is sad to see that many Sikhs have failed to follow this advice. Divisions based on caste/class are still prevalent in the birth place of Sikhism. Lower caste people, in many areas of rural Punjab, even today are not allowed to enter *gurdwaras* of the so-called upper class. This inequality based on parentage continues to be the scourge of underprivileged people, not only in Punjab, but the world over. The sooner it is done away with the better.

"Othay Amlaan De Honay Nay Niberay, Kissay Ni Teri Jaat Puchhni."

[There (in afterlife) only your deeds will be taken into account, no one will ask what your caste was.]

Baba Bulle Shah (1680-1757)
Punjabi Sufi Poet

CHAPTER 17

STATUS OF WOMEN

ੴ

During the Vedic period, it is believed that Indian women enjoyed same status and rights as men. Subsequently, their status began to decline due to outside influences. Islamist plunderers who frequently raided from across the northwestern borders, contributed immensely towards lowering of women's status from 11th century onwards. Since Islam permitted polygamy, the raiding armies captured Indian women and took them away to join their harems. Many were raped and made servants or slaves and exploited in all possible ways, including prostitution. They were treated as mere property, whose only value was as a servant, or for entertainment/enjoyment. They were also considered as seducers who distracted men from spiritual development.

As a result thereof Indian society started seeing the girl as a liability to be kept at home and protected. This led to unwanted customs and traditions like child marriage, *sati, johur, purdah* and denial of school education. *Sati* was a custom where the widow jumped into the pyre lit for her dead husband's cremation, and died with him. *Johur* was similar to *sati* but done en masse.

Such was the status of women when SGGS was being compiled. The authors of SGGS spoke very highly of women and put them on a high pedestal. Guru Nanak shocked the entire society by preaching that women were worthy of praise and were equal to men. He did this five hundred years ago - something the modern world is still fighting for.

This was Guru Nanak's view on women:

ਭੰਡਿ ਜੰਮੀਐ ਭੰਡਿ ਨਿੰਮੀਐ ਭੰਡਿ ਮੰਗਣੁ ਵੀਆਹੁ॥
ਭੰਡਹੁ ਹੋਵੈ ਦੋਸਤੀ ਭੰਡਹੁ ਚਲੈ ਰਾਹੁ॥

Bhand jammiyai bhand nimmiyai bhand mangan viaaho;
bhandoh hovay dosti bhandoh challay raaho.

ਭੰਡਿ ਜਮੀਏ ਭੰਡਿ ਨਿਮੀਏ ਭੰਡਿ ਮੰਗਣੁ ਵੀਆਹੁ॥
ਭੰਡਹੁ ਹੋਵੈ ਦੋਸਤੀ ਭੰਡਹੁ ਚਲੈ ਰਾਹੁ॥

A man is born of a woman, conceived by a woman, and to the
woman he is engaged and married.
He befriends a woman and through her lineage continues.

ਭੰਡੁ ਮੁਆ ਭੰਡੁ ਭਾਲੀਐ ਭੰਡਿ ਹੋਵੈ ਬੰਧਾਨੁ॥ ਸੋ ਕਿਉ ਮੰਦਾ ਆਖੀਐ ਜਿਤੁ ਜੰਮਹਿ ਰਾਜਾਨ॥

Bhand mooya bhand bhaaliyai bhand hovay bandhaan,
so kiu manda aakhiyai jit jammeh raajaan.

ਭੰਡੁ ਮੁਆ ਭੰਡੁ ਭਾਲੀਏ ਭੰਡਿ ਹੋਵੈ ਬੰਧਾਨੁ॥
ਸੋ ਕਿਉ ਮੰਦਾ ਆਖੀਏ ਜਿਤੁ ਜਮਹਿ ਰਾਜਾਨ॥

When his woman (wife) dies man seeks another woman,
relationships are built by women. Why call her bad who
gives birth to kings?

ਭੰਡਹੁ ਹੀ ਭੰਡੁ ਊਪਜੈ ਭੰਡੈ ਬਾਝੁ ਨ ਕੋਇ॥ ਨਾਨਕ ਭੰਡੈ ਬਾਹਰਾ ਏਕੋ ਸਚਾ ਸੋਇ॥

Bhandoh hee bhand oopjai bhandai baajh na koye, Nanak
bhandai baahra eko Sacha soye.

ਭੰਡਹੁ ਹੀ ਭੰਡੁ ਊਪਜੈ ਭੰਡੈ ਬਾਝੁ ਨ ਕੋਇ॥ ਨਾਨਕ ਭੰਡੈ ਬਾਹਰਾ ਏਕੋ ਸਚਾ ਸੋਇ॥

Woman is also born of a woman, without the woman there
would be no one. O Nanak, only the True Lord is beyond the
need of a woman.

M1/473/8

The words "bhandoh challey raho" (through woman the lineage continues) in the first line of the first verse above are significant. Guru Nanak says it is the woman through whom the family lineage continues – not through the man, as commonly believed. Sometimes we may not even know who the father of a child is, but about the mother there is never a doubt. That only a man continues the family name, is a man-made proposition because of which people continue to seek male child for family progression. The truth is that nature has given this gift to woman.

In the second line of above verse Guru Nanak says, "bhand hovey bandhaan" (relationships are built by woman). This shows Guru Nanak's understanding of human psychology. Only in the recent times people in the west, have begun to accept that women are better at developing and maintaining relationships as compared to their male counterparts. In a study conducted in 2018 by scientists at Cambridge University, involving survey of 6,50,000 people, it was established that men and women indeed think differently. It was found that while men were more likely to prefer things and systems, women were more interested in people and emotions. Guru Nanak knew this long ago.

SGGS is very critical of the heinous *sati* system mentioned above. Guru Amar Das on true meaning of *sati*:

ਸਤੀਆ ਏਹਿ ਨ ਆਖੀਅਨਿ ਜੋ ਮੜਿਆ ਲਗਿ ਜਲੰਨ੍ਹਿ ॥
ਨਾਨਕ ਸਤੀਆ ਜਾਣੀਅਨਿੑ ਜਿ ਬਿਰਹੇ ਚੋਟ ਮਰੰਨ੍ਹਿ ॥

Satiya eh na aakhiyan jo marheya lagg jalannih.
Nanak satia jaaniyaneh je birhay choat marannih.

सतीआ एहि न आखीअनि जो मड़िआ लगि जलंन्हि॥
नानक सतीआ जाणीअन्हि जि बिरहे चोट मरंन्हि॥

Do not call them *sati*, who burn themselves along with their dead husbands.

O Nanak, know them as *sati*, who die (within) from the shock of separation (from God).

ਭੀ ਸੋ ਸਤੀਆ ਜਾਣੀਅਨਿ ਸੀਲ ਸੰਤੋਖਿ ਰਹੰਨ੍ਹਿ ॥
ਸੇਵਨਿ ਸਾਈ ਆਪਣਾ ਨਿਤ ਉਠਿ ਸੰਮ੍ਹਾਲੰਨ੍ਹਿ ॥

Bhi so satiya jaaniyan seel santokh rehannih.
Sevan saayee aapna nit uth samhaa-lannih.

भी सो सतीआ जाणीअनि सील संतोखि रहंन्हि ॥
सेवनि साई आपणा नित उठि सम्हालंन्हि ॥

They too are known as *sati*, who remain calm and contented.
And who serve their Lord, and daily awaken to worship Him.

M3/787/8

SGGS equates women with men in another way. Both are given equal opportunity to seek God. In relationship to God women and men are both considered as females and there is only One male in the universe. He is the Husband Lord of all. To say that God is the only male, and all others are females, is just a reflection of the prevalent patriarchal society. It doesn't mean He is actually a 'male' Husband Lord.

Guru Nanak says:

ਠਾਕੁਰੁ ਏਕੁ ਸਬਾਈ ਨਾਰਿ ॥
Thakur ek sabayee naar.
ठाकुरु एकु सबाई नारि ॥

There is only one Husband Lord, all others are women.

M1/933/12

Guru Amar Das expresses similar views:

ਇਸੁ ਜਗ ਮਹਿ ਪੁਰਖੁ ਏਕੁ ਹੈ ਹੋਰ ਸਗਲੀ ਨਾਰਿ ਸਬਾਈ॥
ਸਭਿ ਘਟ ਭੋਗਵੈ ਅਲਿਪਤੁ ਰਹੈ ਅਲਖੁ ਨ ਲਖਣਾ ਜਾਈ॥

Is jagg meh purakh ek hai hor sagli naar sabaayee.
Sabh ghat bhogvai alpat rahay alakh na lakhna jaayee.

इसु जग महि पुरखु एकु है होर सगली नारि सबाई॥
सभि घट भोगवै अलिपतु रहै अलखु न लखणा जाई॥

In this world there is only One Male all others are females.
He indulges in and enjoys all hearts, yet He remains
detached, He cannot be known or described.

M3/591/19

Guru Amar Das again speaks of the relationship with God:

ਮੈ ਕਾਮਣਿ ਮੇਰਾ ਕੰਤੁ ਕਰਤਾਰੁ॥ ਜੇਹਾ ਕਰਾਏ ਤੇਹਾ ਕਰੀ ਸੀਗਾਰੁ॥
ਜਾਂ ਤਿਸੁ ਭਾਵੈ ਤਾਂ ਕਰੇ ਭੋਗੁ॥ ਤਨੁ ਮਨੁ ਸਾਚੇ ਸਾਹਿਬ ਜੋਗੁ॥

Mai kaaman mera kantt Kartaar; jeha karaaye teha
kari sigaar.
Ja tis bhaavay ta karay bhog; tunn munn Saachay Sahib joag.

मै कामणि मेरा कंतु करतारु॥ जेहा कराए तेहा करी सीगारु॥
जां तिसु भावै तां करे भोगु॥ तनु मनु साचे साहिब जोगु॥

I am the bride and my husband is the Creator,
As He desires so I adorn myself.
As it pleases Him, He has a union with me.
My body and mind are merged with my True Lord.

M3/1128/13

When gurus and *bhagats* say they present themselves as women in front of God, it is indeed a true tribute to women, because these enlightened people accept women as their equals.

The above verse seems to indicate that women are surrendering to God for physical and sexual union – that is not correct. God exists in the spiritual domain where there is no physicality, no gender, no sex. He is above sexual need or desire. It should be seen as an urge for spiritual union and complete surrender of the mind.

Guru Nanak reaffirms here that God has no sexual desire and has no woman:

ਨਾ ਤਿਸੁ ਮਾਤ ਪਿਤਾ ਸੁਤ ਬੰਧਪ ਨਾ ਤਿਸੁ ਕਾਮੁ ਨ ਨਾਰੀ॥

Na tis maat pita sut bandhap na tis kaam na naaree.

ना तिसु मात पिता सुत बंधप ना तिसु कामु न नारी॥

God has no mother, father, sons or relatives, He has no sexual desire and has no woman.

M1/597/6

Some people feel that if God is said to be the only male Husband Lord, doesn't it show lower status of women. The answer lies in what Guru Nanak now says here:

ਆਪੇ ਪੁਰਖੁ ਆਪੇ ਹੀ ਨਾਰੀ॥

Aappay purakh aappay hi naaree.

आपे पुरखु आपे ही नारी॥

God himself is male as well as female too.

M1/1020/15

Bhagat Namdev shows concern for women by condemning men who commit adultery:

> ਘਰ ਕੀ ਨਾਰਿ ਤਿਆਗੈ ਅੰਧਾ॥ ਪਰ ਨਾਰੀ ਸਿਉ ਘਾਲੈ ਧੰਧਾ॥
> ਜੈਸੇ ਸਿੰਬਲੁ ਦੇਖਿ ਸੂਆ ਬਿਗਸਾਨਾ॥ ਅੰਤ ਕੀ ਬਾਰ ਮੂਆ ਲਪਟਾਨਾ॥
>
> Ghar ki naar tyagai andhaa, par naaree siu ghaalai dhandha.
> Jaisay simbal dekh sua bigsaana, antt ki baar mua laptaana.
>
> घर की नारि तिआगै अंधा॥ पर नारी सिउ घालै धंधा॥
> जैसे सि्मबलु देखि सूआ बिगसाना॥ अंत की बार मूआ लपटाना॥
>
> The blind fool abandons his own wife,
> and has an affair with another's woman.
> He is like the parrot, who is excited to see the big *simmal* tree,
> but in the end, dies by getting stuck to it.
>
> Namdev/1164/19

Guru Amar Das explains true meaning of husband and wife reflecting equality of the two:

> ਧਨ ਪਿਰੁ ਏਹਿ ਨ ਆਖੀਅਨਿ ਬਹਨਿ ਇਕਠੇ ਹੋਇ॥
> ਏਕ ਜੋਤਿ ਦੁਇ ਮੂਰਤੀ ਧਨ ਪਿਰੁ ਕਹੀਐ ਸੋਇ॥
>
> Dhan pir eh na aakhiyan behan ikkathay hoye,
> Ek jot dui moorti dhan pir kaheeyai soye.
>
> धन पिरु एहि न आखीअनि बहनि इकठे होइ॥
> एक जोति दुइ मूरती धन पिरु कहीऐ सोइ॥
>
> They are not called husband and wife,
> who merely sit together.
> Only those are called husband and wife who have one
> light in two bodies (who are soul-mates).
>
> M3/788/11

Even in the most developed countries of the west, women did not enjoy the same status and rights as men till as late as early part of the 20th century. New Zealand was the first country to give voting rights to women in 1893 followed by Australia in 1902. In USA, Britain and Canada women got the right to vote only after the end of World War I (1919).

Interestingly, one of the leading campaigners for women's right to vote in Britain was a Sikh lady, Princess Sophia Duleep Singh, grand-daughter of Maharaja Ranjit Singh. She was a very popular high socialite in UK. In 1907, she visited her grandfather's erstwhile Sikh kingdom in Punjab. She was greatly impressed when she learnt about justice and equality that prevailed in his empire. She returned to UK and left her high society life, to become a women's rights campaigner. Women in UK got full voting rights in 1928 for which Sophia's contribution was notable.

The reason for lower status of women in the west lies in the Bible and the Church which have been against women's equality. Elizabeth Cady Stanton, 19th century feminist said, "The Bible and the Church have been the greatest stumbling blocks in the way of woman's emancipation." Bible teaches that men are more valuable than women, that women should not seek to have a voice, and that women should not teach or lead. Islam also believes women are inferior. The Quran preaches that supremacy of man is the will of Allah, and that women should live as submissive and obedient wives. In India too there are some sects that still haven't given equal status to women. The *Digambara* sect of Jainism, for example, does not allow a woman to seek enlightenment – she must first be born as a male.

Notwithstanding the above, there is now greater acceptance of girl child, particularly among the more aware societies.

You come across many couples these days who prefer to have daughters rather than sons.

"Freedom cannot be achieved unless women have been emancipated from all kinds of oppression."

Nelson Mandela (1918-2013)
Former PM, South Africa

CHAPTER 18

SEEKER AS HOUSEHOLDER

India has a strong tradition of renunciation by those seeking spiritual awakening. These seekers become *sanyasins* (male) *or sanyasinis* (female) and leave their homes and families for prolonged periods of time – sometimes forever. They go and live in secluded places in distant jungles, mountains or monasteries. They do this in order to focus their attention on meditation and worship, without the distractions of worldly life. Such escape may be fine for those who have no familial duties. Renouncing the world when you still have responsibilities, amounts to shirking your duty.

However, there can be other circumstances where leaving the family could be acceptable - when this is done for a higher good. In Parmahansa Yogananda's book 'Autobiography of a Yogi', Sri Yukteswar tells his disciple Yogananda, "Remember that he who discards his worldly duties can justify himself only by assuming some kind of responsibility towards a much larger family." Guru Nanak went on long journeys to different parts of the world because he was ordained by God to spread His message to maximum people. He could not have done that staying at home. Parmahansa Yogananda left his parents in India and went to USA for similar reasons.

SGGS does not advocate running away from the world to seek God. While you seek Him you must continue to be a good householder - which means being a good father, mother, son, daughter, husband, wife, teacher, friend, and so on. God is to be attained alongside your commitments of the material world, not by running away. This was a revolutionary change in thinking brought about by Guru Nanak because most of the God-realized men during that time were renunciates.

Here are some verses from SGGS that tell us not to escape from the world. Guru Nanak says it is God's greatness that liberation can be achieved while still being a householder:

ਸਤਿਗੁਰ ਕੀ ਐਸੀ ਵਡਿਆਈ॥ ਪੁਤੂ ਕਲਤੂ ਵਿਚੇ ਗਤਿ ਪਾਈ॥

Satgur ki aisee vadeyaayee; putar kalatar vichay gat paayee.

सतिगुर की ऐसी वडिआई॥ पुत्र कलत्र विचे गति पाई॥

Such is the glory of God, one can attain liberation while still living with wife and children.

M1/661/13

Sheikh Farid says, God is to be found within, not in the jungles:

ਫਰੀਦਾ ਜੰਗਲੁ ਜੰਗਲੁ ਕਿਆ ਭਵਹਿ ਵਣਿ ਕੰਡਾ ਮੋੜੇਹਿ॥
ਵਸੀ ਰਬੁ ਹਿਆਲੀਐ ਜੰਗਲੁ ਕਿਆ ਢੂਢੇਹਿ॥

Farida jungle jungle kia bhaveh van kanda moreh.
Vassi rub hiyaliyai jungle kya doodeh.

फरीदा जंगलु जंगलु किआ भवहि वणि कंडा मोड़ेहि॥
वसी रबु हिआलीऐ जंगलु किआ ढूढेहि॥

Farid says, why wander around in jungles, pushing aside wild thorns?
Lord abides in your heart, why search for Him in the jungle?

Farid/1378/17

It is said that when Lord Buddha visited his family after his enlightenment, his wife Yashodhara had just one question for him – was it necessary for him to have abandoned his wife, infant child and his kingdom to achieve enlightenment? Buddha said *no*, he could have easily achieved it even being in the world; but he did not know it then.

In the verse below Guru Ram Das says enlightenment can be attained by regular chanting of Lord's name and that detachment from *maya* can be practiced while remaining a householder:

ਜਪਿ ਮਨ ਰਾਮ ਨਾਮ ਪਰਗਾਸ ॥
ਹਰਿ ਕੇ ਸੰਤ ਮਿਲਿ ਪ੍ਰੀਤਿ ਲਗਾਨੀ ਵਿਚੇ ਗਿਰਹ ਉਦਾਸ ॥

Jupp munn Ram naam pargaas.
Har kay sant mil preet lagaani vichay gireh udaas.

जपि मन राम नाम परगास ॥
हरिके संत मिलि प्रीति लगानी विचे गिरह उदास ॥

O mind, chant Lord's name, to be enlightened.
By meeting Lord's saints, develop love (for God),
and be detached while remaining at home.

M4/1295/3

The word *udaas* mentioned above ordinarily means sad, but in spiritual matters it means 'detached.' 'Detached' itself has a different meaning here from the one commonly understood. Spiritually, you are detached from something or someone when you are neither over-dependent on them nor worried about losing them. You should enjoy benefits of what you have, but if anything is taken away it should not cause any pain or hurt. Take it as God's will and thank Him for whatever He gave you, for whatever period of time. That is being *udaas* or detached.

Guru Nanak describes a true householder:

ਸੋ ਗਿਰਹੀ ਜੋ ਨਿਗ੍ਰਹੁ ਕਰੈ॥ ਜਪੁ ਤਪੁ ਸੰਜਮ ਭੀਖਿਆ ਕਰੈ॥
ਪੁੰਨ ਦਾਨ ਕਾ ਕਰੇ ਸਰੀਰੁ॥ ਸੋ ਗਿਰਹੀ ਗੰਗਾ ਕਾ ਨੀਰੁ॥

So girhee jo nigroh karai, jupp tupp sanjam
bheekheya karai.
Punn daan ka karay sareer, so girhi Ganga ka neer.

सो गिरही जो निग्रहु करै॥ जपु तपु संजमु भीखिआ करै॥
पुंन दान का करे सरीरु॥ सो गिरही गंगा का नीरु॥

True householder is the one who restrains his bodily
passions, who seeks worship, devotion and patience.
Whose body is engaged in good deeds and charity -
he becomes pure like the water of
the Ganges.

M1/952/13

Guru Amar Das on being detached while at home:

ਵਿਚੇ ਗਿਰਹ ਉਦਾਸ ਅਲਿਪਤ ਲਿਵ ਲਾਇਆ॥
ਓਨਾ ਸੋਗੁ ਵਿਜੋਗੁ ਨ ਵਿਆਪਈ ਹਰਿ ਭਾਣਾ ਭਾਇਆ॥
ਨਾਨਕ ਹਰਿ ਸੇਤੀ ਸਦਾ ਰਵਿ ਰਹੇ ਧੁਰਿ ਲਏ ਮਿਲਾਇਆ॥

Vichay girha udaas alpat liv laaya.
Ona sog vijog na viaapayee Har bhaana bhaaya.
Nanak Har seti sadaa rav rahay dhur laye milaaya.

विचे गिरह उदास अलिपत लिव लाइआ॥
ओना सोगु विजोगु न विआपई हरि भाणा भाइआ॥
नानक हरि सेती सदा रवि रहे धुरि लए मिलाइआ॥

Though with the families they are detached, and their minds are with the Lord.

They are not affected by sorrow or separation, and happily accept God's will.

They remain immersed in the Lord, who merges them with Himself.

M3/1249/7

Guru Amar Das now explains the mental state of householders who are seekers:

ਗਿਰਹੀ ਮਹਿ ਸਦਾ ਹਰਿ ਜਨ ਉਦਾਸੀ ਗਿਆਨ ਤਤ ਬੀਚਾਰੀ ॥
ਸਤਿਗੁਰੁ ਸੇਵਿ ਸਦਾ ਸੁਖੁ ਪਾਇਆ ਹਰਿ ਰਾਖਿਆ ਉਰ ਧਾਰੀ ॥

Girahee meh sadaa Har jan udaasee gyan tutt bichaaree.
Satgur sev sadaa sukh paaya Har raakheya ur dhaaree.

गिरही महि सदा हरि जन उदासी गिआन तत बीचारी ॥
सतिगुरु सेवि सदा सुखु पाइआ हरि राखिआ उर धारी ॥

Despite being householder the devotees always remain detached (from worldly life) and contemplate on essence of spiritual knowledge.

Keeping the Lord in their heart, they serve the True Guru and are ever happy.

M3/599/18

Guru Amar Das again on detachment:

ਆਸਾ ਵਿਚਿ ਅਤਿ ਦੁਖੁ ਘਣਾ ਮਨਮੁਖਿ ਚਿਤੁ ਲਾਇਆ ॥
ਗੁਰਮੁਖਿ ਭਏ ਨਿਰਾਸ ਪਰਮ ਸੁਖੁ ਪਾਇਆ ॥
ਵਿਚੇ ਗਿਰਹ ਉਦਾਸ ਅਲਿਪਤ ਲਿਵ ਲਾਇਆ ॥

Aasa vich utt dukh ghana manmukh chit laaya.

Gurmukh bhaye niraas param sukh paaya.

Vichay girah udaas alpat liv laaya.

आसा विचि अति दुखु घणा मनमुखि चितु लाइआ॥

गुरमुखि भए निरास परम सुखु पाइआ॥

विचे गिरहु उदास अलिपत लिव लाइआ॥

The self-oriented people follow their mind, and have
expectations that cause immense pain.
The God-oriented people have no expectations, and they
enjoy supreme happiness.
Even as family men they remain detached and are
attuned to God.

ਓਨਾ ਸੋਗੁ ਵਿਜੋਗੁ ਨ ਵਿਆਪਈ ਹਰਿ ਭਾਣਾ ਭਾਇਆ॥

ਨਾਨਕ ਹਰਿ ਸੇਤੀ ਸਦਾ ਰਵਿ ਰਹੇ ਧੁਰਿ ਲਏ ਮਿਲਾਇਆ॥

Ona sog vijog na viaapayee Har bhaana bhaaya.

Nanak Har seti sadaa rav rahay dhur laye milaaya.

ओना सोगु विजोगु न विआपई हरि भाणा भाइआ॥

नानक हरि सेती सदा रवि रहे धुरि लए मिलाइआ॥

They do not suffer sorrow or separation, because they accept
God's will.
Nanak says they remain immersed in God, who merges them
with Himself.

M3/1249/6

Unless you have a large inheritance you cannot survive in
this world without work. As a householder you have to earn
money to put food on the table. How can you seek God when
your stomach is crying with hunger, when you and your
family's very survival is at stake?

Bhagat Kabir makes this plaint to God:

ਭੂਖੇ ਭਗਤਿ ਨ ਕੀਜੈ ॥ ਯਹ ਮਾਲਾ ਅਪਨੀ ਲੀਜੈ ॥

Bhookhay bhagat na keejai; yeh maala apni leejai.

भूखे भगति न कीजै ॥ यह माला अपनी लीजै ॥

With an empty stomach I cannot worship.
Here, take back Your rosary.

Kabir/656/13

Bhagat Kabir again says, it is not possible to worship when you are starving and are not sure whether you will get your next meal or not. God is not met by giving up food and starving:

ਅੰਨੈ ਬਿਨਾ ਨ ਹੋਇ ਸੁਕਾਲੁ ॥ ਤਜਿਐ ਅੰਨ ਨ ਮਿਲੈ ਗੁਪਾਲੁ ॥
ਕਹੁ ਕਬੀਰ ਹਮ ਐਸੇ ਜਾਨਿਆ ॥ ਧੰਨੁ ਅਨਾਦਿ ਠਾਕੁਰ ਮਨੁ ਮਾਨਿਆ ॥

Annai binaa na hoye sukaal, tajeeyai ann na milai Gopal.
Kahu Kabir hum aisay jaaneya, dhann anaad Thakur
munn maaneya.

अंनै बिना न होइ सुकालु ॥ तजिऐ अंनि न मिलै गुपालु ॥
कहु कबीर हम ऐसे जानिआ ॥ धंनु अनादि ठाकुर मनु मानिआ ॥

Without food there can be no peace, God is not met by giving
up food.
Says Kabir, this is what I have known, blessed is the food
which builds my faith in the Lord.

Kabir/873/5

As a householder you must be honest all the time in your thought, speech and action. Selfish dealings will not get you anywhere and will only add to your bad karma. Guru Nanak says corrupt dealings give immense pain:

ਜਿਨਾ ਰਾਸਿ ਨ ਸਚੁ ਹੈ ਕਿਉ ਤਿਨਾ ਸੁਖੁ ਹੋਇ॥

ਖੋਟੈ ਵਣਜਿ ਵਣੀਜਿਐ ਮਨ ਤਨ ਖੋਟਾ ਹੋਇ॥

ਫਾਹੀ ਫਾਥੇ ਮਿਰਗ ਜਿਉ ਦੁਖੁ ਘਨੋ ਨਿਤ ਰੋਇ॥

Jina raas na such hai kiu tina sukh hoye.

Khotay vanaj vanjiyai munn tunn khota hoye.

Fahee faathay mirg jiu dukh ghano nit roye.

जिना रासि न सचु है किउ तिना सुखु होइ॥

खोटै वणजि वणंजिऐ मनु तनु खोटा होइ॥

फाही फाथे मिरग जिउ दूखु घणो नित रोइ॥

Those who do not find truth acceptable, how can they
find happiness?
With corrupt dealings, the mind and body become corrupt.
Like a deer caught in the trap, they undergo terrible
agony and cry daily.

M1/23/1

Bhagat Kabir says, be very clear about what you choose to be:

ਕਬੀਰ ਜਉ ਗ੍ਰਿਹੁ ਕਰਹਿ ਤ ਧਰਮੁ ਕਰੁ ਨਾਹੀ ਤ ਕਰੁ ਬੈਰਾਗੁ॥

ਬੈਰਾਗੀ ਬੰਧਨੁ ਕਰੈ ਤਾ ਕੋ ਬਡੋ ਅਭਾਗੁ॥

Kabir jao grih kareh ta dharma kar nahi ta kar bairaag.

Bairaagi bandhan karai ta ko barho abhaag.

कबीर जउ ग्रिहु करहि त धरमु करु नाही त करु बैरागु॥

बैरागी बंधनु करै ता को बडो अभागु॥

Kabir says, if you are a householder, then you must practice
righteousness, otherwise it is better you became a renunciate.
It will be your great misfortune if having become a renunciate,
you still get entangled in worldly affairs.

Kabir/1377/13

As a seeker and a householder your earnings must be clean. Like you need clean air to breathe, clean water to drink and clean food to eat, similarly, you need clean money to live a virtuous life. Your dealings must be honest and truthful, all the time. It won't do if you indulge in cheating and hurting people most of the time and then seek God's forgiveness once in a while. Laws of God don't operate that way. All your deeds will be accounted for.

If your urge for meeting God is strong enough you will find Him while you are a householder. All the Sikh Gurus attained high spiritual status while at home. Those who went on long journeys did so only to preach the Lord's message, as ordained by Him. All of them were married and had children, except Guru Har Krishan who died young.

Being an honest householder and a serious worshipper is not easy. But don't worry, God will help you all the way. Your worship and hard work will be suitably rewarded.

Guru Nanak says:

ਜਿਨੀ ਨਾਮੁ ਧਿਆਇਆ ਗਏ ਮਸਕਤਿ ਘਾਲਿ॥
ਨਾਨਕ ਤੇ ਮੁਖ ਉਜਲੇ ਕੇਤੀ ਛੁਟੀ ਨਾਲਿ॥

Jini naam dhayaaya gaye masakat ghaal.
Nanak tay mukh ujlay keti chhutti naal.

जिनी नामु धिआइआ गए मसकति घालि॥
नानक ते मुख उजले केती छुटी नालि॥

Those who meditate on the Name, and leave the world after working hard;
O Nanak, in the Lord's Court, their faces glow (due to spiritual bliss), and many others are saved with them.

M1/8/12

A householder as a seeker is a more noble person because he does both, work as well as worship; whereas a renunciate can only worship and cannot indulge in worldly affairs.

"A devotee who can call on God while living a householder's life is a hero indeed. God thinks: 'He is blessed indeed who prays to me in the midst of his worldly duties. He is trying to find me, overcoming a great obstacle – pushing away, as it were, a huge block of stone weighing a ton.' Such a man is a real hero."

Ramakrishna Parmahansa (1836-1886)
Indian Spiritual Guru

CHAPTER 19

GRACE

ੴ

Grace in the spiritual sense means God's benevolence, forgiveness, gift, blessings, intervention etc., where it seems God goes out of the way to help someone. There are numerous references to God's grace in SGGS. The Punjabi words used for grace include *nadar, karam, mehar, kirpa, daya,* and so on.

There are two essentials for success in life, more so in spiritual life - first, your own deeds & actions, and second, God's grace. We will explore deeds and actions in the chapter titled, 'Karam.' Here we'll focus on God's grace which He showers upon those He is pleased with.

You must do everything to prepare yourselves for God's benevolence. How do we do that? By worshipping, doing worthy deeds and acquiring godlike qualities. Seekers of God must pursue Him with their utmost; though they will attain Him only when He decides to shower His grace. Do not worry if there is delay, the journey itself will be highly satisfying.

Guru Amar Das on God's grace coming to those He is pleased with:

ਜਿਸ ਨੋ ਨਦਰਿ ਕਰੇ ਸੋ ਪਾਏ ॥

Jis no nadar karay so paaye.

जिस नो नदरि करे सो पाए॥

> To whomsoever He grants His grace, he receives.
>
> M3/114/15

Guru Amar Das again:

> ਸਾਚੇ ਸਾਹਿਬਾ ਕਿਆ ਨਾਹੀ ਘਰਿ ਤੇਰੈ॥
> ਘਰਿ ਤ ਤੇਰੈ ਸਭੁ ਕਿਛੁ ਹੈ ਜਿਸੁ ਦੇਹਿ ਸੁ ਪਾਵਏ॥
>
> Saachay sahiba kia naahi ghar teyrai; ghar ta teyrai
> sabh kichh hai jis dehay su paavay.
>
> साचे साहिबा किआ नाही घरि तेरै॥
> घरि त तेरै सभु किछु है जिसु देहि सु पावए॥
>
> O my True Lord, what is it that You don't have?
> You have everything, only they receive, unto whom You give.
>
> M3/917/7

Guru Ram Das says, whatever you may try, you can't receive
God's love without His benevolence:

> ਕੋਈ ਕਰੈ ਉਪਾਵ ਅਨੇਕ ਬਹੁਤੇਰੇ ਬਿਨੁ ਕਿਰਪਾ ਨਾਮੁ ਨ ਪਾਵੈ॥
>
> Koyee karai upaav anek bahuteray bin kirpa naam na paavai.
>
> कोई करै उपाव अनेक बहुतेरे बिनु किरपा नामु न पावै॥
>
> However hard one may try, His Name (His love) is not
> obtained without His grace.
>
> M4/172/17

The above verses indicate that God's grace comes to a
select few. Is God then selective in deciding who will be

granted His grace? No, He showers His Grace on everyone. As
Guru Nanak says:

ਜੈਸੀ ਨਦਰਿ ਕਰੇ ਤੈਸਾ ਹੋਇ॥ ਵਿਣੁ ਨਦਰੀ ਨਾਨਕ ਨਹੀ ਕੋਇ॥

Jaisee nadar karay taisa hoye, vin nadri Nanak nahi koye.

जैसी नदरि करे तैसा होइ॥ विणु नदरी नानक नही कोइ॥

As He grants His grace so it happens.
Nanak says there is no one without His grace.

M1/661/9

Guru Arjan Dev reiterates that God is showering His grace
on all:

ਪੂਰਨ ਪੂਰਿ ਰਹੇ ਦਇਆਲ॥ ਸਭ ਉਪਰਿ ਹੋਵਤ ਕਿਰਪਾਲ॥

Pooran poor rahay dayaal, sabh oopar hovat kirpaal.

पूरन पूरि रहे दइआल॥ सभ ऊपरि होवत किरपाल॥

The Complete Lord remains merciful to all,
He is gracious to all.

M5/292/14

Here Guru Amar Das says He showers His grace all the time:

ਅੰਮ੍ਰਿਤੁ ਸਦਾ ਵਰਸਦਾ ਬੁਝਨਿ ਬੁਝਣਹਾਰ॥
ਗੁਰਮੁਖਿ ਜਿਨ੍ਹੀ ਬੁਝਿਆ ਹਰਿ ਅੰਮ੍ਰਿਤੁ ਰਖਿਆ ਉਰਿ ਧਾਰਿ॥

Amrit sadaa varsda bhoojan bhoojanhaar.

Gurmukh jinhee bujheya Har amrit rakheya ur dhaar.

अमृतु सदा वरसदा बूझनि बूझणहार॥
गुरमुखि जिन्ही बुझिआ हरि अमृतु रखिआ उरि धारि॥

> The ambrosial nectar (God's grace) rains down continuously,
> the knowledgeable know this.
> God-oriented people who have realized this, embrace the
> Lord's grace.
>
> M3/1281/17

There seems to be a paradox here. On one hand we are saying God grants His grace to the selected ones, and on the other, that there is no one without His grace. Actually, God showers His grace on everyone, but the problem is with us, we are not prepared, to accept His grace. When it rains it falls all over, but only those vessels collect water which have the right side up. If our vessels are upside down, how will we collect the water? Same goes for God's grace. If our minds are not tuned towards God, we will not receive His grace, though it falls on everyone. Jesus said, "The harvest is plenteous, but the labourers are few." (Matthew 9:37). Those who have their vessel right side up are indeed very rare.

That's exactly what Guru Nanak says:

> ਉਂਧੈ ਭਾਂਡੈ ਕਛੁ ਨ ਸਮਾਵੈ ਸੀਧੇ ਅੰਮ੍ਰਿਤੁ ਪਰੈ ਨਿਹਾਰ ॥
>
> Oondhay bhaandai kachhu na samaavai seedhay amrit
> parai nihaar.
>
> ऊंधै भांडै कछु न समावै सीधै अम्रितु परै निहार ॥
>
> Nothing is collected in a vessel that is turned upside down.
> Amrit (God's love) pours into the one that is right side up.
>
> M1/504/3

Effort on our part is very essential, though it may not seem to produce the result. Gautam Buddh struggled for many years searching for the truth but he did not get the answer during the period of his struggle. It came to him when he gave up. Did his effort bring enlightenment? Yes and no. Without the effort he would not have been prepared to receive God's grace. Yet enlightenment came only when God willed it. But he was fully prepared.

You would have noticed that sometimes when you are trying hard to remember something like a name, a place, etc., you keep struggling but it doesn't come to you. When you are tired you give up and relax. Then that thing suddenly comes to your mind. The effort prepared you to receive the answer but it did not produce the result. The answer came on its own.

Guru Arjan Dev says to receive grace you must be consumed with desire for God's love:

ਜਿਨ ਕਉ ਲਗੀ ਪਿਆਸ ਅੰਮ੍ਰਿਤੁ ਸੇਇ ਖਾਹਿ ॥

Jin kau laggi peyaas amrit sei khaahay.

जिन कउ लगी पिआस अम्रितु सेइ खाहि॥

Only those who are thirsty, get to relish the nectar (God's love).

M5/962/2

The reason why grace does not come to most of us is that we actually don't want it. Our expectations are more in the material world whereas God's grace mainly pertains to spiritual benevolence. What do most people understand from the following lines by Guru Arjan Dev which are often heard:

ਲਖ ਖੁਸੀਆ ਪਾਤਿਸਾਹੀਆ ਜੇ ਸਤਿਗੁਰੁ ਨਦਰਿ ਕਰੇਇ ॥

Lakh khusia paatsaahiya jay Satgur nadar karay.

लख खुसीआ पातिसाहीआ जे सतिगुरु नदरि करेइ॥

> Hundreds of thousands of pleasures and high positions are
> obtained if the True Guru bestows His Grace.
>
> M5/44/7

Most people think the pleasures here refer to material
wealth and high positions refer to political and physical power.
Not so. The pleasures and high positions mentioned here are
those we enjoy on spiritual awakening i.e. spiritual bliss and
high spiritual status.

Now few verses on what happens when you receive God's grace.

Guru Nanak:

> ਨਾਨਕ ਨਦਰਿ ਕਰੇ ਜਿਸੁ ਉਪਰਿ ਸਚਿ ਨਾਮਿ ਵਡਿਆਈ ॥
>
> Nanak nadar karay jis oopar sach naam vadeyaayee.
>
> नानक नदरि करे जिसु उपरि सचि नामि वडिआई॥
>
> Nanak says, those upon whom He showers His grace, obtain
> the glorious greatness of True Name.
>
> M1/147/4

Guru Amar Das says, when grace comes, all other pleasures
are forgotten:

> ਕਹੈ ਨਾਨਕੁ ਹੋਰਿ ਅਨ ਰਸ ਸਭਿ ਵੀਸਰੇ ਜਾ ਹਰਿ ਵਸੈ ਮਨਿ ਆਇ ॥
>
> Kahai Nanak hor un rus sabh veesray ja Har vassai munn aaye.
>
> कहै नानकु होरि अन रस सभि वीसरे जा हरि वसै मनि आइ॥
>
> Says Nanak, all other pleasures are forgotten when God
> comes to dwell in the mind.
>
> M3/921/13

Guru Arjan Dev says grace can do wonders:

ਕਰਿ ਕਿਰਪਾ ਅਪਨੇ ਜਨ ਰਾਖੇ ॥ ਜਨਮ ਜਨਮ ਕੇ ਕਿਲਬਿਖ ਲਾਥੇ ॥

Kar kirpa apnay jann raakhay janam janam kay
kilbikh laathay.

करि किरपा अपने जन राखे ॥ जनम जनम के किलबिख लाथे ॥

By His grace God looks after His people; sins of all past lives
are washed away.

M5/202/15

The power of God's grace is so strong that it can override
your past and present karma. Dr Brian Weiss, MD, in his
book 'Through Time Into Healing' says, "Grace, however, can
supersede karma. Grace is divine intervention, a loving hand
reaching down from the heavens to help us, to ease our burden
and our suffering."

Guru Arjan Dev says the same thing:

ਗੁਰ ਪੂਰੇ ਕੇ ਚਰਣ ਗਹੇ ॥ ਕੋਟਿ ਜਨਮ ਕੇ ਪਾਪ ਲਹੇ ॥
ਰਤਨ ਜਨਮੁ ਇਹੁ ਸਫਲ ਭਇਆ ॥ ਕਹੁ ਨਾਨਕ ਪ੍ਰਭ ਕਰੀ ਮਇਆ ॥

Gur pooray kay charan gahay; kot janam kay paap lahay.
Ratan janam eho safal bhaiya; kahu Nanak Prabh teri maiya.

गुर पूरे के चरण गहे ॥ कोटि जनम के पाप लहे ॥
रतन जनमु इहु सफल भइआ ॥ कहु नानक प्रभ करी मइआ ॥

Those who take shelter at Complete Guru's feet, their sins of
hundreds and thousands of previous lives are mitigated.
Their priceless life has become successful, Nanak says, God
has showered His grace.

M5/387/10

Guru Arjan Dev again on mitigation of negative karma:

ਜਿਸ ਨੋ ਤੇਰੀ ਨਦਰਿ ਨ ਲੇਖਾ ਪੁਛੀਐ ॥
ਜਿਸ ਨੋ ਤੇਰੀ ਖੁਸੀ ਤਿਨਿ ਨਉ ਨਿਧਿ ਭੁੰਚੀਐ ॥

Jis no teri nadar na lekha puchheeyai; jis no teri khusi tin nau
nidh bhuncheeyai.

जिस नो तेरी नदरि न लेखा पुछ्ठीऐ ॥
जिस नो तेरी खुसी तिनि नउ निधि भुंचीऐ ॥

On whom Your Grace is showered, is not called upon to give
account of his actions.
One with whom You are pleased, enjoys the nine treasures.

M5/961/15

As per ancient Indian thought there are nine treasures of god of wealth which include things like family, flowers, precious stones, clothes, conch shell, delicious eatables, skills in arts and weaponry etc. Possession of these things is supposed to make you happy. But Sikhism does not believe that material things can give you true happiness. Guru Arjan Dev uses this term (nine treasures) only to say that the joy equivalent to all the treasures is relished by a person whom God grants His grace.

God-realization is the highest reward one can think of, but there are very few takers. People want everything from God but they are not sure whether they want Him. Meeting Him or realizing Him is the biggest spiritual achievement one can imagine, the highest form of Grace. What more is left to gain?

There are select few on whom God chooses to grant His grace and sets the stage for meeting them. This should be a matter of greatest joy one can ever imagine. But some unfortunate ones get scared. They can't comprehend what they will do if God actually stood in front of them. They shudder at the thought of meeting Him and suddenly develop cold feet - just as the opportunity of many lifetimes is knocking at their door. Instead of running away, one should surrender to Him and let anything happen. You don't know after how many rebirths this opportunity will come again. People get scared because the experience involves transformative process they've never experienced before.

Do not be afraid of God, love and seek Him instead. Be ready to meet Him, because one day you will – in this life or later. That will be the day of His grace coming to you, the day of your liberation.

"Your worst days are never so bad that you are beyond the reach of God's grace. And your best days are never so good that you are beyond the need of God's grace."

Jerry Bridges (1929-2016)
American Author

CHAPTER 20

MIND

Since ancient times the wise ones have been telling us that real success in life lies in controlling and winning over the mind. Most of the time our mind is not under our control - it keeps running away in different directions. Uncontrolled mind is the cause of most of our problems. What exactly is mind? Let's explore.

Before we go into what SGGS says about mind let us see the science's view. Science believes that brain and mind are like a computer where brain is the physical hardware and mind is like the invisible operating software. They record everything that happens to us right from our childhood. Most of these recordings take place at the conscious level, but some are subliminal, i.e. we are not consciously aware of such imprints. These recordings determine our feelings, emotions, memory, intelligence, imagination, reasoning, judgment and so on. These are the things that make up our personality and distinguish one person from another.

This, however, is not adequate explanation of the mind and falls short in many ways. There have been many cases where, consequent to an organ transplant, the recipients developed thoughts, feelings and capabilities of the donors. In 2016 a University of Melbourne study reported of a 63-year-old man, with a very limited artistic ability, who underwent a heart transplant. He was amazed to find that, after the operation, his artistic ability increased dramatically. Reason? The heart donor was a keen artist. In another case an 8-year-old girl who received a 10-year-old girl's heart began to have vivid dreams of a man trying to kill her. It was found that the donor was murdered and the recipient who had the nightmares described the killer in such detail that the police were able to find and convict him. There was yet another case where fondness for beer and chicken nuggets of a kidney donor was transferred to the recipient who did not relish these things before. If mind is limited to brain, how could this happen? Perhaps brain is not the only place where our thoughts and memories are stored.

Then there have been many studies on reincarnation where people have accurately remembered their past lives. Where did these memories come from? You may have also experienced the phenomenon of déjà vu, where you re-live a situation like visiting a place or meeting someone, but you are quite sure you haven't had that experience in this life before.

We have also known of many cases of telepathy amongst humans and animals. It is often seen that when the master is getting ready to take out his dog, it starts getting excited even when he is in a different room and can't see or hear the master. There have been cases where cats quietly disappeared just before their appointment with the vet. How does that happen? Obviously mind is much more than mere recordings in our brain.

Our *rishis* who studied and observed the mind closely, knew of these characteristics of the mind. The authors of SGGS were also aware of this and took a broader view of the mind. They found the missing link to be the invisible soul. It connects the mind to information and energy outside the mind and the body. Science, however, does not believe in soul or God – because it cannot see them. Science and spirituality have different competencies. Deepak Chopra in his book, 'Life After Death' says, "Just as religion had no competency in physics and chemistry, science has no competency in spiritual issues."

Soul or *atma* is part of God (*Parmatma* - Supreme Soul) which is detached from God to dwell in the physical body. Human endeavour lies in inner cleansing of the soul, over hundreds of reincarnations, before it awakens and re-merges with Supreme Soul.

Now some quotations from SGGS. In the following verse, Guru Amar Das puts a poser to the learned pandit and extols him to focus more on study of the mind:

ਇਹੁ ਮਨੁ ਗਿਰਹੀ ਕਿ ਇਹੁ ਮਨੁ ਉਦਾਸੀ॥ ਕਿ ਇਹੁ ਮਨੁ ਅਵਰਨੁ ਸਦਾ ਅਵਿਨਾਸੀ॥

Ihu munn girhee ki ihu munn udaasi; ki ih munn avaran
sadaa avinaasi.

इहु मनु गिरही कि इहु मनु उदासी॥ कि इहु मनु अवरनु सदा अविनासी॥

Is this mind a householder, or is this mind detached (from *maya*)?
Is this mind above class distinction, is it eternal and immortal?

ਕਿ ਇਹੁ ਮਨੁ ਚੰਚਲੁ ਕਿ ਇਹੁ ਮਨੁ ਬੈਰਾਗੀ॥ ਇਸੁ ਮਨ ਕਉ ਮਮਤਾ ਕਿਥਹੁ ਲਾਗੀ॥

Ki ihu munn chanchal ki ihu munn bairaagi; is munn ko
mamta kithahu laagi.

कि इहु मनु चंचलु कि इहु मनु बैरागी॥ इसु मन कउ ममता किथहु लागी॥

Is this mind fickle, or is this mind detached?
From where has this mind acquired attachment (to *maya*)?

ਪੰਡਿਤ ਇਸੁ ਮਨ ਕਾ ਕਰਹੁ ਬੀਚਾਰੁ॥ ਅਵਰੁ ਕਿ ਬਹੁਤਾ ਪੜਹਿ ਉਠਾਵਹਿ ਭਾਰੁ॥

Pandit is munn ka karho vichaar; avar ki bahuta parhay
uthaaveh bhaar.

पंडित इसु मन का करहु बीचारु॥ अवरु कि बहुता पड़हि उठावहि भारु॥

O pandit, reflect on this mind.
Why read so much else, and carry such a heavy burden?

M3/1261/4

In the verse below Guru Amar Das asks the mind to recognize its true self. The second part of the verse also tells us that a quiet mind is a sign of spiritual growth. All meditation is aimed at that:

ਮਨ ਤੂੰ ਜੋਤਿ ਸਰੂਪੁ ਹੈ ਆਪਣਾ ਮੂਲੁ ਪਛਾਣੁ ॥
ਮਨ ਹਰਿ ਜੀ ਤੇਰੈ ਨਾਲਿ ਹੈ ਗੁਰਮਤੀ ਰੰਗੁ ਮਾਣੁ ॥

Munn tu jyot saroop hai aapna mool pachhaan.
Munn har ji teray naal hai gurmati rung maan.

मन तूं जोति सरूपु है आपणा मूलु पछाणु ॥
मन हरि जी तेरै नालि है गुरमती रंगु माणु ॥

O mind, you are the image of divine light, recognize your
true essence. O my mind, the Lord is with you,
enjoy His love with Guru's advice.

ਮੂਲੁ ਪਛਾਣਹਿ ਤਾਂ ਸਹੁ ਜਾਣਹਿ ਮਰਣ ਜੀਵਣ ਕੀ ਸੋਝੀ ਹੋਈ ॥
ਗੁਰ ਪਰਸਾਦੀ ਏਕੋ ਜਾਣਹਿ ਤਾਂ ਦੂਜਾ ਭਾਉ ਨ ਹੋਈ ॥

Mool pachhaaneh ta seh jaaneh maran jeevan ki sojhi hoyee.
Gur parsadi eko jaaneh ta dooja bhao na hoyee.

मूलु पछाणहि तां सहु जाणहि मरण जीवण की सोझी होई ॥
गुर परसादी एको जाणहि तां दूजा भाउ न होई ॥

When you recognize your true essence, you will know your
Husband Lord, and then you will understand death and life.
By Guru's grace know the One, then you shall not be
attracted to any other.

ਮਨਿ ਸਾਂਤਿ ਆਈ ਵਜੀ ਵਧਾਈ ਤਾ ਹੋਆ ਪਰਵਾਣੁ ॥
ਇਉ ਕਹੈ ਨਾਨਕੁ ਮਨ ਤੂੰ ਜੋਤਿ ਸਰੂਪੁ ਹੈ ਅਪਣਾ ਮੂਲੁ ਪਛਾਣੁ ॥

Munn saant aayee vaji vadhaayee ta hoa parvaan.
Eeu kahay Nanak munn tu jyot saroop hai apna mool pachhaan.

मनि सांति आई वजी वधाई ता होआ परवाणु॥
इउ कहै नानकु मन तूं जोति सरूपु है अपणा मूलु पछाणु॥

When the mind becomes calm, celebrations resound, then
you shall be accepted (in Lord's court).
Thus says Nanak, O my mind, you are the very image of
divine light, recognize your true essence.

M3/441/3

The *atma*, though temporarily separated from *Parmatma*,
retains contact with it, as well as with everything else in the
universe. This is how our mind is able to access information from
anywhere even when there is no physical or electronic contact.
This connection is at the spirit level, which science doesn't accept.

In spiritual matters cleverness of the mind does not work.
The mind needs to be tamed, if God is to be known, as the
following two verses tell us:

ਚਤੁਰਾਈ ਨਹ ਚੀਨਿਆ ਜਾਇ॥ ਬਿਨੁ ਮਾਰੇ ਕਿਉ ਕੀਮਤਿ ਪਾਇ॥
Chaturayee nah cheeneya jaaye; bin maaray kiu
keemat paaye.
चतुराई नह चीनिआ जाइ॥ बिनु मारे किउ कीमति पाइ॥

God cannot be known through cleverness (of the mind).
Without death (surrender) of the mind, we cannot know
its value.

M1/221/12

ਮਨ ਕੀ ਮਤਿ ਤਿਆਗਹੁ ਹਰਿ ਜਨ ਹੁਕਮੁ ਬੂਝਿ ਸੁਖੁ ਪਾਈਐ ਰੇ॥
ਜੋ ਪ੍ਰਭੁ ਕਰੈ ਸੋਈ ਭਲ ਮਾਨਹੁ ਸੁਧਿ ਦੁਖਿ ਓਹੀ ਧਿਆਈਐ ਰੇ॥

Munn ki matt tiagaho har jun hukam boojh sukh paeeyai ray.
Jo prabh karai soee bhal maanohu sukh dukh ohee
dhiaayee-ai ray.

ਮਨ ਕੀ ਮਤਿ ਤਿਆਗਹੁ ਹਰਿ ਜਨ ਹੁਕਮੁ ਬੂਝਿ ਸੁਖੁ ਪਾਈਐ ਰੇ॥
ਜੋ ਪ੍ਰਭੁ ਕਰੈ ਸੋਈ ਭਲ ਮਾਨਹੁ ਸੁਖਿ ਦੁਖਿ ਓਹੀ ਧਿਆਈਐ ਰੇ॥

Leave aside the cleverness of your mind, O Lord's creatures,
happiness is to be found in understanding and accepting
His command.
Whatever God does, believe that to be good for you – worship
Him, whether in pleasure or in pain.

M5/209/14

If not controlled, the mind has a habit of going all over, thinking all sorts of things, mostly negative. It is either thinking of regrets, mistakes and lost opportunities of the past, or worries of the future - often of things that will never happen. Spiritual teacher Eckhart Tolle, in his book 'The Power of Now', says, "So the single most vital step on your journey toward enlightenment is this; learn to disidentify yourself from the mind." Well, it cannot be 'total' disidentification, because some of mind's functioning is required for day to day planning and living. However, do not allow it to take you for a ride all over the place, all the time.

Guru Ram Das asks the mind to stop wandering and get back home, to be with the Lord and enjoy His blessings:

ਮੇਰੇ ਮਨ ਪਰਦੇਸੀ ਵੇ ਪਿਆਰੇ ਆਉ ਘਰੇ॥
ਹਰਿ ਗੁਰੁ ਮਿਲਾਵਹੁ ਮੇਰੇ ਪਿਆਰੇ ਘਰਿ ਵਸੈ ਹਰੇ॥
ਰੰਗਿ ਰਲੀਆ ਮਾਣਹੁ ਮੇਰੇ ਪਿਆਰੇ ਹਰਿ ਕਿਰਪਾ ਕਰੇ॥
ਗੁਰੁ ਨਾਨਕ ਤੁਠਾ ਮੇਰੇ ਪਿਆਰੇ ਮੇਲੇ ਹਰੇ॥

Meray munn pardesi vay piaray aao gharay; Har Guru
milaavoh meray piaray garh vasai Haray.

Rung ralia maanoh meray piaray Har kirpa karay;
Guru Nanak tutha meray piaray melay Haray.

मेरे मन परदेसी वे पिआरे आउ घरे॥
हरि गुरू मिलावहु मेरे पिआरे घरि वसै हरे॥
रंगि रलीआ माणहु मेरे पिआरे हरि किरपा करे॥
गुरु नानकु तुठा मेरे पिआरे मेले हरे॥

O my wandering mind, please return home. Meet the Lord with
Guru's blessings O my dear, and God will dwell in your heart.

Make merry and enjoy, O dear, as the Lord bestows
His grace on you.

Nanak says, those with whom the Guru is pleased,
they meet the Lord.

M4/451/16

Guru Teg Bahadur tells us of uselessness of effort if the
mind is not under control:

ਤੀਰਥ ਕਰੈ ਬ੍ਰਤ ਫੁਨਿ ਰਾਖੈ ਨਹ ਮਨੂਆ ਬਸਿ ਜਾ ਕੋ॥
ਨਿਹਫਲ ਧਰਮੁ ਤਾਹਿ ਤੁਮ ਮਾਨਹੁ ਸਾਚੁ ਕਹਤ ਮੈ ਯਾ ਕਉ॥

Teerath karai barat phun raakhai nah manua bas ja ko.
Nihphal dharam taahay tum manoh saach kehat mai ya kao.

तीरथ करै ब्रत फुनि राखै नह मनूआ बसि जा को॥
निहफल धरमु ताहि तुम मानहु साचु कहत मै या कउ॥

A person who goes on pilgrimage, does fasting, but does not
have control over his mind;

Believe that religion/duty for such a man is useless,
I tell him this Truth.

M9/831/3

This beautiful verse by Guru Amar Das is again addressed to the mind, telling it to always remain with God:

ਏ ਮਨ ਮੇਰਿਆ ਤੂ ਸਦਾ ਰਹੁ ਹਰਿ ਨਾਲੇ ॥
ਹਰਿ ਨਾਲਿ ਰਹੁ ਤੂ ਮੰਨ ਮੇਰੇ ਦੂਖ ਸਭਿ ਵਿਸਾਰਣਾ ॥
ਅੰਗੀਕਾਰੁ ਓਹੁ ਕਰੇ ਤੇਰਾ ਕਾਰਜ ਸਭਿ ਸਵਾਰਣਾ ॥

Aye munn mereya tu sadaa rahu Har naalay.
Har naal rahu tu munn meray dookh sabh visaarna.
Angikaar oh karay tera karaj sabh savaarna.

ए मन मेरिआ तू सदा रहु हरि नाले ॥
हरि नालि रहु तू मंन मेरे दूख सभि विसारणा ॥
अंगीकारु ओहु करे तेरा कारज सभि सवारणा ॥

O my mind, always remain with the Lord.
By remaining with Him, all sufferings will depart.
He will embrace you, and all your problems/issues will be resolved.

ਸਭਨਾ ਗਲਾ ਸਮਰਥੁ ਸੁਆਮੀ ਸੋ ਕਿਉ ਮਨਹੁ ਵਿਸਾਰੇ ॥
ਕਹੈ ਨਾਨਕੁ ਮੰਨ ਮੇਰੇ ਸਦਾ ਰਹੁ ਹਰਿ ਨਾਲੇ ॥

Sabhna gala samrath suamee so kiu manoh visaaaray.
Kahai Nanak munn meray sada rahu Har naalay.

सभना गला समरथु सुआमी सो किउ मनहु विसारे ॥
कहै नानकु मंन मेरे सदा रहु हरि नाले ॥

Lord is the master of every thing, so why let Him go from your mind?
Says Nanak, O my mind, always remain with the Lord.

M3/917/4

There can be no spiritual progress until the mind is silenced and brought under control. Chatter of the mind can be silenced with meditation or by living in the present moment. Mind's silence is a precondition for God to reside in the heart.

Where mind is in control, God will not come, and where God resides, there is no mind. When you are under mind's control you see nothing but yourself, but when mind is shut you see God everywhere - you have arrived.

"If a man can control his mind he can find the way to enlightenment, and all wisdom and virtue will naturally come to him."

Lord Buddha (563-483 BC)
Founder Buddhism

CHAPTER 21

HUMILITY

ੴ

In the chapter on ego we saw how it is man's biggest problem which keeps him entangled in the material world; and it is also the biggest barrier in spiritual development. One of the most effective ways of getting rid of ego is to develop its antidote - humility. Embracing humility is a major step towards overcoming the burden of ego. To have humility means being humble and modest, not being proud or arrogant. It certainly doesn't mean weakness or meekness. The Punjabi word for it is *nimrata*.

In the material world where success is governed by cut-throat competition, humility may not seem to be a desirable trait. However, humility is not submissiveness. Combined with firmness it can also be an effective tool for managing people. For those who have chosen the spiritual path, humility is a highly valued quality that will take you far. While ego, pride and arrogance are qualities of the head, humility comes from the heart. It is the fundamental virtue. Saint Augustine said, "Humility is the foundation of all the other virtues hence, in the soul in which this virtue does not exist there cannot be any other virtue except in mere appearance."

The need for being humble is repeatedly highlighted in SGGS. Many Gurus and other authors of the holy book have written about it. Let's first see what Guru Nanak says:

ਹਮ ਨਹੀ ਚੰਗੇ ਬੁਰਾ ਨਹੀ ਕੋਇ॥ ਪ੍ਰਣਵਤਿ ਨਾਨਕੁ ਤਾਰੇ ਸੋਇ॥

Hum nahi changay bura nahi koye; Pranvat Nanak taaray soye.

हम नही चंगे बुरा नही कोइ॥ प्रणवति नानकु तारे सोइ॥

I am not good, no one is bad; Nanak prays and the
Lord liberates.

M1/728/14

Guru Nanak reiterates:

ਨਾ ਹਮ ਚੰਗੇ ਆਖੀਅਹ ਬੁਰਾ ਨ ਦਿਸੈ ਕੋਇ॥
ਨਾਨਕ ਹਉਮੈ ਮਾਰੀਐ ਸਚੇ ਜੇਹੜਾ ਸੋਇ॥

Na hum changay aakhee-ah bura na deesai koye.
Nanak haumai maareeyai sachay jehra soye.

ना हम चंगे आखीअह बुरा न दिसै कोइ॥
नानक हउमै मारीऐ सचे जेहड़ा सोइ॥

Don't call me good, I see none who is bad.
O Nanak, he who kills his ego, becomes
True (enlightened).

M1/1015/12

Guru Arjan Dev says, happy are those who are humble and
have shed their ego:

ਸੁਖੀ ਬਸੈ ਮਸਕੀਨੀਆ ਆਪੁ ਨਿਵਾਰਿ ਤਲੇ॥ ਬਡੇ ਬਡੇ ਅਹੰਕਾਰੀਆ ਨਾਨਕ ਗਰਬਿ ਗਲੇ॥

Sukhi bassai maskeeniya aap nivaar talay. Badday badday
ahankaariya Nanak garbh galay.

सुखी बसै मसकीनीआ आपु निवारि तले॥ बडे बडे अहंकारीआ नानक गरबि गले॥

The humble people subdue their ego and
abide in peace.
The highly proud people, O Nanak,
are destroyed by their own pride.

M5/278/5

Another quote from Guru Arjan Dev:

ਆਪਸ ਕਉ ਜੋ ਜਾਨੈ ਨੀਚਾ॥ ਸੋਊ ਗਨੀਐ ਸਭ ਤੇ ਊਚਾ॥

Aapas kao jo jaanai neecha, sou ganiyai sabh tay oocha.

आपस कउ जो जाणै नीचा॥ सोऊ गनीऐ सभ ते ऊचा॥

He who believes he is lowly, consider him to be the
highest of all.

M5/266/7

Guru Nanak brings out the lesson on humility giving
example of a *simmal* tree (*bombax ceiba* or cotton tree) which
is thick & tall and appears to be full of pride, though has little
to offer:

ਸਿੰਮਲ ਰੁਖੁ ਸਰਾਇਰਾ ਅਤਿ ਦੀਰਘ ਅਤਿ ਮੁਚੁ॥
ਓਇ ਜਿ ਆਵਹਿ ਆਸ ਕਰਿ ਜਾਹਿ ਨਿਰਾਸੇ ਕਿਤੁ॥
ਫਲ ਫਿਕੇ ਫੁਲ ਬਕਬਕੇ ਕੰਮਿ ਨ ਆਵਹਿ ਪਤ॥
ਮਿਠਤੁ ਨੀਵੀ ਨਾਨਕਾ ਗੁਣ ਚੰਗਿਆਈਆ ਤਤੁ॥

Simmal rukh sraayera att dheeragh att much.
Oey jay aaveh aas kar jaahe niraassay kitt.
Phal phikkay phul bakbakay kumm na aaveh patt.
Mithat neevi Nanaka gunh changeyaia tatt.

सिमल रुखु सराइरा अति दीरघ अति मुचु॥
ओइ जि आवहि आस करि जाहि निरासे किंतु॥
फल फिके फुल बकबके कमि न आवहि पत॥
मिठतु नीवी नानका गुण चंगिआईआ ततु॥

The *simmal* tree is straight like an arrow,
it is very tall and thick.
(Birds) come to it with great expectation but
go back disappointed.
Its fruit is bland, the flowers tasteless,
and the leaves are of no use.
Humility is sweet, O Nanak, it is the essence of good virtue.

M1/470/12

Simmal tree seems to be proud without any reason. On
the other hand a fruit-bearing tree which ought to be more
proud, often bends in humility and offers its fruit to anyone
who would take it. Also, when the strong wind blows, the trees
that don't bend are the first to be broken, while those which
do are saved. Same with people, those who bend in humility
can't be beaten easily.

Bhagat Kabir gives a very appropriate example of what the
mighty elephant cannot do but a humble ant can:

ਹਰਿ ਹੈ ਖਾਂਡੁ ਰੇਤੁ ਮਹਿ ਬਿਖਰੀ ਹਾਥੀ ਚੁਨੀ ਨ ਜਾਇ॥
ਕਹਿ ਕਬੀਰ ਗੁਰਿ ਭਲੀ ਬੁਝਾਈ ਕੀਟੀ ਹੋਇ ਕੈ ਖਾਇ॥

Har hai khaand reyt meh bikhri haathi chuni na jaaye.
Keh Kabir gur bhali bujhaayee keeti hoye kai khaaye.

हरि है खांडु रेतु महि बिखरी हाथी चुनी न जाइ॥
कहि कबीर गुरि भली बुझाई कीटी होइ कै खाइ॥

> God is like sugar scattered in the sand, the elephant cannot pick it up.
> Says Kabir, Guru has explained this, become like a humble ant and relish the sugar (godliness).
>
> Kabir/1377/8

As long as you are full of ego and think you are big like the elephant, you will not be able to gather the love of God. However, if you are humble like the small ant, His love is all yours. Elephant and ant here are only symbolic of big and small ego.

Here is a verse by Sheikh Farid on his humbleness:

> ਫਰੀਦਾ ਕਾਲੇ ਮੈਡੇ ਕਪੜੇ ਕਾਲਾ ਮੈਡਾ ਵੇਸੁ ॥
> ਗੁਨਹੀ ਭਰਿਆ ਮੈ ਫਿਰਾ ਲੋਕੁ ਕਹੈ ਦਰਵੇਸੁ ॥
>
> Farida kaalay maiday kapray kaala maida ves.
> Gunhee bhareya main fira lok kahai darves.
>
> फरीदा काले मैडे कपड़े काला मैडा वेसु ॥
> गुनही भरिआ मै फिरा लोकु कहै दरवेसु ॥
>
> Says Farid, my attire is black, my appearance is black.
> I wander around full of sins, yet people call me a saint.
>
> Farid/1381/3

Black attire and black appearance are connected to sinful life. In the olden days, blackening of a criminal's face was a form of punishment meted out by local headmen. One still hears of this practice sometimes, though not very common.

Sheikh Farid again:

> ਨਿਵਣੁ ਸੁ ਅਖਰੁ ਖਵਣੁ ਗੁਣੁ ਜਿਹਬਾ ਮਣੀਆ ਮੰਤੁ ॥
> ਏ ਤ੍ਰੈ ਭੈਣੇ ਵੇਸ ਕਰਿ ਤਾਂ ਵਸਿ ਆਵੀ ਕੰਤੁ ॥
>
> Nivan su akhar khavan gunh jih-ba mania muntt;
> Ei trai bhainay ves kar ta vas aavee kuntt.
>
> ਨਿਵਣੁ ਸੁ ਅਖਰੁ ਖਵਣੁ ਗੁਣੁ ਜਿਹਬਾ ਮਣੀਆ ਮੰਤੁ ॥
> ਏ ਤ੍ਰੈ ਭੈਣੇ ਵੇਸ ਕਰਿ ਤਾਂ ਵਸਿ ਆਵੀ ਕੰਤੁ ॥
>
> Humility is the word, tolerance is the trait, and polite speak
> is the mantra. O sister, if you adopt these three,
> the Lord will embrace you.
>
> Farid/1384/15

And now a verse from Bhagat Ravidas:

> ਤੂ ਜਾਨਤ ਮੈ ਕਿਛੁ ਨਹੀ ਭਵ ਖੰਡਨ ਰਾਮ ॥ ਸਗਲ ਜੀਅ ਸਰਨਾਗਤੀ ਪ੍ਰਭ ਪੂਰਨ ਕਾਮ ॥
>
> Tu jaanat mai kichhu nahi bhav khandan Ram; sagal jia
> sarnaagati Prabh pooran kaam.
>
> ਤੂ ਜਾਨਤ ਮੈ ਕਿਛੁ ਨਹੀ ਭਵ ਖੰਡਨ ਰਾਮ ॥ ਸਗਲ ਜੀਅ ਸਰਨਾਗਤੀ ਪ੍ਰਭ ਪੂਰਨ ਕਾਮ ॥
>
> You know I am nothing, O Lord, the destroyer of fear.
> All souls are under Your shelter, and You resolve all affairs.
>
> Ravidas/858/4

To be able to say that you are nothing, or that you know nothing is the hall mark of real humility. The more frequently a person says, "I know nothing" the more spiritually enlightened he is likely to be. After his enlightenment Socrates said, "The only thing I know is that I know nothing." Similarly,

Leo Tolstoy said, "The only thing we know is that we know nothing – and that is the highest flight of human wisdom." When you contemplate deeply on the vastness of God's creation you indeed are dumbstruck, and obliged to accept that you really are nothing and know nothing. To make them realize of their nothingness Buddha, as also Gorakhnath, asked their disciples to become *bhickshus* (beggars) and go home to home seeking alms. As a beggar you can't have any ego or pride; you must accept humility.

Some more quotations by Guru Arjan Dev on humility:

ਤੂ ਸਮਰਥੁ ਸਦਾ ਹਮ ਦੀਨ ਭੇਖਾਰੀ ਰਾਮ ॥
ਮਾਇਆ ਮੋਹਿ ਮਗਨੁ ਕਢਿ ਲੇਹੁ ਮੁਰਾਰੀ ਰਾਮ ॥

Tu samrath sadaa humm deen bhekhaari Ram.
Maya moh magan kadh lehu muraari Ram.

तू समरथु सदा हम दीन भेखारी राम ॥
माइआ मोहि मगनु कढि लेहु मुरारी राम ॥

You are ever so powerful, I am a poor beggar, O Lord.
I am entangled in the love of *maya*, get me out of it O Lord!

M5/547/8

ਮੈ ਨਿਰਗੁਨ ਗੁਨੁ ਨਾਹੀ ਕੋਇ ॥ ਕਰਨ ਕਰਾਵਨਹਾਰ ਪ੍ਰਭ ਸੋਇ ॥

Mai nirgun gunh naahi koye; karan karaavanhaar Prabh soye.

मैं निरगुन गुणु नाही कोइ ॥ करन करावनहार प्रभ सोइ ॥

I am virtue-less, I have no virtues at all; God is the creator and the doer of everything.

M5/388/1

ਸਾਧ ਕੀ ਸੋਭਾ ਅਤਿ ਮਸਕੀਨੀ॥ ਸੰਤ ਵਡਾਈ ਹਰਿ ਜਸੁ ਚੀਨੀ॥

Saadh ki sobha utt maskeeni; sant vadaayee Har jas cheeni.

साध की सोभा अति मसकीनी॥ संत वडाई हरि जसु चीनी॥

The glory of Saints lies in their extreme humility.
Greatness of Saints lies in their praise of the Lord.

M5/676/15

Finally a verse by Bhatt Kal in praise of Guru Angad Dev:

ਸਦਾ ਅਕਲ ਲਿਵ ਰਹੈ ਕਰਨ ਸਿਉ ਇਛਾ ਚਾਰਹ॥
ਦ੍ਰਮ ਸਪੂਰ ਜਿਉ ਨਿਵੈ ਖਵੈ ਕਸੁ ਬਿਮਲ ਬੀਚਾਰਹ॥

Sadaa akal liv rahai karan siu ichhaa chaareh.
Drum sapoor jiu nivai khavai kas bimal bichaareh.

सदा अकल लिव रहै करन सिउ इछा चारह॥
द्रुम सपूर जिउ निवै खवै कसु बिमल बीचारह॥

(O Guru Angad) you are always in remembrance of God,
you do as you wish.
Like a fruit bearing tree, you bow in humility and bear the
burden of humanity; it's a pure thought.

Kal/1392/1

Humility should come as result of knowledge, wisdom, and strength of character, not out of ignorance and weakness. Humility can be a very subtle thing. The moment you say you've got it, you've lost it. When you say I am humble, the chances are that it's your ego speaking, rather than your humility. Test and study your responses in day to day situations to develop humility. For example, you go to a store to buy something.

The salesman is engaged in some other chores and does not attend to you for some time. What is your response? Is it, "How dare you make me wait, don't you know who I am?" Or, "Could you please listen to me, I'm in a bit of a hurry." I don't have to tell which response is from the ego and which out of humility. Practice humility all the time. Jesus Christ said, "Blessed are the meek, for they shall inherit the earth." (Matthew 5:5). Meek, in the New Bible, is translated as humble. Humble people are the ones who are more awakened spiritually, and they shall rule.

If we look at history we notice that all the mighty, powerful and proud men like Alexander, Genghis Khan, Mogul Emperors, Adolf Hitler etc., hardly have any relevance now. The humble and spiritual people like Gautam Buddh, Jesus Christ, Prophet Mohammad, and Guru Nanak, still rule the hearts and minds of people the world over - and will continue to do so.

For the descendants of mighty Jahangir and Aurangzeb, who martyred Sikh Gurus, Guru Arjan Dev and Guru Teg Bahadur, it is becoming difficult to even maintain the graves of these proud tyrants. But look at the number of *gurdwaras*, hospitals, schools, colleges, orphanages, old age homes and other institutions built in gurus' names. These humble gurus continue to be loved and remembered by millions in India and abroad. There is no dearth of money with institutions running in their memory.

First Mughal Emperor Babur (1483-1530), and first Sikh guru, Guru Nanak (1469-1539), were contemporaries. One was a proud warrior, the other a humble fakir. One conquered people, the other liberated them. See where they stand today. The lesson is, 'If you want to own a piece of land become like Babur; if you want the whole creation become like Guru Nanak.'

A small anecdote with a lesson in humility. Once Tulsidas (author of *Ramchritmanas*) learnt that Rahim (one of Akbar's nine jewels) often gave alms to the poor, but always looked down while giving. Tulsidas sent Rahim a couplet which said:

"Aisee Deynee Dayan Jiun Kit Seekhay Ho Sayan,
Jiun Jiun Kar Ooncheyo Kari, Tayon Tayon Neechay Nayan."

[Where have you learnt to give (alms) like this, O great man? As your hands go up (to give), your eyes begin to look down.]

With utmost humility Rahim replied:

"Denhaar Koee Aur Hai, Bhejat Jo Din Rayan.
Log Brahm Hum Par Karay, Taasi Nichay Nayan."

[The Giver is someone else (God), who keeps giving
day and night.
People mistakenly think that I give, that's why
I look down in embarrassment.]

Some people often say that God is responsible for all good things in their lives, and they themselves are responsible for all suffering. This taking responsibility for their suffering is spoken out of supposed humility; but it can't be so - either God is responsible for everything in your life or nothing. Make Him in charge of everything, then trust Him – He likes it that way.

"Humility is the greatest quality that a man can have, and arrogance is undoubtedly the worst."

Maulana W Khan (1925 - 2021)
Indian Islamic Scholar,
Peace Activist

CHAPTER 22

SEVA

ੴ

When it comes to *seva* (voluntary service), followers of SGGS are always in the forefront and never let go an opportunity to help. Whenever there is a natural, or man-made calamity, anywhere in the world, you will see Sikh volunteers getting there the fastest to arrange food, water, medicines, clothing, shelter and whatever else may be required.

Even at religious functions in *gurdwaras* and other places, you will notice many Sikh volunteers doing *seva* by helping with cooking, serving food, cleaning utensils, wiping floors, taking care of shoes (which have to be removed before entering the main precincts) and doing other chores. It is not uncommon to see well-to-do people sitting on the floor cleaning and polishing shoes of the poor. All this is voluntary work done in adherence to the teachings enshrined in SGGS.

The practice of community service has its origins in Guru Nanak serving food to hungry people. His father once gave him money to buy goods from the town which could be sold for profit. On his way he met some holy people who hadn't eaten for days, so he spent all the money on their food. When he returned home empty-handed his father was furious because of the lost opportunity to make some profit. Young Nanak's only defense was, "What could be more profitable business than providing food to the hungry?" From this grew the custom of community service. The practice was later institutionalized by the successor gurus and it continues to this day in the form of *langar* (free food kitchen) that runs in every *gurdwara*. This service has now expanded into other areas of assistance, like healthcare, education, old age care, and so on.

Physical service is also called *kaar seva. Kaar* means hand, therefore, *kaar seva* is service done with your hands. Whenever there is a need for physical labour for things like construction work, renovations, cleaning or de-silting water bodies etc., there is no dearth of *kaar sevaks*, (also known as *sevadaars*) who respond overwhelmingly. All *seva* is considered as an opportunity to serve and is without any remuneration. In the Sikh spirit of Oneness of the world, service is not limited to helping Sikhs alone - it is for anyone who is in need.

Now some verses on community service that motivate followers of SGGS. Guru Nanak writes:

ਇਤੁ ਤਨਿ ਲਾਗੈ ਬਾਣੀਆ॥ ਸੁਖੁ ਹੋਵੈ ਸੇਵ ਕਮਾਣੀਆ॥ ਸਭ ਦੁਨੀਆ ਆਵਣ ਜਾਣੀਆ॥

It tunn laagai baaniya, sukh hovai sev kamaaniya, sabh duniya aavan jaaniya.

इतु तनि लागै बाणीआ॥ सुखु होवै सेव कमाणीआ॥ सभ दुनीआ आवण जाणीआ॥

Those who are touched by the *gurbani*, earn happiness by doing service. They realize the temporariness of the world.

ਵਿਚਿ ਦੁਨੀਆ ਸੇਵ ਕਮਾਈਐ॥ ਤਾ ਦਰਗਹ ਬੈਸਣੁ ਪਾਈਐ॥ ਕਹੁ ਨਾਨਕ ਬਾਹ ਲੁਡਾਈਐ॥

Vich duniya sev kamaeeyai, ta dargah baisan paaeeyai, kahu Nanak baah ludaayeeyai.

विचि दुनीआ सेव कमाईऐ॥ ता दरगह बैसणु पाईऐ॥ कहु नानक बाह लुडाईऐ॥

In this world earn by doing service, you shall then find a place in Lord's court; Nanak says, you thence swing your arms (in joy).

M1/25/19

Guru Amar Das on focusing attention on service and *gurban*i:

> ਕਰਮੁ ਹੋਵੈ ਸਤਿਗੁਰੁ ਮਿਲਾਏ॥ ਸੇਵਾ ਸੁਰਤਿ ਸਬਦਿ ਚਿਤੁ ਲਾਏ॥
> ਹਉਮੈ ਮਾਰਿ ਸਦਾ ਸੁਖੁ ਪਾਇਆ ਮਾਇਆ ਮੋਹੁ ਚੁਕਾਵਣਿਆ॥
>
> Karam hovai Satguru milaaye, seva surat sabad chit laaye,
> haumai maar sada sukh paaya maya moh chkuvaneya.
>
> करमु होवै सतिगुरू मिलाए॥ सेवा सुरति सबदि चितु लाए॥
> हउमै मारि सदा सुखु पाइआ माइआ मोहु चुकावणिआ॥
>
> By God's grace man meets the Lord; due to his focus on
> service and his mind on the *shabad* (word of *gurbani*);
> His ego is finished and he is ever so happy,
> his love for *maya* is ended.
>
> M3/109/19

Guru Amar Das again says, service brings happiness:

> ਸੇਵਾ ਤੇ ਸਦਾ ਸੁਖੁ ਪਾਇਆ ਗੁਰਮੁਖਿ ਸਹਜਿ ਸਮਾਵਣਿਆ॥
>
> Seva tay sadaa sukh paayaa gurmukh sehaj samaavaneya.
>
> सेवा ते सदा सुखु पाइआ गुरमुखि सहजि समावणिआ॥
>
> Because of their service, the God-oriented people are ever
> happy and unwavering.
>
> M3/125/19

Guru Arjan Dev's advice on service along with worship:

> ਸਾਧਸੰਗਿ ਭਇਓ ਜਨਮੁ ਪਰਾਪਤਿ॥ ਕਰਿ ਸੇਵਾ ਭਜੁ ਹਰਿ ਹਰਿ ਗੁਰਮਤਿ॥
>
> Saadhsangh bhaeyo janam praapat, kar seva bhaj Har Har gurmat.
>
> साधसंगि भइओ जनमु परापति॥ करि सेवा भजु हरि हरि गुरमति॥

> You have been born into the company of the holy; as per
> Guru's advice, serve (humanity) and worship the Lord.
>
> M5/176/14

Guru Ram Das prays here that he be made to serve God's servants. Serving is a superior work, he says:

> ਜੋ ਜਨ ਧਿਆਵਹਿ ਹਰਿ ਹਰਿ ਨਾਮਾ ॥
> ਤਿਨ ਦਾਸਨਿ ਦਾਸ ਕਰਹੁ ਹਮ ਰਾਮਾ ॥
> ਜਨ ਕੀ ਸੇਵਾ ਉਤਮ ਕਾਮਾ ॥
>
> Jo jann dhiaaveh Har Har naama,
> tin daasan daas karoh humm Raama,
> jann ki seva ootam kaama.
>
> जो जन धिआवहि हरि हरि नामा ॥
> तिन दासनि दास करहु हम रामा ॥
> जन की सेवा ऊतम कामा ॥
>
> Those who meditate on Lord's name,
> O Lord, make me serve such servants.
> Serving people is the highest deed.
>
> M4/164/6

As per SGGS, the followers are expected to share a part of their income for charitable purposes. Guru Gobind Singh had this included in Sikh code of conduct, where he quantified the donation amount as *dasvandh* (one tenth) of the income. As a result of this, as also their general tendency to help others, Sikhs contribute liberally. This makes them the highest per capita donors for charity in the world.

Service/sharing, along with worship and honest work are the three fundamentals of SGGS philosophy.

Guru Nanak speaks of working and sharing:

> ਘਾਲਿ ਖਾਇ ਕਿਛੁ ਹਥਹੁ ਦੇਇ ॥ ਨਾਨਕ ਰਾਹੁ ਪਛਾਣਹਿ ਸੇਇ ॥
>
> Ghaal khaaye kichhu hathoh dei;
> Nanak raahu pachhaaneh saye.
>
> घालि खाइ किछु हथहु देइ ॥ नानक राहु पछाणहि सेइ ॥
>
> He who earns by the sweat of his brow, and shares some;
> Nanak says he knows the way (to salvation).
>
> M1/1245/19

There are many references in SGGS on serving saintly/enlightened people. Bhagat Kabir on serving a saint and God:

> ਕਬੀਰ ਸੇਵਾ ਕਉ ਦੁਇ ਭਲੇ ਏਕੁ ਸੰਤੁ ਇਕੁ ਰਾਮੁ ॥
>
> Kabir seva kou doye bhalay ek sant ik Raam.
>
> कबीर सेवा कउ दुइ भले एकु संतु इकु रामु ॥
>
> Kabir says, serving a saint and God are both
> good deeds.
>
> Kabir/1373/6

As we have seen earlier, in today's world it is not easy to find a truly enlightened saint whom we could serve on a regular basis. Our best bet is to serve God's deprived children and those going through difficult times.

There are three ways to serve i.e., with *tunn, munn* and *dhunn* (all rhyming with 'run'). *Tunn* is the body which means the physical work. *Munn* is the mind which implies the mental/devotional aspect of self-less and unconditional service – without expectations. *Dhunn* is wealth which means monetary contribution. More important than the amount you give, is the concern you have for the recipients. One hundred rupees given by a daily wager could bring more spiritual benefit than a million rupees given by a materialist business tycoon.

Guru Arjan Dev on the need to make service selfless:

ਸੇਵਾ ਕਰਤ ਹੋਇ ਨਿਹਕਾਮੀ॥ ਤਿਸ ਕਉ ਹੋਤ ਪਰਾਪਤਿ ਸੁਆਮੀ॥
ਅਪਨੀ ਕ੍ਰਿਪਾ ਜਿਸੁ ਆਪਿ ਕਰੇਇ॥ ਨਾਨਕ ਸੋ ਸੇਵਕੁ ਗੁਰ ਕੀ ਮਤਿ ਲੇਇ॥

Seva karat hoye nihkaami, tis kou hoat praapat Suami.
Apni kripa jis aap karay, Nanak so sevak gur ki mutt laye.

सेवा करत होइ निहकामी॥ तिस कउ होत परापति सुआमी॥
अपनी क्रिपा जिसु आपि करेइ॥ नानक सो सेवकु गुर की मति लेइ॥

He who serves selflessly, attains God.
On whom He showers His grace, Nanak says,
he receives Lord's wisdom.

M5/286/19

Benefit from service cannot be derived if it is done to satisfy the ego. In fact true service should make you feel humble not proud. If you get an opportunity to serve, don't boast about it – instead thank God humbly for giving you a chance to help someone. Also thank the recipient of your service for making you do a noble deed.

Guru Amar Das says service done to boost your ego, is all a waste of time as it serves no purpose:

ਹਉਮੈ ਵਿਚਿ ਸੇਵਾ ਨ ਹੋਵਈ ਤਾ ਮਨੁ ਬਿਰਥਾ ਜਾਇ॥
Haumai vich seva na hovayee ta munn birtha jaaye.
हउमै विचि सेवा न होवई ता मनु बिरथा जाइ॥

> You cannot serve under the influence of ego,
> because such service goes waste.
>
> M3/560/12

A piece of advice by Guru Amar Das for those who do not serve:

> ਅਨਦਿਨੁ ਸਦਾ ਵਿਸਟਾ ਮਹਿ ਵਾਸਾ ਬਿਨੁ ਸੇਵਾ ਜਨਮੁ ਗਵਾਵਣਿਆ ॥
>
> Andin sadaa vista meh vaasa bin seva janam gwaavaneya.
>
> अनदिनु सदा विसटा महि वासा बिनु सेवा जनमु गवावणिआ ॥
>
> Those who do not serve, live in filth all the time and they
> waste away their life.
>
> M3/119/13

Besides helping the community, there are a number of verses in SGGS that urge you to serve God.

Guru Arjan Dev on serving God:

> ਮੇਰੇ ਮਨ ਸਤਗੁਰ ਕੀ ਸੇਵਾ ਲਾਗੁ ॥ ਜੋ ਦੀਸੈ ਸੋ ਵਿਣਸਣਾ ਮਨ ਕੀ ਮਤਿ ਤਿਆਗੁ ॥
>
> Meray munn Satgur ki seva laag; jo deesai so vinsana, munn
> ki mutt teyaag.
>
> मेरे मन सतगुर की सेवा लागु ॥ जो दीसै सो विणसणा मन की मति तिआगु ॥
>
> O my mind, get to serve the Lord; whatever is visible will
> disappear, shed the mind's cleverness.
>
> M5/50/5

How do you serve God? By worshipping Him and by helping and protecting His creation. We have taken too many liberties with nature and have harmed it in innumerable ways. In our urge to create and own more wealth we have destroyed/polluted jungles, mountains, rivers, oceans, air, glaciers and animal kingdom. Protecting and restoring nature is one of the best ways to serve God. Helping humanity in need is also a great service to God.

Seva rendered by Sikh volunteers during Covid-19 pandemic, particularly during the early period of mass migration, was exceptional. In Delhi alone Sikh organizations were providing free food to over a hundred thousand people every day, sometimes touching much higher numbers. Where it was not possible for individuals to come to the *gurdwaras*, meals were delivered wherever they were located. In addition, food and accommodation was also arranged for doctors, nurses, and other medical staff working under Delhi administration.

Similar *seva* is still being performed all over India, as well as in other nations having Sikh population. It is being appreciated by the world immensely, and it is also helping people know Sikhism better. A message from Prince Charles said, "In the United Kingdom, as elsewhere, Sikhs are playing a vital role on the frontline of this crisis, whether in hospitals or other key roles, or through the remarkable work that is being done by *gurdwaras* to support local communities and the most vulnerable. In all this, it seems to me, Sikhs so marvelously embody the values on which Guru Nanak founded your religion......". Canadian PM, Justin Trudeau said, "Everyday Sikh Canadians make our cities and our neighbourhoods stronger and right now when people need help the most, you're stepping up once again."

To serve people who are not as fortunate as you, is indeed a noble deed. It must help you develop humility which, as we saw earlier, is a great virtue to possess.

To conclude, a simple statement by Guru Arjan Dev on benefit of service:

ਸੇਵਕ ਕਉ ਗੁਰੁ ਸਦਾ ਦਇਆਲ ॥

Sevak kao Gur sadaa dayaal.

सेवक कउ गुरु सदा दइआल ॥

Guru is always kind to those who serve.

M5/286/14

"I don't know what your destiny will be, but one thing I do know: the only ones among you who will be really happy are those who have sought and found how to serve."

Albert Schweitzer (1875-1965)
French Theologian

CHAPTER 23

REMEMBRANCE

ੴ

As far as remembering God is concerned, most of us are like the Sunday-morning Christian, who remembers God only on a Sunday morning when he visits the church, and commits all forms of sin rest of the time. Most of us don't remember God even while visiting the place of worship. Our minds are too occupied with other mundane things. Such visits should be utilized mainly for remembering God, thanking Him and for seeking His wisdom.

Some people spend lot of time chanting 'Waheguru Waheguru' or 'Ram Ram.' Such chanting even whole day, will get you nowhere if remembrance of God is not there. The mind has the habit of quietly drifting away without warning. It should be truly focused on God during such chanting.

You should feel the presence of God in everything you do. The more we remember God, the more peace will come to us. The time spent in remembrance will also keep us away from bad karma and the consequences thereof. Even when we are engaged in daily activities like working, eating, resting, traveling, playing etc., the thought of God must never leave us.

There is great significance given to God remembrance in SGGS. Here is a simple but crucial lesson from Guru Nanak:

ਗੁਰਾ ਇਕ ਦੇਹਿ ਬੁਝਾਈ॥ ਸਭਨਾ ਜੀਆ ਕਾ ਇਕੁ ਦਾਤਾ ਸੋ ਮੈ ਵਿਸਰਿ ਨ ਜਾਈ॥

Gura ik deh bhujaayee, sabhna jia ka ik daataa so mai visar na jaayee.

गुरा इक देहि बुझाई॥ सभना जीआ का इकु दाता सो मै विसरि न जाई॥

My guru has explained this one thing; there is only One Benefactor of all beings, may I never forget Him.

M1/2/10

'May I never forget Him,' this advice from Guru Nanak is priceless. Following this simple edict of remembering God all the time, will take you closer to God and you would earn great amount of His love.

Guru Amar Das tells us about the wastefulness of life without remembrance:

ਸਤਿਗੁਰੁ ਨ ਸੇਵਿਓ ਸਬਦੁ ਨ ਰਖਿਓ ਉਰ ਧਾਰਿ॥
ਧਿਗੁ ਤਿਨਾ ਕਾ ਜੀਵਿਆ ਕਿਤੁ ਆਏ ਸੰਸਾਰਿ॥

Satguru na seveyo sabad na rakheyo ur dhaar.
Dhig tina ka jeeveya kit aaye sansaar.

सतिगुरू न सेविओ सबदु न रखिओ उर धारि॥
धिगु तिना का जीविआ कितु आए संसारि॥

Those who do not remember the True Guru, and do not keep the Word enshrined in their mind;
Shame on their living, what have they come into this world for?

M3/1414/3

Guru Nanak tells us how remembrance can remove all worries and bring happiness:

ਚਿੰਤਤ ਹੀ ਦੀਸੈ ਸਭੁ ਕੋਇ॥ ਚੇਤਹਿ ਏਕੁ ਤਹੀ ਸੁਖੁ ਹੋਇ॥

Chintat hee deesai sabh koye; chayteh ek tahee sukh hoye.

ਚਿੰਤਤ ਹੀ ਦੀਸੈ ਸਭੁ ਕੋਇ॥ ਚੇਤਹਿ ਏਕੁ ਤਹੀ ਸੁਖੁ ਹੋਇ॥

Everyone appears to be in worry.
Remember the One, only then will there be happiness.

M1/932/16

In the verse below Guru Amar Das tells us not to forget the Lord even for a moment:

ਇਕੁ ਤਿਲੁ ਪਿਆਰਾ ਵਿਸਰੈ ਭਗਤਿ ਕਿਨੇਹੀ ਹੋਇ॥
ਮਨੁ ਤਨੁ ਸੀਤਲੁ ਸਾਚ ਸਿਉ ਸਾਸੁ ਨ ਬਿਰਥਾ ਕੋਇ॥

Ik til piyaara visrai bhagat kinehee hoye.
Munn tunn seetal saach siu saas na birtha koye.

ਇਕੁ ਤਿਲੁ ਪਿਆਰਾ ਵਿਸਰੈ ਭਗਤਿ ਕਿਨੇਹੀ ਹੋਇ॥
ਮਨੁ ਤਨੁ ਸੀਤਲੁ ਸਾਚ ਸਿਉ ਸਾਸੁ ਨ ਬਿਰਥਾ ਕੋਇ॥

If one forgets the Beloved Lord even for a moment, what kind of worship is that?
The mind and body are soothed by the remembrance of True Lord, not a single breath should go waste.

M3/35/5

Guru Amar Das reiterates:

ਇਕੁ ਦਮੁ ਸਾਚਾ ਵੀਸਰੈ ਸਾ ਵੇਲਾ ਬਿਰਥਾ ਜਾਇ॥
ਸਾਹਿ ਸਾਹਿ ਸਦਾ ਸਮਾਲੀਐ ਆਪੇ ਬਖਸੇ ਕਰੇ ਰਜਾਇ॥

Ik dumm saacha veesrai sa vela birtha jaaye.
Sah sah sadaa samaliyai aapay bakhsay karay rajaaye.

इकु दमु साचा वीसरै सा वेला बिरथा जाइ॥
साहि साहि सदा समालीऐ आपे बखसे करे रजाइ॥

If one forgets the True Lord even for a moment, that moment
has gone waste.
Remember Him with every breath you take, He will bless you,
as He wishes.

M3/506/14

Guru Arjan Dev on all-time remembrance:

ਉਠਤ ਬੈਠਤ ਸੋਵਤ ਜਾਗਤ ਇਹੁ ਮਨੁ ਤੁਝਹਿ ਚਿਤਾਰੈ॥
ਸੁਖ ਦੂਖ ਇਸੁ ਮਨ ਕੀ ਬਿਰਥਾ ਤੁਝ ਹੀ ਆਗੈ ਸਾਰੈ॥

Oothat baithat sovat jaagat ih munn tujhay chitaaray.
Sookh dookh is munn ki birtha Tujh hee aagay saaray.

ऊठत बैठत सोवत जागत इहु मनु तुझहि चितारै॥
सूख दूख इसु मन की बिरथा तुझ ही आगै सारै॥

While standing or sitting, asleep or awake, this mind always
remembers You.
The state of my mind, my happiness and my sorrow, is all
known to You.

M5/820/11

That is how God is to be remembered; all the time. It is called
'unremembered remembrance' where you don't have to make
a special effort to remember God, but it is automatically there
all the time. That is the ultimate in remembrance, but it takes
time and requires practice. You can start by remembering
Him, as frequently as you can. Think of Him when you wake
up in the morning, before you go to sleep, when you eat, when
you leave for work, when you reach back home and so on. Keep

increasing your remembrance till it becomes unremembered remembrance and His thought is always with you.

In the verses below Bhagat Namdev gives interesting similes of remembrance during various daily chores. That is how God is to be remembered:

ਆਨੀਲੇ ਕੁੰਭੁ ਭਰਾਈਲੇ ਉਦਕ ਰਾਜ ਕੁਆਰਿ ਪੁਰੰਦਰੀਏ॥
ਹਸਤ ਬਿਨੋਦ ਬੀਚਾਰ ਕਰਤੀ ਹੈ ਚੀਤੁ ਸੁ ਗਾਗਰਿ ਰਾਖੀਅਲੇ॥

Aaneelay kumbh bharayeelay oodak raaj kuaar purandareeye.
Hast binod bichaar karti hai cheet su gaagar raakheeyele.

आनीले कुमभु भराईले ऊदक राज कुआरि पुरंदरीए॥
हसत बिनोद बीचार करती है चीतु सु गागरि राखीअले॥

Young girl of the city takes a pitcher, and is filling it with water.
She laughs, plays, and chats with friends, but her attention is always on the pitcher.

ਮੰਦਰੁ ਏਕੁ ਦੁਆਰ ਦਸ ਜਾ ਕੇ ਗਊ ਚਰਾਵਨ ਛਾਡੀਅਲੇ॥
ਪਾਂਚ ਕੋਸ ਪਰ ਗਊ ਚਰਾਵਤ ਚੀਤੁ ਸੁ ਬਛਰਾ ਰਾਖੀਅਲੇ॥

Mandar ek duaar dus ja kay gaoo charaavan chhaadiyelay.
Paanch kos par gaoo charavat cheet su bachhra raakhiyelay.

मंदरु एकु दुआर दस जा के गऊ चरावन छाडीअले॥
पांच कोस पर गऊ चरावत चीतु सु बछरा राखीअले॥

From the house of ten gates the cow is let loose to graze.
It grazes up to five *kos* (old unit of distance) away, but her attention is always on the young calf.

कहत नामदेउ सुनहु तिलोचन बालकु पालन पउढीअले॥
अंतरि बाहरि काज बिरुधी चीतु सु बारिक राखीअले॥

Kahat Namdeo sunoh Tilochan baalak paalan paudiyelay.
Antir bahar kaaj biroodhee cheet su barik raakhiyelay.

कहत नामदेउ सुनहु तिलोचन बालकु पालन पउढीअले॥
अंतरि बाहरि काज बिरूधी चीतु सु बारिक राखीअले॥

Says Namdev, listen O Tilochan, the child is placed in
the cradle.
The mother is busy moving in and out of the house, but her
attention is always on the child.

Namdev/972/15

We may not remember God but He remembers us all the time,
and provides us with all the necessities of life. We must not forget
Him because no one can give us true contentment and happiness
as He can. We must remember Him throughout the day and the
night. Spiritual guru, Lahiri Mahasaya said, "If you don't invite
God to be your summer guest, He won't come in the winter of your
life." Remember to invite Him every day, every hour, every minute.

Here Guru Arjan Dev asks his mind not to let go remembrance
even for a moment:

ਮਨ ਮੇਰੇ ਸਤਿਗੁਰ ਸੇਵਾ ਸਾਰੁ॥
ਕਰੇ ਦਇਆ ਪ੍ਰਭੁ ਆਪਣੀ ਇਕ ਨਿਮਖ ਨ ਮਨਹੁ ਵਿਸਾਰੁ॥

Munn meray Satgur seva saar.
Karay daya Prabh aapnee ik nimakh na manoh visaar.

मन मेरे सतिगुर सेवा सारु॥
करे दइआ प्रभु आपणी इक निमख न मनहु विसारु॥

O my mind, be in service of True Guru.
God will grant His grace, do not forget Him even for a moment.

M5/48/4

Guru Arjan Dev further says that true happiness comes to
those places where God is remembered:

ਘਰ ਮੰਦਰ ਖੁਸੀਆ ਤਹੀ ਜਹ ਤੂ ਆਵਹਿ ਚਿਤਿ॥

ਦੁਨੀਆ ਕੀਆ ਵਡਿਆਈਆ ਨਾਨਕ ਸਭਿ ਕੁਮਿਤ॥

Ghar mandar khusia tehee jeh tu aaveh chit.

Duniya keeya vadeayeea Nanak sabh kumit.

घर मंदर खुसीआ तही जह तू आवहि चिति॥

दुनीआ कीआ वडिआईआ नानक सभि कुमित॥

Happiness is found in those homes and temples where
You are remembered.

(Where You are not remembered) all the world's praises,
O Nanak, are like bad friends.

M5/319/10

Guru Amar Das says why forget Him who has given us
our body and soul and because of whom we are respectfully
accepted in the Lord's court:

ਸੋ ਕਿਉ ਵਿਸਰੈ ਜਿਸ ਕੇ ਜੀਅ ਪਰਾਨਾ॥ ਸੋ ਕਿਉ ਵਿਸਰੈ ਸਭ ਮਾਹਿ ਸਮਾਨਾ॥

ਜਿਤੁ ਸੇਵਿਐ ਦਰਗਹ ਪਤਿ ਪਰਵਾਨਾ॥

So kiu visrai jis kay jia praana. So kiu visrai sabh
maahay smaana.

Jit saviye dargeh patt parvaana.

सो किउ विसरै जिस के जीअ पराना॥ सो किउ विसरै सभ माहि समाना॥

जितु सेविऐ दरगह पति परवाना॥

Why forget Him, who owns our soul and our life?
Why forget Him, who pervades everything?

And by serving whom we are accepted in the
Lord's court with honour.

M3/159/17

Finally this verse from Guru Ram Das:

> ਨਾਨਕ ਜਿਸੁ ਬਿਨੁ ਘੜੀ ਨ ਜੀਵਣਾ ਵਿਸਰੇ ਸਰੈ ਨ ਬਿੰਦ॥
> ਤਿਸੁ ਸਿਉ ਕਿਉ ਮਨ ਰੂਸੀਐ ਜਿਸਹਿ ਹਮਾਰੀ ਚਿੰਦ॥
>
> Nanak, jis bin gharee na jeevna visray sarai na bind.
> Tis siu kiu munn roosiye jiseh hamaaree chind.
>
> नानक जिसु बिनु घड़ी न जीवणा विसरे सरै न बिंद॥
> तिसु सिउ किउ मन रूसीऐ जिसहि हमारी चिंद॥
>
> O Nanak, without whom, we can't live for a moment and by
> forgetting Him, we cannot manage even a second.
> Why allow our mind to be annoyed with Him,
> who cares for us?
>
> M4/1250/11

The main lesson from above verses is that if we keep the thought of God at the back of our mind, all the time, He may consider us worthy of His grace. God doesn't expect much from us; only remembrance, gratitude and *seva*. Bhagwat Gita says, "For one who remembers me without deviation, I am easy to obtain." (9.14)

If you forget God, you only create hurdles in your spiritual journey. How can you realize God if you don't remember Him? One way to remember God is to admire His miraculous creation. If you look deeply, almost everything, every activity, is a miracle; but we do not see it as such because it has become common phenomenon. A miniscule cell in the womb of a woman becomes a wondrous human being. Isn't that a miracle? But we don't give it a second thought because it is happening everywhere all the time. How do we breathe, how does the whole body function? Ponder over it and you will find that all the functions of the body are indeed breathtaking miracles. A small seed grows into a tall majestic tree. Isn't that a miracle? Clouds floating in the sky, the rainbow, the sunshine, the birds flying high, the blossoming of flowers, the jungles, the mountains, the rivers, the stars are all miracles. Remember God with awe when you observe such things - and they are there everywhere. Albert Einstein rightly said, "There are only two ways to live your life. One is as though nothing is a miracle. The other is as though everything is a miracle." Look at everything in the creation with some intensity and you will see miracles everywhere. That will remind you of God.

Remember to remember Him – all the time.

"To have that constant remembrance of God is to be intensely happy. Nothing can describe that divine joy."

Paramahansa Yogananda (1893-1952)
Indian Spiritual Guru

Bhagat Ravidas (1450-1520)	Hindu, UP, Shoe Maker	40
Bhagat Sain (1343-1440)	Hindu, Punjab, Barber	1
Bhagat Dhanna (1415-1475)	Hindu, Rajasthan, Farmer	4
Bhagat Peepa (1426-1562)	Hindu, Rajasthan/UP, King	1
Bhagat Parmanand (1483-1593)	Hindu, Maharashtra	1
Bhagat Surdas (1479-1580)	Hindu, UP, Poet	1
Bhagat Bhikhan (1480-1573)	Muslim, UP, Sufi Saint	2
Bhagat Sadhna (b. 1180)	Muslim, Sindh/Punjab Butcher	1
Bhagat Beni (Period not known)	Muslim, Punjab	3

Bhatts (11)

Bhatts were traditional poets and singers who eked out a living by eulogizing kings and other important people. When the influence of Sikh Gurus began they became followers of Sikhism and started writing and singing praises of the Gurus. Their writings appear in SGGS at pages from 1389 to 1409. There is some confusion about the exact number of Bhatts whose writings appear in SGGS because of some similar sounding names. However, there is a general belief that following eleven Bhatts contributed: Kalh/Kalhshaar, Jalap, Kirat, Bhikha, Salh, Bhalh, Nalh, Gayand, Mathura, Balh, and Harbans.

Other Contributors (4)

These are, Bhai Mardana (3), Baba Sundar (6), Bhai Satta (1) and Bhai Balwand (1).

* Guru Gobind Singh did not include his own poetry in SGGS. However, there is one couplet which was written by him which is mentioned as *Salok Mahalla 10* in some old

hand-written scripts of SGGS. In the present version the couplet is part of writings of his father Guru Teg Bahadur under *Salok Mahalla 9.*

When Guru Teg Bahadur was imprisoned by Aurangzeb in Delhi, and just before he was martyred for the cause of Kashmiri pandits, the Guru sent a couplet to his son to seek his response as a test of his readiness to take over *Guruship* from him. The couplet he sent in a letter was:

ਬਲੁ ਛੁਟਕਿਓ ਬੰਧਨ ਪਰੇ ਕਛੂ ਨ ਹੋਤ ਉਪਾਇ॥
ਕਹੁ ਨਾਨਕ ਅਬ ਓਟ ਹਰਿ ਗਜ ਜਿਉ ਹੋਹੁ ਸਹਾਇ॥

Bal chhutkeo bandhan paray kachhu na hoat upaaye.
Kahu Nanak abb oat Har gaj jehu hoho sahaaye.

बलु छुटकिओ बंधन परे कछू न होत उपाइ॥
कहु नानक अब ओट हरि गज जिउ होहु सहाइ॥

My strength is gone and I am shackled, there seems to be no way out.
Says Nanak, O Lord give me Your support and help me as You helped the elephant (from a story in the *Puraanas* in which God helped the elephant).

M9/1429/6

Then as a young boy of nine, Gobind Rai (later to become Guru Gobind Singh) replied:

ਬਲੁ ਹੋਆ ਬੰਧਨ ਛੁਟੇ ਸਭੁ ਕਿਛੁ ਹੋਤ ਉਪਾਇ॥
ਨਾਨਕ ਸਭੁ ਕਿਛੁ ਤੁਮਰੈ ਹਾਥ ਮੈ ਤੁਮ ਹੀ ਹੋਤ ਸਹਾਇ॥

Bal hoa bandhan chhutay sabh kichhu hoat upaaye.
Nanak, sabh kichhu tumrai haath mai tum hee hoat sahaaye.

CHAPTER 24

SUFFERING

ੴ

In the course of our lives we all undergo suffering of some kind or the other, which brings us immense pain and misery. It may be a physical pain or an emotional one, or both. For some the intensity of this pain could be very high while for others it may not be so. Also, for some it may last a long time, sometimes encompassing a whole life, while others have it for shorter periods.

Though no one wants it but suffering will surely come, says Guru Nanak:

ਸੁਖ ਕਉ ਮਾਗੈ ਸਭੁ ਕੋ ਦੁਖੁ ਨ ਮਾਗੈ ਕੋਇ ॥
ਸੁਖੈ ਕਉ ਦੁਖੁ ਅਗਲਾ ਮਨਮੁਖਿ ਬੂਝ ਨ ਹੋਇ ॥

Sukh kau maagai sabh ko dukh na maagai koye.
Sukhai kau dukh agla manmukh bhooj na hoye.

सुख कउ मागै सभु को दुखु न मागै कोइ ॥
सुखै कउ दुखु अगला मनमुखि बूझ न होइ ॥

Everyone seeks pleasure, no one wants suffering.
Self-oriented (selfish) people do not understand that pleasure
will be followed by suffering.

M1/57/12

Suffering and pleasure come to us as God given. As seen earlier, we are given human body to have every type of experience, good and bad, which cannot be had while in the spirit world, because we don't have physical body there. Before we are reincarnated we are given the choice of determining what kind of experiences we would like in our next life. We make the decision based on the karma we have accumulated. If we are required to suffer because of our negative karma, we may deliberately choose to do it, for mitigating our sins and for speedy spiritual progress. Hence the suffering we go through may be the result of our own choosing. Spiritual progress and learning is the fastest during our life on earth.

When faced with suffering, people react differently, depending upon their spiritual understanding and the intensity of suffering. Those who are aware of God's plan would welcome it and consider it as an opportunity to redeem themselves. Others find it as an unnecessary punishment and turn rebellious, blaming everyone, even God - but not themselves. Such reaction only makes their life more miserable.

You must accept suffering as God's will and see it as an opportunity to facilitate your spiritual progress. Gary Zukav, in his best-selling book, 'Seat Of The Soul' says, "The pains that you suffer, the loneliness that you encounter, the experiences that are disappointing or distressing, the addictions and seeming pitfalls of your life are each doorways to awareness. Each offers you an opportunity to see beyond the illusion that serves the balancing and growth of your soul."

In the verse below Guru Nanak explains how suffering is actually the remedy, while pleasure is the disease:

ਦੁਖੁ ਦਾਰੂ ਸੁਖੁ ਰੋਗੁ ਭਇਆ ਜਾ ਸੁਖੁ ਤਾਮਿ ਨ ਹੋਈ ॥

Dukh daaru sukh rog bhaya ja sukh taam na hoyee.

दुखु दारू सुखु रोगु भइआ जा सुखु तामि न होई ॥

> Suffering is remedy while pleasure is the disease,
> because where there is only pleasure, there is no
> desire for God.
>
> M1/469/9

When indulgence in pleasure of the material world becomes overriding, we have no time for God, we just forget Him. He is kept in the back of our mind, to be called upon for help when we hit a bad patch. That is bad planning. It is always a good idea to keep friendship with God all the time.

Guru Nanak says even suffering is God's gift:

> ਕੇਤਿਆ ਦੂਖ ਭੂਖ ਸਦ ਮਾਰ॥ ਏਹਿ ਭਿ ਦਾਤਿ ਤੇਰੀ ਦਾਤਾਰ॥
>
> Keteya dookh bhookh sadd maar; eh bhi daat teri daataar.
>
> केतिआ दूख भूख सद मार॥ एहि भि दाति तेरी दातार॥
>
> So many people constantly suffer pain and hunger;
> O Lord these too are your gifts.
>
> M1/5/13

Now Guru Nanak says suffering and pleasure are two sides of the same coin - one is born out of the other:

> ਦੂਖਾ ਤੇ ਸੁਖ ਉਪਜਹਿ ਸੂਖੀ ਹੋਵਹਿ ਦੂਖ॥
> ਜਿਤੁ ਮੁਖਿ ਤੂ ਸਾਲਾਹੀਅਹਿ ਤਿਤੁ ਮੁਖਿ ਕੈਸੀ ਭੂਖ॥
>
> Dukha tay sukh oopjeh sukhi hoveh dookh.
> Jit mukh tu salaahieh tit mukh kaisee bhookh.
>
> दूखा ते सुख ऊपजहि सूखी होवहि दूख॥
> जितु मुखि तू सालाहीअहि तितु मुखि कैसी भूख॥

> Pleasure is born out of pain while pain grows out of pleasure.
> Those who always praise Your virtues, they no more have any other desires.
>
> M1/1328/1

End of desire is the beginning of contentment and joy that leads to awakening.

In our worldly experiences God ensures a balance between pain and pleasure. We have to experience both – that is the truth. That's why Bhagat Kabir says he doesn't seek pleasure because he knows pain will surely follow:

> ਸੁਖ ਮਾਂਗਤ ਦੁਖ ਆਗੈ ਆਵੈ॥ ਸੋ ਸੁਖ ਹਮਹੁ ਨ ਮਾਂਗਿਆ ਭਾਵੈ॥
>
> Sukh maangat dukh aagai aavai; so sukh hamho na maangya bhaavai.
>
> सुखु मांगत दुखु आगै आवै॥ सो सुखु हमहु न मांगिआ भावै॥
>
> When I seek pleasure, pain comes along; I do not find it worthwhile to seek such pleasure.
>
> Kabir/330/6

Why is suffering necessary? Because it makes you appreciate the value of peace and joy. Suffering is also the mechanism God has put in place to remind you when you have forgotten Him, and drifted from the true purpose of your life.

Now some verses on how to deal with suffering. Guru Amar Das asks the mind to be with the Lord all the time:

> ਏ ਮਨ ਮੇਰਿਆ ਤੂ ਸਦਾ ਰਹੁ ਹਰਿ ਨਾਲੇ॥
> ਹਰਿ ਨਾਲਿ ਰਹੁ ਤੂ ਮੰਨ ਮੇਰੇ ਦੂਖ ਸਭਿ ਵਿਸਾਰਣਾ॥

Aye munn mereya tu sadaa raho Har naalay.
Har naal raho tu munn meray dookh sabh visaarna.

ए मन मेरिआ तू सदा रहु हरि नाले॥
हरि नालि रहु तू मंन मेरे दूख सभि विसारणा॥

O my mind, remain with the Lord all the time.
Remain with the Lord, all your sufferings will disappear.

M3/917/4

Guru Arjan Dev implores us to accept suffering as God's will and to worship Him all the time:

ਮਨ ਕੀ ਮਤਿ ਤਿਆਗਹੁ ਹਰਿ ਜਨ ਹੁਕਮੁ ਬੁਝਿ ਸੁਖੁ ਪਾਈਐ ਰੇ॥
ਜੋ ਪ੍ਰਭੁ ਕਰੈ ਸੋਈ ਭਲ ਮਾਨਹੁ ਸੁਖਿ ਦੁਖਿ ਓਹੀ ਧਿਆਈਐ ਰੇ॥

Munn ki mutt tiagoh Har jann hukam bhooj sukh paayeeyai ray.
Jo Prabbh karai soee bhal maanoh sukh dukh ohee dhyaaeeyai ray.

मन की मति तिआगहु हरि जन हुकमु बूझि सुखु पाईऐ रे॥
जो प्रभु करै सोई भल मानहु सुखि दुखि ओही धिआईऐ रे॥

Leave aside your mind's advice, O Lord's people, understand God's will if you want to be happy.
Whatever God does accept that to be good, worship Him during pleasure and pain.

M5/209/14

In the next two verses, Guru Arjan Dev tells us to come under God's shelter to mitigate our suffering:

ਜਾ ਕੈ ਹਰਿ ਵਸਿਆ ਮਨ ਮਾਹੀ॥ ਤਾ ਕਉ ਦੁਖੁ ਸੁਪਨੈ ਭੀ ਨਾਹੀ॥

Ja kai Har vaseya munn maahi, ta kou dukh supnay bhi naahi.

जा कै हरि वसिआ मन माही॥ ता कउ दुखु सुपनै भी नाही॥

Those who have the Lord enshrined in their minds, they do not suffer even in their dreams.

M5/193/5

ਪ੍ਰਭ ਕੀ ਸਰਨਿ ਸਗਲ ਭੈ ਲਾਥੇ ਦੁਖ ਬਿਨਸੇ ਸੁਖੁ ਪਾਇਆ॥

Prabh ki saran sagal bhai laathay, dukh binsay sukh paaya.

प्रभ की सरणि सगल भै लाथे दुख बिनसे सुखु पाइआ॥

When you come under God's shelter all suffering departs and you embrace happiness.

M5/615/17

Guru Teg Bahadur cautions us to cater for bad times:

ਜਤਨ ਬਹੁਤ ਸੁਖ ਕੇ ਕੀਏ ਦੁਖ ਕੋ ਕੀਓ ਨ ਕੋਇ॥

Jatan bahut sukh kay kiye dukh ko kio na koye.

जतन बहुत सुख के कीए दुख को कीओ न कोइ॥

We do everything for getting pleasure, but nothing for dealing with pain.

M9/1428/11

We should not leave worshipping only for bad times. Do it in good times too so that bad times don't come to us - if they do, we are better prepared to handle them. During the Covid-19 pandemic people suddenly started praying and begging God to save them. Had they worshipped Him during happy days and, refrained from all forms of sin committed against nature and mankind, God would not have inflicted this punishment. It was the collective karma playing out.

Guru Arjan Dev says, one should not only accept suffering as God's will but must find it sweet and desirable. He himself displayed this under most trying conditions. As we know, he was martyred in 1606 on orders of Mughal Emperor Jehangir for his ever increasing popularity among the masses. The Guru was asked to convert to Islam but he refused. He was arrested and taken to Lahore where, under the supervision of Diwan Chandu, he was tortured to death. He was made to sit on a hot plate and burning hot sand was poured over his body. Some influential people of Lahore including his friend Mian Meer, could not see this cruelty and offered to intervene, but the Guru rejected their offer saying his suffering was God's will which he must accept. There was no complaint and no remorse expressed by him during the torture. He instead recited this own verse from SGGS:

ਤੇਰਾ ਕੀਆ ਮੀਠਾ ਲਾਗੈ ॥ ਹਰਿ ਨਾਮੁ ਪਦਾਰਥੁ ਨਾਨਕੁ ਮਾਂਗੈ ॥

Tera kia meetha laagai, Har naam padarath Nanak maangai.

तेरा कीआ मीठा लागै ॥ हरि नामु पदारथु नानकु मांगै ॥

Whatever you do, I find it pleasing.
Nanak seeks the gift of Lord's Name.

M5/394/4

Guru Arjan Dev accepted his suffering willingly in the same spirit as Socrates had done by drinking the hemlock poison, and as Jesus Christ accepted the cross. Instead of cursing or hating those responsible for his death, Jesus sought forgiveness for them saying, "Father forgive them, for they know not what they do." (Luke 23:34)

Suffering is good for you and brings immense benefit of enriching the soul. However, what brings equal benefit, if not more, is helping others in their time of suffering. We must share others' burden as much as we can, particularly of those in dire need. Sometimes it may involve as little effort as giving a smile to someone looking for a bit of respect and recognition. I am reminded of a closing line used every day by Pat Gates, host of 'Breakfast Show' on Voice of America in the sixties and seventies. She would conclude every show by saying, "If you see someone without a smile, give him one of yours." Helping someone could be as simple as that.

"If your goal is to avoid pain and escape suffering, I would not advise you to seek higher levels of consciousness or spiritual evolution."

M Scott Peck, MD (1936-2005)
American Psychiatrist & Author

CHAPTER 25

HOLY COMPANY

ੴ

If you want to succeed in your spiritual endeavour, be in the company of saints and sages who have already trodden that path. People around you have great influence on your life, and the kind of company you keep largely determines who you are. If you associate with kind and compassionate people you too will become kind and compassionate. On the other hand if you are in the company of arrogant, egoistic and selfish people, that is the kind of person you are more likely to become. It is therefore not only important to keep good company but equally important to shun bad one.

The need for good company is mentioned in SGGS several hundred times. I have selected few quotations. Here Guru Nanak says good company makes you God-oriented:

ਜਿਨ ਕੈ ਮਨਿ ਵਸਿਆ ਸਚੁ ਸੋਈ ॥ ਤਿਨ ਕੀ ਸੰਗਤਿ ਗੁਰਮੁਖਿ ਹੋਈ ॥

Jin kai munn vasseya such soyee, tin ki sangat gurmukh hoyee.

जिन कै मनि वसिआ सचु सोई॥ तिन की संगति गुरमुखि होई॥

Company of those in whom the True Lord resides; makes you God-oriented.

M1/228/2

Bhagat Kabir says, mind goes all over, what it gets depends on the company it has:

ਕਬੀਰ ਮਨੁ ਪੰਖੀ ਭਇਓ ਉਡਿ ਉਡਿ ਦਹ ਦਿਸ ਜਾਇ॥
ਜੋ ਜੈਸੀ ਸੰਗਤਿ ਮਿਲੈ ਸੋ ਤੈਸੋ ਫਲੁ ਖਾਇ॥

Kabir munn pankhee bhayeo ud ud deh dis jaaye.
Jo jaisee sangat milai so taiso phal khaaye.

कबीर मनु पंखी भइओ उडि उडि दह दिस जाइ॥
जो जैसी संगति मिलै सो तैसो फलु खाइ॥

Kabir says, the mind is like a bird which flies in ten different directions. What it receives depends on the company it finds.

Kabir/1369/1

Here Guru Nanak tells us to keep company of the under privileged and lowly people because God is closer to them:

ਨੀਚਾ ਅੰਦਰਿ ਨੀਚ ਜਾਤਿ ਨੀਚੀ ਹੂ ਅਤਿ ਨੀਚੁ॥
ਨਾਨਕੁ ਤਿਨ ਕੈ ਸੰਗਿ ਸਾਥਿ ਵਡਿਆ ਸਿਉ ਕਿਆ ਰੀਸ॥
ਜਿਥੈ ਨੀਚ ਸਮਾਲੀਅਨਿ ਤਿਥੈ ਨਦਰਿ ਤੇਰੀ ਬਖਸੀਸ॥

Neecha andar neech jaat neechi hu utt neech.
Nanak tin kai sung saath vadeya siu kia rees.
Jithai neech samaliyan tithai nadar teri bakhsees.

नीचा अंदरि नीच जाति नीची हू अति नीचु॥
नानकु तिन कै संगि साथि वडिआ सिउ किआ रीस॥
जिथै नीच समालीअनि तिथै नदरि तेरी बखसीस॥

Seek company of the lowest of the low class, the very lowest of the low.
Be in company of such meek people; why emulate big people?
Where the lowly are cared for, Lord's grace is showered upon there.

M1/15/8

Guru Arjan Dev on company of holy saints:

ਉਨ ਸੰਤਨ ਕੈ ਮੇਰਾ ਮਨੁ ਕੁਰਬਾਨੇ॥ ਜਿਨ ਤੂੰ ਜਾਤਾ ਜੋ ਤੁਧੁ ਮਨਿ ਭਾਨੇ॥
ਤਿਨ ਕੈ ਸੰਗਿ ਸਦਾ ਸੁਖੁ ਪਾਇਆ ਹਰਿ ਰਸ ਨਾਨਕ ਤ੍ਰਿਪਤਿ ਅਘਾਨਾ ਜੀਉ॥

Un santan kai mera munn kurbaanay; jin toon jaataa jo tudh
munn bhaanay.
Tin kai sung sadaa sukh paaya Har ras Nanak tripat aghaana jio.

उन संतन कै मेरा मनु कुरबाने॥ जिन तूं जाता जो तुधु मनि भाने॥
तिन कै संगि सदा सुखु पाइआ हरि रस नानक त्रिपति अघाना जीउ॥

I sacrifice myself unto those saints who have known You, and
whom You love.
In their company I have found ever lasting peace, says
Nanak, they are filled with Lord's love.

M5/100/11

Guru Amar Das says a congregation is holy if True Guru
is present (in the minds of those attending) and you cannot
attain salvation without the word of *gurbani:*

ਸਤਿਗੁਰ ਬਾਝਹੁ ਸੰਗਤਿ ਨ ਹੋਈ॥ ਬਿਨੁ ਸਬਦੇ ਪਾਰੁ ਨ ਪਾਏ ਕੋਈ॥

Satgur baajhoh sangat na hoyee; bin sabday paar na
paaye koyee.

सतिगुर बाझहु संगति न होई॥ बिनु सबदे पारु न पाए कोई॥

Without the True Guru, there is no holy congregation.
Without the *shabad* (word of *gurbani*), no one can
cross over.

M3/1068/16

In this prayer Guru Ram Das humbly seeks good company:

ਜਿਨੀ ਗੁਰਮੁਖਿ ਨਾਮੁ ਸਲਾਹਿਆ ਤਿਨਾ ਸਭ ਕੋ ਕਹੈ ਸਾਬਾਸਿ॥
ਤਿਨ ਕੀ ਸੰਗਤਿ ਦੇਹਿ ਪ੍ਰਭ ਮੈ ਜਾਚਿਕ ਕੀ ਅਰਦਾਸਿ॥

Jini gurmukh naam salaaheya tinna sabh ko kahai saabaas.
Tin ki sangat deh prabh mai jaachik ki ardaas.

जिनी गुरमुखि नामु सलाहिआ तिना सभ को कहै साबासि॥
तिन की संगति देहि प्रभ मै जाचिक की अरदासि॥

God-oriented people who praise the *Naam*, are applauded
by everyone.
Grant me their company, O Lord, I make this prayer as
a beggar.

M4/42/4

Guru Arjan Dev on the mind being filled with love when you
are in good company:

ਸਾਧਸੰਗਤਿ ਮਨਿ ਵਸੈ ਸਾਚੁ ਹਰਿ ਕਾ ਨਾਉ॥
ਸੇ ਵਡਭਾਗੀ ਨਾਨਕਾ ਜਿਨਾ ਮਨਿ ਇਹੁ ਭਾਉ॥

Saadhsangat munn vasai saach Har ka nao; say vad-bhaagee
Nanaka jin munn eho bhaao.

साधसंगति मनि वसै साचु हरि का नाउ॥
से वडभागी नानका जिना मनि इहु भाउ॥

In the company of the Holy, the True Name of the Lord comes
to dwell in the mind.
Very fortunate are those, O Nanak, whose minds are filled
with Lord's love.

M5/51/6

The oft quoted lines of Guru Arjan Dev where he says your only
purpose in life is to meet the holy saints and to worship the Lord:

ਅਵਰਿ ਕਾਜ ਤੇਰੈ ਕਿਤੈ ਨ ਕਾਮ॥ ਮਿਲੁ ਸਾਧਸੰਗਤਿ ਭਜੁ ਕੇਵਲ ਨਾਮ॥

Awar kaaj tayrai kitai na kaam; mil sadhsangat bhaj keval naam.

अवरि काज तेरै कितै न काम॥ मिलु साधसंगति भजु केवल नाम॥

Nothing else will benefit you (spiritually); join the holy company, and meditate on the Lord's name.

M5/12/6

Guru Arjan Dev says finding company of holy saints is a matter of great fortune as it takes you closer to God:

ਵਡੈ ਭਾਗਿ ਪਾਇਆ ਸਾਧਸੰਗੁ॥ ਪਾਰਬ੍ਰਹਮ ਸਿਉ ਲਾਗੋ ਰੰਗੁ॥

Vaddai bhaag paayeaa saadhsangh, Parbrahm siu laago rung.

वडै भागि पाइआ साधसंगु॥ पारब्रहम सिउ लागो रंगु॥

By good fortune, one finds company of the holy.
(Because of that) their love for the Supreme Lord blossoms forth.

M5/178/5

If you walk through a garden you will pick up some fragrance of the flowers - just being close to them. Similarly, closeness to holy people is bound to influence you positively.

Bhagat Kabir says, in a jungle the sandalwood plant also spreads its fragrance to nearby plants:

ਓਇ ਭੀ ਚੰਦਨੁ ਹੋਇ ਰਹੇ ਬਸੇ ਜੁ ਚੰਦਨ ਪਾਸਿ॥

Oey bhi chandan hoye rahay basay jo chandan paas.

ओइ भी चंदनु होइ रहे बसे जु चंदन पासि॥

> Even those plants become like sandalwood which are in close
> proximity of the sandalwood tree.
>
> Kabir/1365/2

Sri Ramakrishna Paramahansa was a renowned Indian saint of 19th century. He did not read any books, but he surprised people with his knowledge of spirituality and religion. When asked by a disciple how he acquired so much knowledge he replied, "I have not read but I have heard the learned. I have made a garland of their knowledge..." He accumulated all knowledge and wisdom from company of his gurus and other holy people.

It is difficult to find holy people for daily company. You can at least choose friends and associates who are good. Look for following qualities:

Are God-oriented.

Not entrapped in maya.

Are honest and truthful.

Believe in Oneness of creation.

Are humble.

Worship only God.

Are kind and grateful.

Have love and compassion for the poor.

Contribute/participate in community service.

Understand true meaning of religion.

Respect all religions and faiths.

Promote harmony, not hatred.

Have constant remembrance of God.

Treat all human beings as equal.

Count their blessings every day and thank God.

Accept ownership of their problems.

Respect women.

Read spiritual literature.

Sing and listen to gurbani kirtan.

Appreciate and enjoy nature.

Believe in universal brotherhood.

Do not indulge in meaningless rituals.

Having seen what kind of people we should have for our company, let us now see the kind of *kusangat* (bad company) we must avoid. We should be as concerned in rejecting bad company, as we are in selecting good one, because bad selection can ruin us.

Here Bhagat Kabir says, be in the company of a saint, and avoid a non-believer:

ਕਬੀਰ ਸੰਗਤਿ ਕਰੀਐ ਸਾਧ ਕੀ ਅੰਤਿ ਕਰੈ ਨਿਰਬਾਹੁ ॥
ਸਾਕਤ ਸੰਗੁ ਨ ਕੀਜੀਐ ਜਾ ਤੇ ਹੋਇ ਬਿਨਾਹੁ ॥

Kabir, sangat kareeyai saadh ki untt karai nirbaaho.
Saakat sangh na keejeeyai jaa tay hoye binaaho.

कबीर संगति करीऐ साध की अंति करै निरबाहु ॥
साकत संगु न कीजीऐ जा ते होइ बिनाहु ॥

Kabir says, be in the company of a holy person
because he will see you through.
Don't have company of a non-believer; that could
ruin you.

Kabir/1369/8

Guru Teg Bahadur advises us to stay away from bad habits
and bad company:

ਸਾਧੋ ਮਨ ਕਾ ਮਾਨੁ ਤਿਆਗਉ॥ ਕਾਮੁ ਕ੍ਰੋਧੁ ਸੰਗਤਿ ਦੁਰਜਨ ਕੀ ਤਾ ਤੇ ਅਹਿਨਿਸਿ ਭਾਗਉ॥

Saadho munn ka maan tayaagou, kaam karodh sangat durjan
ki ta tay ahenis bhaagao.

साधो मन का मानु तिआगउ॥ कामु क्रोधु संगति दुरजन की ता ते अहिनिसि भागउ॥

O holy people, leave aside your mind's pride, and stay away,
day and night, from lust, anger and bad company.

M9/219/1

Guru Angad Dev's advice for shunning company of foolish
people:

ਨਾਲਿ ਇਆਣੇ ਦੋਸਤੀ ਕਦੇ ਨ ਆਵੈ ਰਾਸਿ॥

Naal iaanay dosti kaday na aavai raas.

नालि इआणे दोसती कदे न आवै रासि॥

Friendship with a stupid person never works out.

M2/474/12

Guru Amar Das also speaks of ill-effects of bad company:

ਕੁਸੰਗਤਿ ਬਹਹਿ ਸਦਾ ਦੁਖੁ ਪਾਵਹਿ ਦੁਖੋ ਦੁਖ ਕਮਾਇਆ॥

Kusangat beheh sadaa dukh paaveh dukho dukh kamaaeya.

कुसंगति बहहि सदा दुखु पावहि दुखो दुखु कमाइआ॥

Those who join bad company always suffer, and earn more
and more pain.

M3/1068/15

Now Guru Nanak's advice on staying away from a stupid person:

ਮੰਦਾ ਕਿਸੈ ਨ ਆਖੀਐ ਪੜਿ ਅਖਰੁ ਏਹੋ ਬੁਝੀਐ ॥
ਮੂਰਖੈ ਨਾਲਿ ਨ ਲੁਝੀਐ ॥

Manda kissai na aakheeyai parh akhar eho boojheeyai;
moorkhai naal na loojheeyai.

मंदा किसै न आखीऐ पड़ि अखरु एहो बुझीऐ ॥
मूरखै नालि न लुझीऐ ॥

From your readings, learn not to call anyone bad;
and not to get into a scuffle with a stupid person.

M1/473/13

This closing line from Guru Arjan Dev sums up the usefulness of good company:

ਮੇਰੇ ਮਾਧਉ ਜੀ ਸਤਸੰਗਤਿ ਮਿਲੇ ਸੁ ਤਰਿਆ ॥

Mayray Madho ji satsangat milay so tareyaa.

मेरे माधउ जी सतसंगति मिले सु तरिआ ॥

O my Lord, those who find holy company,
sail across.

M5/10/10

It is evident that to achieve spiritual success, company and guidance of enlightened people is desirable. But where do you find such company? Even if you do, how do you find time to be with them? You are too busy as a worshipper and a householder. In such a scenario, your best option is to make authors of SGGS and their *bani* your spiritual companions – read *gurbani* and listen to it on TV, radio, mobile or computer. Visit *gurdwaras* and join in singing *gurbani shabads*.

"Tell me with whom you associate and I will tell you who you are."

JW von Goethe (1749-1832)
German Writer & Statesman

CHAPTER 26

RELATIONSHIP WITH GOD

੧ੳ

Most of us do not enjoy good relationship with God, because we either don't understand Him, or don't have faith in Him, or simply don't believe He exists. We do not think and act in a manner that God expects from us, therefore, we fail to receive joys and pleasures which come when He is pleased. We are not even sure that we need Him at all. Leslie White, US Anthropologist said, "One of the first steps to reaching the heart of God and gaining a closer relationship with Him is admitting that you need Him in your life." You must first accept that you need God and that you need Him all the time. We often treat God as 'something' to be called up only in an emergency.

What kind of relationship we should have with God? One common belief is that we are all children of God and the relationship is that of a father and a child. While SGGS endorses this relationship, it does not limit it to that of father and child alone, but speaks of one that is more broad-based. If God is everything to us, as indeed He is, then the relationship should be much more expansive. Let's study different types of relationships that are referred to in SGGS. We start with father-child relationship which is mentioned in many verses. Here are few of them.

Guru Ram Das prays to the Lord that He look after him as His child:

ਹਮ ਬਾਰਿਕ ਦੀਨ ਕਰਹੁ ਪ੍ਰਤਿਪਾਲਾ॥

Hum baarik deen karahu pritipaala.

हम बारिक दीन करहु प्रतिपाला॥

I am a poor child, please look after me.

M4/94/13

Guru Arjan Dev makes a similar comment as son of God:

ਸੋਈ ਕਰਾਇ ਜੋ ਤੁਧੁ ਭਾਵੈ॥ ਮੋਹਿ ਸਿਆਣਪ ਕਛੂ ਨ ਆਵੈ॥
ਹਮ ਬਾਰਿਕ ਤਉ ਸਰਣਾਈ॥ ਪ੍ਰਭਿ ਆਪੇ ਪੈਜ ਰਖਾਈ॥

Soyee karaaye jo tudh bhavai; mohay sianap kachhu na aavai.

Hum barik tao sarnaayee; Prabh aapay paij rakhaayee.

सोई कराइ जो तुधु भावै॥ मोहि सिआणप कछू न आवै॥
हम बारिक तउ सरणाई॥ प्रभि आपे पैज रखाई॥

You make me do whatever You like,
I have no wisdom of my own.
We are children under Your protection,
You yourself give us dignity.

M5/626/17

The relationship expands here. He is now both, father as well as mother, says Guru Ram Das:

ਹਮ ਬਾਰਿਕ ਕਿਛੁ ਨ ਜਾਣਹੁ ਹਰਿ ਮਾਤ ਪਿਤਾ ਪ੍ਰਤਿਪਾਲਾ॥

Hum baarik kichhu na jaanohu Har maat pita pritpaala.

हम बारिक किछु न जाणहू हरि मात पिता प्रतिपाला॥

I am a child I know nothing, God looks after me as both,
mother and father.

M4/985/17

Guru Arjan Dev also says the same thing:

ਮੇਰਾ ਮਾਤ ਪਿਤਾ ਹਰਿ ਰਾਇਆ ॥
ਕਰਿ ਕਿਰਪਾ ਪ੍ਰਤਿਪਾਲਣ ਲਾਗਾ ਕਰੀ ਤੇਰਾ ਕਰਾਇਆ ॥

Mera maat pita Har raayeyaa;
kar kirpa pritpaalan laaga kari tera karaaya.

मेरा मात पिता हरि राइआ ॥
करि किरपा प्रतिपालण लागा करीं तेरा कराइआ ॥

The Lord is both, my mother and my father.
With Your graciousness You look after me,
I do as You tell me.

M5/626/18

The relationship with God is also that of a friend and
companion, which means we can be very close to Him and
speak to Him on all personal and private issues, as we would
do with a close friend.

Guru Amar Das says:

ਸਤਗੁਰੁ ਸੇਵਿ ਗੁਣ ਨਿਧਾਨੁ ਪਾਇਆ ਤਿਸ ਦੀ ਕੀਮ ਨ ਪਾਈ ॥
ਹਰਿ ਪ੍ਰਭੁ ਸਖਾ ਮੀਤੁ ਪ੍ਰਭੁ ਮੇਰਾ ਅੰਤੇ ਹੋਇ ਸਖਾਈ ॥

Satgur sev gunh nidhaan paayeya tis di keem na paayee.
Har Prabh sakha meet Prabh mera unttay hoye sakhaayee.

सतगुरु सेवि गुण निधानु पाइआ तिस दी कीम न पाई॥
हरि प्रभु सखा मीतु प्रभु मेरा अंते होइ सखाई॥

Serving the True Guru, one attains highest virtues;
His value cannot be estimated.
God is my friend and companion, in the end He is the
one who will see me through.

M3/32/9

In the verse below, Guru Amar Das says, besides being
mother and father, God is also his relative and brother:

ਮੇਰਾ ਪਿਤਾ ਮਾਤਾ ਹਰਿ ਨਾਮੁ ਹੈ ਹਰਿ ਬੰਧਪੁ ਬੀਰਾ॥

Mera pita maata Har naam hai Har bandhap beera.

मेरा पिता माता हरि नामु है हरि बंधपु बीरा॥

The Lord's Name is my father and mother; the Lord is also
my relative and my brother.

M3/163/6

Guru Ram Das also endorses the relationship of mother,
father, companion and friend:

ਮੈ ਹਰਿ ਬਿਨੁ ਅਵਰੁ ਨ ਕੋਈ ਬੇਲੀ ਮੇਰਾ ਪਿਤਾ ਮਾਤਾ ਹਰਿ ਸਖਾਇਆ॥

Mai Har bin avar na koyee beli mera pita maata Har sakhaayaa.

मै हरि बिनु अवरु न कोई बेली मेरा पिता माता हरि सखाइआ॥

Other than the True Lord I have no companion, He alone is
my father, mother, friend and companion.

M4/882/3

Next relationship is that of Master and servant - God is the Master and we all are His servants. Guru Arjan Dev says the Lord ensures respect and dignity of His servants:

ਜੀਉ ਪਾਇ ਪਿੰਡੁ ਜਿਨਿ ਸਾਜਿਆ ਦਿਤਾ ਪੈਨਣੁ ਖਾਣੁ ॥
ਅਪਣੇ ਦਾਸ ਕੀ ਆਪਿ ਪੈਜ ਰਾਖੀ ਨਾਨਕ ਸਦ ਕੁਰਬਾਣੁ ॥

Jiu paaye pind saajeyaa ditta painan khaan.
Apnay daas ki aap paij raakhi Nanak sadd kurbaan.

जीउ पाइ पिंडु जिनि साजिआ दिता पैनणु खाणु ॥
अपणे दास की आपि पैज राखी नानक सद कुरबाणु ॥

He who fashioned the body and placed the soul within,
who gives clothing and food;
He Himself preserves the honour of His servants,
says Nanak, I am ever ready to sacrifice
myself (unto Him).

M5/619/19

Here the relationship is that of doctor and patient. This is important because only God can cure us of all physical and mental ailments. Guru Amar Das says:

ਸਤਿਗੁਰ ਬਾਝਹੁ ਵੈਦੁ ਨ ਕੋਈ ॥

Satgur baajhoh vaid na koyee.

सतिगुर बाझहु वैदु न कोई ॥

Other than the True Guru, no one is my
physician (No one can cure me).

M3/1016/10

Guru Arjan Dev also says the same:

ਮੇਰਾ ਬੈਦੁ ਗੁਰੁ ਗੋਵਿੰਦਾ ॥

ਹਰਿ ਹਰਿ ਨਾਮੁ ਅਉਖਧੁ ਮੁਖਿ ਦੇਵੈ ਕਾਟੈ ਜਮ ਕੀ ਫੰਧਾ ॥

Mera baid Guru Govinda.

Har Har naam aukhad mukh devai kaatai jumm ki phanda.

मेरा बैदु गुरू गोविंदा ॥

हरि हरि नामु अउखधु मुखि देवै काटै जम की फंधा ॥

My physician is my Guru, the Lord.

He gives me medicine of the Lord's Name, and cuts away the noose of death (releases me from cycle of birth & death).

M5/618/3

There is also the relationship of *ishq* (love) with the Beloved God. This type of love is much spoken of in the Sufi tradition of Islam and is extensively used in Sufi poetry. Sufism believes in two forms of love i.e., *ishq-e-majazi* and *ishq-e-haqiqi*. *Ishq-e-majazi* is the ordinary form of love with things that are temporary in nature. This includes love of another person like a beloved, a parent, a child, a teacher and so on. This is also the love of material possessions. These objects of love are of the physical world of time and will perish one day. *Ishq-e-haqiqi* is the love with something that is *haqiqat* (real), permanent, true, and beyond time; that is the love with the Beloved Lord. This form of love involves extreme spiritual yearning for God.

Listening to Sufi poetry of *ishq-e-haqiqi* one sometimes confuses it with poetry of ordinary love. For example, Sufi poet Amir Khusro says, *"Khusro Baaji Prem Ki Maen Kheloon Pi Ke Sungh. Jeet Gaee To Piya Merey Haary Pi Ke Sungh."* (I play the game of love with my Beloved. If I win He is mine, if I lose then I am His.) One thinks this is the love of a woman for her man, but Khusro is actually speaking of his love for God.

Even the poetry of SGGS seems to often indicate an ordinary yearning of a woman for physical union with her husband – as we saw in chapter on 'Status of Women'. But the poetic expression is actually an urge for spiritual union with the Lord. God is in the spiritual domain, while sexual union can only be experienced in physical form.

Let's see some verses of SGGS that speak of this *ishq-e-haqiqi* love. Guru Ram Das on true love for the True Beloved:

ਗੁਰਮੁਖਿ ਸਚੀ ਆਸਕੀ ਜਿਤੁ ਪ੍ਰੀਤਮੁ ਸਚਾ ਪਾਈਐ ॥

Gurmukh sachee aaskee jit Preetam Sachaa paayeeai.

गुरमुखि सची आसकी जितु प्रीतमु सचा पाईऐ ॥

The God-oriented man's true love gets him the True Beloved.

M4/1422/8

Guru Amar Das says, all suffering and pain is over when you meet the Beloved Lord:

ਮਿਤੁ ਘਨੇਰੇ ਕਰਿ ਥਕੀ ਮੇਰਾ ਦੁਖੁ ਕਾਟੈ ਕੋਇ ॥
ਮਿਲਿ ਪ੍ਰੀਤਮ ਦੁਖੁ ਕਟਿਆ ਸਬਦਿ ਮਿਲਾਵਾ ਹੋਇ ॥

Mitar ghaneray kar thakki mera dukh kaatai koye.
Mil Pritam dukh kateya sabad milaava hoye.

मित्र घणेरे करि थकी मेरा दुखु काटै कोइ ॥
मिलि प्रीतम दुखु कटिआ सबदि मिलावा होइ ॥

I am tired of making friendships, someone please
end my suffering.
On meeting my Beloved Lord, my suffering is over; I have
made union with the *shabad* (guru's word).

M3/37/7

Guru Arjan Dev makes a passionate plea to the Beloved God to spare some time for him:

ਕਰਮਹੀਣ ਧਨ ਕਰੈ ਬਿਨੰਤੀ ਕਦਿ ਨਾਨਕ ਆਵੈ ਵਾਰੀ ॥
ਸਭਿ ਸੁਹਾਗਣਿ ਮਾਣਹਿ ਰਲੀਆ ਇਕ ਦੇਵਹੁ ਰਾਤਿ ਮੁਰਾਰੀ ॥

Karamheen dhann karai binantee kad Nanak aawai vaaree.
Sabh suhagan maaneh rallia ik devoh raat Muraree.

करमहीण धन करै बिनंती कदि नानक आवै वारी ॥
सभि सुहागणि माणहि रलीआ इक देवहु राति मुरारी ॥

This luck-less woman pleads, says Nanak, when will my turn come?
All married women are making merry, O Lord please
spare one night for me.

M5/959/15

I reiterate, this is to be taken as a plea for spiritual union with God - not for a sexual embrace.

Guru Arjan Dev says, God as Husband Lord will give us whatever we seek; we should have faith in Him:

ਜੋ ਮਾਗਉ ਸੋਈ ਸੋਈ ਪਾਵਉ ਅਪਨੇ ਖਸਮ ਭਰੋਸਾ ॥
ਕਹੁ ਨਾਨਕ ਗੁਰੁ ਪੂਰਾ ਭੇਟਿਓ ਮਿਟਿਓ ਸਗਲ ਅੰਦੇਸਾ ॥

Jo magao soyee soyee paavao apnay khasam bharosa.
Kaho Nanak gur poora bheteyo miteyo sagal andesa.

जो मागउ सोई सोई पावउ अपने खसम भरोसा ॥
कहु नानक गुरु पूरा भेटिओ मिटिओ सगल अंदेसा ॥

Whatever you ask you shall receive; if you have faith in your
Husband Lord.
Nanak says, I have met the Complete Guru (God), and all my
doubts are dispelled.

M5/619/11

Guru Ram Das tells us that God is His own Master, as also His own Servant:

ਹਰਿ ਧਿਆਵਹੁ ਸੰਤਹੁ ਜੀ ਸਭਿ ਦੂਖ ਵਿਸਾਰਣਹਾਰਾ ॥
ਹਰਿ ਆਪੇ ਠਾਕੁਰੁ ਹਰਿ ਆਪੇ ਸੇਵਕੁ ਜੀ ਕਿਆ ਨਾਨਕ ਜੰਤ ਵਿਚਾਰਾ ॥

Har dhiyaavoh santoh ji sabh dookh visaranhaara.
Har aapay thakur aapay sevak ji kia Nanak jantt vichaara.

हरि धिआवहु संतहु जी सभि दूख विसारणहारा ॥
हरि आपे ठाकुरु हरि आपे सेवकु जी किआ नानक जंत विचारा ॥

**Worship the Lord, O Saints; He is the Dispeller of all sorrow.
The Lord Himself is His own Master, and His own Servant,
O Nanak, the poor beings are at His mercy.**

M4/10/19

Being His own master and own servant means He is self-contained and self-sustaining. He doesn't need a relationship with us; it is we who need Him.

Finally, Guru Nanak says those who forget their Husband Lord drift to lower category:

ਖਸਮੁ ਵਿਸਾਰਹਿ ਤੇ ਕਮਜਾਤਿ ॥ ਨਾਨਕ ਨਾਵੈ ਬਾਝੁ ਸਨਾਤਿ ॥

Khasam visaareh tay kamjaat; Nanak naavai baajh sunaat.

खसमु विसारहि ते कमजाति ॥ नानक नावै बाझु सनाति ॥

**Those who forget their Husband Lord drift to sub-human class.
O Nanak, without the Name, they are outcasts.**

M1/10/1

As we see, God is not just our father, He is related to us in every possible way. He is everything and all-in-one for us. Important thing is that we must build our own direct relationship with Him.

A true guru's help is of utmost importance, but the effort has to mainly come from us. In whatever we do we must ask ourselves whether what we are doing will be liked by God or not. Don't ask the priest or anyone else, make your own judgment and commune with God directly from the heart. When in doubt seek guidance from SGGS.

We often fail to understand what kind of actions will be appreciated by God. Many of the rituals we follow to please God are not what He wants. For example, I have seen many people pluck flowers early in the morning (often stealing) to place them before an idol or picture of a deity - believing it will please God. But God's plan was different. He wanted to have the flowers fully blossom on the plant where people could appreciate the beauty and fragrance of His creation, where equally beautiful butterflies could sit in peace, where bees could collect the honey for people to relish. By plucking the flowers these people actually interfere with His plan and earn His ill-will (bad karma), instead of goodwill. They spoil their relationship with God instead of building it.

If you ask people what kind of attitude they have towards God, a very common reply is, "Well, I am a God-fearing person." This is fine and in line with Guru Nanak's statement:

ਨਾਨਕ ਜਿਨੑ ਮਨਿ ਭਉ ਤਿਨੑਾ ਮਨਿ ਭਾਉ ॥

Nanak jinah munn bhou tinha munn bhaao.

नानक जिन्ह मनि भउ तिन्हा मनि भाउ॥

Those who have fear (of Him) in their mind, they also have love (for Him).

M1/465/14

Once you start progressing on your godly path, the fear of God will gradually turn into love of God. Why should you fear Him? You should be afraid of Him only if you are living a sinful life. If you live an honest man's life you have no reason to fear God.

Be God-loving not God-fearing.

"My relationship with God is very personal. I think you can be on first name terms with Him, you know, and tell Him what your troubles are, and ask for help. I do it all the time and it works for me."

Wernher von Braun (1912-1977)
NASA Engineer

CHAPTER 27

KIRTAN

ੴ

It has been found that singing has tremendous benefits. It works like a tranquilizer which has soothing effect on our nerves and uplifts our spirits. Singing creates musical vibrations in the body that enhance our physical and mental wellbeing. The effect of singing is cumulative, which means the more we sing the more harmony we have. It is believed that singing also has a positive impact on the functioning of our heart. Overall, singing has similar benefits as those of meditation – silencing the mind. Group singing, we learn is even more beneficial. And when we sing religious and spiritual songs in chorus, the benefits are far greater. Singing of *gurbani* or other religious songs, accompanied by musical instruments is called *kirtan*. Audiences often join in such singing.

We are learning of these benefits today, but founders of most religions seem to have known this many centuries ago, because almost all religious traditions encourage spiritual singing - with the exception of a few, like the mainstream Islam. On the sidelines, Islam however, has a strong tradition of singing in *Qawali* and *Sufi* forms. Even in the mainstream Islam, singing is being better tolerated now, if it is aimed at spiritual wellbeing.

SGGS lays great stress on *kirtan*. This is so because Guru Nanak, the founder of Sikhism, himself enjoyed spiritual singing. Some lovingly call him 'The Singing Guru'. Whenever he connected with God and received His message he would ask his companion Mardana to start playing the *rabaab* and he would fully immerse in singing God's word. This singing tradition was followed by successive gurus. Most of the *gurbani* in SGGS is, therefore, written in poetry form set under musical compositions in thirty-one *ragas*. There are more than one thousand references to singing God's praises in SGGS.

Today, *gurbani kirtan* is an important part of every Sikh religious function. In many *gurdwaras* singing of *gurbani* in the morning and evening is a daily feature. In *Harmandir Sahib*, the sanctum sanctorum of Sikhs in Amritsar, *kirtan* continues the whole day.

Guru Nanak sets the tone for singing right in the beginning of SGGS, where he tells us to sing God's praises:

> ਜਿਨਿ ਸੇਵਿਆ ਤਿਨਿ ਪਾਇਆ ਮਾਨੁ ॥ ਨਾਨਕ ਗਾਵੀਐ ਗੁਣੀ ਨਿਧਾਨੁ ॥
>
> Jin seveya tin paaya maan; Nanak gaaveeyai gunhee nidhaan.
>
> जिनि सेविआ तिनि पाइआ मानु॥नानक गावीऐ गुणी निधानु॥
>
> **Those who worship Him attain the honour; O Nanak, sing (of Him), who is full of virtues.**
>
> M1/2/7

In the following verse Guru Nanak is intrigued about what happens in God's court, and then goes on to describe a beautiful scene where mesmerizing singing is going on:

> ਸੋ ਦਰੁ ਕੇਹਾ ਸੋ ਘਰੁ ਕੇਹਾ ਜਿਤੁ ਬਹਿ ਸਰਬ ਸਮਾਲੇ ॥
>
> ਵਾਜੇ ਨਾਦ ਅਨੇਕ ਅਸੰਖਾ ਕੇਤੇ ਵਾਵਣਹਾਰੇ ॥
>
> ਕੇਤੇ ਰਾਗ ਪਰੀ ਸਿਉ ਕਹੀਅਹਿ ਕੇਤੇ ਗਾਵਣਹਾਰੇ ॥

So dar kehaa so ghar kehaa jit beh sarb smaalay.

Vaajay naad anek asankha ketay vavanhaaray.

Ketay raag pari siu kahieh ketay gaavanhaaray.

सो दरु केहा सो घरु केहा जितु बहि सरब समाले॥

वाजे नाद अनेक असंखा केते वावणहारे॥

केते राग परी सिउ कहीअनि केते गावणहारे॥

What kind of door is that, what kind of house is that in which
You sit and take care of everything?
Countless musical instruments are playing and there are so
many players.
So many harmonious ragas are being sung,
and there are so many singers.

M1/6/4, M1/8/14 & M1/347/4

The above verse continues to describe how in the heavenly abode different lower gods, goddesses, angels and others sing God's praises.

Music in Lord's court has also been mentioned by people recollecting their after-life experiences under hypnosis. Pioneering research on such experiences was conducted by Michael Newton, PhD, and reported in his book, "Journey of Souls." Many of his subjects reported about music playing in spirit world. When asked about what kind of sounds were heard there, one of the subjects said, "An...echo...of music...musical tingling...wind chimes...vibrating with my movements...so relaxing." He further said, "...the waves of musical notes here are so beautiful...bells...strings...such tranquility." This is quite in line with what Guru Nanak has described.

We live in most difficult times. As per ancient Indian scriptures time is divided into four *yugas* (ages); *Satya, Treta, Dwapar* and *Kali Yuga*. In terms of character, wisdom, life span and quality of life *Satya Yuga* was the best and the present *Kali Yuga* is the worst.

Guru Arjan Dev tells us that *kirtan* is most needed in these bad times:

ਕਲਜੁਗ ਮਹਿ ਕੀਰਤਨੁ ਪਰਧਾਨਾ॥ ਗੁਰਮੁਖਿ ਜਪੀਐ ਲਾਇ ਧਿਆਨਾ॥

Kaljug meh kirtan pardhaana, gurmukh japeeyai laaye dhiaana.

कलजुग महि कीरतनु परधाना॥ गुरमुखि जपीऐ लाइ धिआना॥

In the dark age of *Kali Yuga, kirtan* is of supreme importance.
O God-oriented people, you must chant (God's virtues),
with focused attention.

M5/1075/19

The key point here is, chanting must be done with 'focused attention' on God. Not much will be gained from just singing or chanting with the mind occupied with too many worldly issues.

Guru Arjan Dev on liberation through *kirtan*:

ਜੈਸੋ ਗੁਰਿ ਉਪਦੇਸਿਆ ਮੈ ਤੈਸੋ ਕਹਿਆ ਪੁਕਾਰਿ॥
ਨਾਨਕੁ ਕਹੈ ਸੁਨਿ ਰੇ ਮਨਾ ਕਰਿ ਕੀਰਤਨੁ ਹੋਇ ਉਧਾਰੁ॥

Jaiso gur updeseya mai taisay kaheya pukaar.
Nanak kahai sunn ray mana kar kirtan hoye udhaar.

जैसो गुरि उपदेसिआ मै तैसो कहिआ पुकारि॥
नानकु कहै सुनि रे मना करि कीरतनु होइ उधारु॥

As the Guru has taught me, so I speak out.
Says Nanak, listen O my mind, do *kirtan* for attaining liberation.

M5/214/10

The following verse of Guru Amar Das further implores us to sing *gurbani*:

ਆਵਹੁ ਸਿਖ ਸਤਿਗੁਰੂ ਕੇ ਪਿਆਰਿਹੋ ਗਾਵਹੁ ਸਚੀ ਬਾਣੀ ॥

ਬਾਣੀ ਤ ਗਾਵਹੁ ਗੁਰੂ ਕੇਰੀ ਬਾਣੀਆ ਸਿਰਿ ਬਾਣੀ ॥

ਜਿਨ ਕਉ ਨਦਰਿ ਕਰਮੁ ਹੋਵੈ ਹਿਰਦੈ ਤਿਨਾ ਸਮਾਣੀ ॥

Aavoh Sikh Satguru kay piareho gaavoh sachi bani.

Bani ta gavaho guru keri baaniya sirr bani.

Jin kau nadar karam hovai hirday tinaa samaani.

आवहु सिख सतिगुरू के पिआरिहो गावहु सची बाणी ॥

बाणी त गावहु गुरू केरी बाणीआ सिरि बाणी ॥

जिन कउ नदरि करमु होवै हिरदै तिना समाणी ॥

Come, O beloved Sikhs of the True Guru, sing the true *bani*.

Sing Guru's *bani*, the supreme *bani* of all *banis*.

Those who are blessed, it (the *bani*) finds a place
in their hearts.

M3/920/4

Singing must be done with humility. While singing, do not let your ego spoil the show. If you sing to bloat your ego, you will fail to derive any benefit. The aim of your singing must only be to seek God's love.

This is what Guru Amar Das says:

ਇਕਿ ਗਾਵਤ ਰਹੇ ਮਨਿ ਸਾਦੁ ਨ ਪਾਇ ॥ ਹਉਮੈ ਵਿਚਿ ਗਾਵਹਿ ਬਿਰਥਾ ਜਾਇ ॥

ਗਾਵਣਿ ਗਾਵਹਿ ਜਿਨ ਨਾਮ ਪਿਆਰੁ ॥ ਸਾਚੀ ਬਾਣੀ ਸਬਦ ਬੀਚਾਰੁ ॥

Ik gaavat rahay munn saad na paaye, haumai vich gaaveh
birtha jaaye.

Gaavan gaaveh jin naam piyaar, saachi bani sabad bichaar.

ਇਕਿ ਗਾਵਤ ਰਹੇ ਮਨਿ ਸਾਦੁ ਨ ਪਾਇ॥ ਹਉਮੈ ਵਿਚਿ ਗਾਵਹਿ ਬਿਰਥਾ ਜਾਇ॥

ਗਾਵਣਿ ਗਾਵਹਿ ਜਿਨ ਨਾਮ ਪਿਆਰੁ॥ ਸਾਚੀ ਬਾਣੀ ਸਬਦ ਬੀਚਾਰੁ॥

Some people keep singing, but their minds do not
find it pleasurable.
If you sing in ego, it all goes waste.
Those who love the Name and sing, they contemplate
on the true *bani*.

M3/158/16

Bhagat Kabir speaks of purity in spiritual singing and appreciates those who sing:

ਸੋ ਨਿਰਮਲੁ ਨਿਰਮਲ ਹਰਿ ਗੁਨ ਗਾਵੈ॥ ਸੋ ਭਾਈ ਮੇਰੈ ਮਨਿ ਭਾਵੈ॥

So nirmall nirmal Har gunh gaavai, so bhaayee merai
munn bhaavai.

सो निरमलु निरमल हरि गुन गावै॥ सो भाई मेरै मनि भावै॥

He who sings virtues of the Pure Lord becomes pure.
O brothers, such people appeal to my heart.

Kabir/328/13

Kirtan can take us to the highest level of spiritual development. Guru Nanak, as we know, sang his way to enlightenment. Guru Ram Das tells us about the same thing:

ਹਰਿ ਹਰਿ ਜਸੁ ਗਾਇਆ ਪਰਮ ਪਦੁ ਪਾਇਆ ਤੇ ਊਤਮ ਜਨ ਪਰਧਾਨ ਜੀਉ॥

Har Har jus gaaya param padh paaya tay ootam jann pardhaan jio.

हरि हरि जसु गाइआ परम पदु पाइआ ते ऊतम जन परधान जीउ॥

> Those who sing Lord's praises, obtain supreme spiritual
> status, and they become the most respected.
>
> M4/446/10

Guru Teg Bahadur tells us that, without *kirtan,* the life is
being wasted:

> ਗੁਨ ਗੋਬਿੰਦ ਗਾਇਓ ਨਹੀ ਜਨਮੁ ਅਕਾਰਥ ਕੀਨੁ ॥
> ਕਹੁ ਨਾਨਕ ਹਰਿ ਭਜੁ ਮਨਾ ਜਿਹ ਬਿਧਿ ਜਲ ਕਉ ਮੀਨੁ ॥
>
> Gunn Gobind gaayeo nahi janam akaarath keen.
> Kahu Nanak Har bhaj mana jih bidh jal kao meen.
>
> गुन गोबिंद गाइओ नही जनमु अकारथ कीनु ॥
> कहु नानक हरि भजु मना जिह बिधि जल कउ मीनु ॥
>
> You have not sung of Lord's virtues, you have wasted your life.
> Nanak says, O my mind, immerse yourself in the Lord, like
> the fish (immerses itself) in water.
>
> M9/1426/11

If you can't sing then you must listen to *gurbani kirtan,*
which also has tremendous benefits. Research has found that
listening to music releases dopamine in the brain which is
a feel-good chemical. Listening to *gurbani* is also a form of
meditation which brings about spiritual upliftment.

Guru Nanak says by singing and listening you get rid of
your suffering and bring home happiness:

> ਗਾਵੀਐ ਸੁਣੀਐ ਮਨਿ ਰਖੀਐ ਭਾਉ ॥ ਦੁਖੁ ਪਰਹਰਿ ਸੁਖੁ ਘਰਿ ਲੈ ਜਾਇ ॥
>
> Gaaviye suniye munn rakheeyai bhao,
> dukh parhar sukh ghar lai jaaye.

ਗਾਵੀਐ ਸੁਣੀਐ ਮਨਿ ਰਖੀਐ ਭਾਉ॥ ਦੁਖੁ ਪਰਹਰਿ ਸੁਖੁ ਘਰਿ ਲੈ ਜਾਇ॥

Sing, listen and keep Him in your heart with love, your sorrows will depart and you will take home happiness.

M1/2/8

Guru Nanak continues:

ਨਾਨਕ ਭਗਤਾ ਸਦਾ ਵਿਗਾਸੁ॥ ਸੁਣਿਐ ਦੂਖ ਪਾਪ ਕਾ ਨਾਸੁ॥

Nanak bhagta sadaa vigaas, suniyai dookh paap ka naas.

नानक भगता सदा विगासु॥ सुणिऐ दूख पाप का नासु॥

Says Nanak, the worshippers are always in blissful state, by listening you get rid of your sorrow and sins.

M1/2/18

The above verse continues to list many more benefits of listening to *kirtan.*

Gurbani kirtan is almost always sung with accompaniment of musical instruments. It started with Bhai Mardana's *rabaab* accompanying Guru Nanak's singing. The successor gurus followed this tradition, and also experimented with other string instruments like the *sarangi* and *dilruba.* Many other instruments were tried over a period of time - before the arrival of the harmonium.

Harmonium was invented in France in 1842 by Alexandre Debain and was brought to India by British missionaries. The original design was like a piano with a foot pump and a keyboard played with both hands. The current Indian version which could be played while sitting on the floor - with one hand pumping air and the other playing - was created by

Dwarkanath Ghose. Due to its melodious sound and ease of play, it has become the most popular musical instrument in India, particularly for religious singing; though it is also the choice of many singers of other genres. For *gurbani kirtan* too it is now the preferred instrument, along with the *tablas (a set of two small drums)*.

What all can be sung in *kirtan*? Well, on your own you can sing anything in gratitude and praise of God, but in a *gurdwara*, singing *bani* of only the following is permitted:

SGGS.

Guru Gobind Singh.

Bhai Gurdas, a Sikh scholar and scribe for Adi Granth.

Bhai Nand Lal, poet in the court of Guru Gobind Singh.

The aim of *kirtan* is to get to a stage where one can hear the *anahad naad*, a natural musical sound that resonates in the universe. All sound that we normally hear is created by striking or friction between two or more objects, but *anahad naad* is God created un-struck and frictionless sound, which is heard with spiritual advancement.

We have seen that there is great emphasis on singing in SGGS, but what about dancing? Some religions and sects encourage dancing. You often see people dancing in *mandirs* and at other religious gatherings. Osho's followers also dance and sway a lot. In Sufism too there is a tradition of meditational dancing, particularly among the Dervishes in Turkey. But SGGS does not encourage it – that's why you do not find anyone dancing in a *gurdwara* or at any other Sikh religious congregation.

This is what Guru Amar Das says about dancing:

ਭਗਤਿ ਕਰਹਿ ਮੂਰਖ ਆਪੁ ਜਣਾਵਹਿ॥ ਨਚਿ ਨਚਿ ਟਪਹਿ ਬਹੁਤੁ ਦੁਖੁ ਪਾਵਹਿ॥
ਨਚਿਐ ਟਪਿਐ ਭਗਤਿ ਨ ਹੋਇ॥ ਸਬਦਿ ਮਰੈ ਭਗਤਿ ਪਾਏ ਜਨੁ ਸੋਇ॥

Bhagat kareh moorakh aap janaaveh; nach nach tuppeh
bahut dukh paaveh.
Nacheya tappeya bhagat na hoye, sabad marai bhagat paaye
jann soye.

भगति करहि मूरख आपु जणावहि॥ नचि नचि टपहि बहुतु दुखु पावहि॥
नचिऐ टपिऐ भगति न होइ॥ सबदि मरै भगति पाए जनु सोइ॥

Stupid people worship to show off; they dance and jump -
only to suffer immense pain.
You cannot worship by dancing and jumping around.
Only he can worship who connects with the word and
loses himself.

M3/159/1

Dancing and jumping around only gives some pleasure to
the mind, nothing more, as Guru Nanak says:

ਨਚਣੁ ਕੁਦਣੁ ਮਨ ਕਾ ਚਾਉ॥

Nachan kuddan munn kaa chao.

नचणु कुदणु मन का चाउ॥

Dancing and jumping around is merely for pleasing of the
mind.

M1/465/14

SGGS is not against dancing per se, it only says dancing has little spiritual value, unlike singing and listening to *kirtan*.

"Kirtan allows us to enter into a mystery world - a world where all the logic of our minds, all the condition and learning are left outside. And in this mystery, we create a temple inside of our hearts, a place of refuge, a place of love, a place of just being."

Jai Uttal (b. 1951)
American Musician

KARAM

K*aram* is the Punjabi word for karma. It has three different meanings. First, it means all actions and deeds we do in our daily lives. Second, it is our fate or destiny (*kismet*) that we create with our deeds - this can be good or bad. Third, is derived from Arabic language, meaning God's grace (like Allah's *karam*). In this chapter we will look into the first two meanings of *karam*, while the third has been covered in the chapter on 'Grace'.

There is a law of karma which has been known the world over since ancient times. The law is, "As you sow so shall you reap." Authors of SGGS fully endorsed this law which is frequently quoted in the holy book.

It is generally believed that we arrive in this world empty-handed and depart empty-handed. This is not entirely true, particularly in the spiritual context. We come with our destiny imprinted on our souls, based on our deeds of previous lives. During our current life, depending on nature of our deeds, we either mitigate our sins or collect more. On departure from this life we carry the account of our *karam*, which helps determine our destiny in the next life. Good deeds and thoughts are therefore necessary.

Guru Nanak states the law of *karam*:

ਪੁੰਨੀ ਪਾਪੀ ਆਖਣੁ ਨਾਹਿ ॥ ਕਰਿ ਕਰਿ ਕਰਣਾ ਲਿਖਿ ਲੈ ਜਾਹੁ ॥
ਆਪੇ ਬੀਜਿ ਆਪੇ ਹੀ ਖਾਹੁ ॥ ਨਾਨਕ ਹੁਕਮੀ ਆਵਹੁ ਜਾਹੁ ॥

Punni paapi aakhan nahi, kar kar karna likh lai jaaho.
Aapay beej aapay hee khaaho, Nanak hukami aavoh jaaho.

पुंनी पापी आखणु नाहि ॥ करि करि करणा लिखि लै जाहु ॥
आपे बीजि आपे ही खाहु ॥ नानक हुकमी आवहु जाहु ॥

Virtue and sin are not merely for the sake of saying
(they truly control your destiny). Whatever you do,
is recorded (in your destiny).
As you sow so you reap; Nanak says, by divine
order you come and go.

M1/4/13

Guru Nanak asks us here to take full responsibility for our deeds:

ਦਦੈ ਦੋਸੁ ਨ ਦੇਊ ਕਿਸੈ ਦੋਸੁ ਕਰੰਮਾ ਆਪਣਿਆ ॥
ਜੋ ਮੈ ਕੀਆ ਸੋ ਮੈ ਪਾਇਆ ਦੋਸੁ ਨ ਦੀਜੈ ਅਵਰ ਜਨਾ ॥

Daddai dos na deyoo kissai dos karama aapaneya.
Jo mai kia so mai paaya dos na deejai avar jana.

ददै दोसु न देऊ किसै दोसु करमा आपणिआ ॥
जो मै कीआ सो मै पाइआ दोसु न दीजै अवर जना ॥

I don't blame anyone else, the blame lies in my own deeds.
As I sowed so I reaped, I don't blame any
other person.

M1/433/13

Bhagat Trilochan also tells us that good and bad comes to us as per our own deeds:

ਨਾਰਾਇਨ ਨਿੰਦਸਿ ਕਾਇ ਭੂਲੀ ਗਵਾਰੀ॥ ਦੁਕ੍ਰਿਤੁ ਸੁਕ੍ਰਿਤੁ ਥਾਰੋ ਕਰਮ ਰੀ॥

Narayan nindis kaaye bhooli gawaari,
dukrit sukrit thaaro karam ri.

नाराइण निंदसि काइ भूली गवारी॥ दुक्रितु सुक्रितु थारो करमु री॥

Why denigrate God you stupid rustic? Bad and good
(in your life) is as per your own deeds.

Trilochan/695/2

Guru Amar Das cautions those who do not understand the divine order (*hukam*) and whose deeds are controlled by their untrustworthy minds:

ਹੁਕਮੁ ਨ ਜਾਣਹਿ ਬਪੁੜੇ ਭੂਲੇ ਫਿਰਹਿ ਗਵਾਰ॥
ਮਨਹਠਿ ਕਰਮ ਕਮਾਵਦੇ ਨਿਤ ਨਿਤ ਹੋਹਿ ਖੁਆਰੁ॥
ਅੰਤਰਿ ਸਾਂਤਿ ਨ ਆਵਈ ਨਾ ਸਚਿ ਲਗੈ ਪਿਆਰੁ॥

Hukam na jaaneh bappuray bhoolay phiray gawaar.
Manhath karam kamaavday nit nit hoye khuaar.
Antar saant na aavaee na sach laggai piyaar.

हुकमु न जाणहि बपुड़े भूले फिरहि गवार॥
मनहठि करम कमावदे नित नित होहि खुआरु॥
अंतरि सांति न आवई ना सचि लगै पिआरु॥

Stupid people do not understand the divine order, they
wander around lost.
They work under the forced influence of their minds and suffer daily.
They do not get inner peace and do not earn the love of the
True One.

M3/66/9

Guru Amar Das cautions those who work for their ego:

ਹਉਮੈ ਕਰਮ ਕਮਾਵਦੇ ਜਮਡੰਡੁ ਲਗੈ ਤਿਨ ਆਇ॥
ਜਿ ਸਤਿਗੁਰ ਸੇਵਨਿ ਸੇ ਉਬਰੇ ਹਰਿ ਸੇਤੀ ਲਿਵ ਲਾਇ॥

Haumai karam kamaavday jamdand lagai tin aaye.
Jay Satgur sevan say oobray Har seti liv laaye.

हउमै करम कमावदे जमडंडु लगै तिन आइ॥
जि सतिगुरु सेवनि से उबरे हरि सेती लिव लाइ॥

Those who work for ego satisfaction are struck by the
messenger of death.
Those who take shelter under the True Guru are
uplifted and saved.

M3/65/10

Guru Nanak says, it is good and bad deeds that determine
your closeness to God:

ਚੰਗਿਆਈਆ ਬੁਰਿਆਈਆ ਵਾਚੈ ਧਰਮੁ ਹਦੂਰਿ॥
ਕਰਮੀ ਆਪੋ ਆਪਣੀ ਕੇ ਨੇੜੈ ਕੇ ਦੂਰਿ॥

Changeaaiya bureaaiya vaachai dharam hadoor.
Karmi aapo aapni kay nerai kay door.

चंगिआईआ बुरिआईआ वाचै धरमु हदूरि॥
करमी आपो आपणी के नेड़ै के दूरि॥

Your good and bad deeds are evaluated by the king of
death in the presence of the Lord.
As per your deeds you either get closer to God,
or move further away.

M1/8/11

Sheikh Farid tells us of a foolish farmer whose expectations do not match his deeds:

ਫਰੀਦਾ ਲੋੜੈ ਦਾਖ ਬਿਜਉਰੀਆਂ ਕਿਕਰਿ ਬੀਜੈ ਜਟੁ ॥
ਹੰਢੈ ਉੰਨ ਕਤਾਇਦਾ ਪੈਧਾ ਲੋੜੈ ਪਟੁ ॥

Farida lorai daakh Bijurian kikkar beejai jatt.

Hanndai unn kataayeda paidha lorai patt.

फरीदा लोड़ै दाख बिजउरीआं किकरि बीजै जटु ॥
हंढै उंन कताइदा पैधा लोड़ै पटु ॥

Farid says, the farmer wants famous raisins of Bijaur region
(now in Khyber Pakhtunkhwa province of Pakistan) but sows
the seed of *kikkar* (*babool*, or *acacia nilotica*).
He spins wool all the time but wants to wear silk.

Farid/1379/2

The results you get will be dependent on actions you take. How can you harvest best quality raisins if you sow *kikkar* seed? How can you hope to wear silk if you spin only wool all the time?

Here is an interesting example by Bhagat Kabir of a monkey who gets caught because of his greedy behaviour:

ਜਿਉ ਕਪਿ ਕੇ ਕਰ ਮੁਸਟਿ ਚਨਨ ਕੀ ਲੁਬਧਿ ਨ ਤਿਆਗੁ ਦਇਓ ॥
ਜੋ ਜੋ ਕਰਮ ਕੀਏ ਲਾਲਚ ਸਿਉ ਤੇ ਫਿਰਿ ਗਰਹਿ ਪਰਿਓ ॥

Jiu kup kay kar must chanan ki lubhadh na tiaag daeyo.

Jo jo karam kiye laalach siu tay phir gareh pareyo.

जिउ कपि के कर मुसटि चनन की लुबधि न तिआगु दइओ ॥
जो जो करम कीए लालच सिउ ते फिरि गरहि परिओ ॥

> Like a monkey whose fist is full of black gram inside a jar,
> which he won't let go because he is too greedy (gets captured
> in the bargain).
> (Similarly) all deeds done in greed by a man become a noose
> around his neck (as bad karma).
>
> Kabir/336/12

This is about an old trick used by monkey-catchers, who leave some gram in a tight-necked jar to lure the monkey. The monkey puts his hand inside the jar and grabs a fistful of gram. Now his hand wouldn't come out unless he releases the gram, but he is too greedy to do that. The monkey-catcher grabs him. For a fistful of gram the monkey loses his freedom. Many men behave similarly, committing acts in greed which create bad *karam*.

The sinners who have collected bad *karam* seem to have no way out but to pay for their sins; in this life or in the future ones. God however, is ever so merciful and is ever-ready to give you a chance. His doors are always open for those willing to change and surrender completely. Their bad *karam* can be cleared instantaneously.

Here is Guru Nanak offering you an escape from your bad *karam*:

> ਅਉਖਧ ਮੰਤ੍ਰ ਮੂਲੁ ਮਨ ਏਕੈ ਜੇ ਕਰਿ ਦ੍ਰਿੜੁ ਚਿਤੁ ਕੀਜੈ ਰੇ॥
> ਜਨਮ ਜਨਮ ਕੇ ਪਾਪ ਕਰਮ ਕੇ ਕਾਟਨਹਾਰਾ ਲੀਜੈ ਰੇ॥
>
> Aokhad mantar mool munn ekai jay kar drireh chit keejai ray.
> Janam janam kay paap karam kay kaatanhaara leejai ray.
>
> अउखध मंत्र मूलु मन एकै जे करि द्रिड़ु चितु कीजै रे॥
> जनम जनम के पाप करम के काटनहारा लीजै रे॥

This is the prime mantra, put your mind on Him with full
devotion and determination.
Take your bad *karam* of all lives to Him, the Destroyer
(of bad karma).

M1/156/3

Guru Arjan Dev also tells us how, by serving the Lord,
record of bad *karam* can be made inoperative and one can get
out of the cycle of birth and death:

ਹਰਿ ਦਰੁ ਸੇਵੇ ਅਲਖ ਅਭੇਵੇ ਨਿਹਚਲੁ ਆਸਣੁ ਪਾਇਆ ॥
ਤਹ ਜਨਮ ਨ ਮਰਣੁ ਨ ਆਵਣ ਜਾਣਾ ਸੰਸਾ ਦੂਖੁ ਮਿਟਾਇਆ ॥

Har dar sevay alakh ahbevay nihchal aasan paaya.
Teh janam na maran na aavan jaana sansa dookh mitaaya.

हरि दरु सेवे अलख अभेवे निहचलु आसणु पाइआ ॥
तह जनम न मरणु न आवण जाणा संसा दूखु मिटाइआ ॥

He who serves at the door of the Unknowable Lord
attains a stable position.
Then there is no birth and death, no coming and
going, all anxiety and pain are removed.

ਚਿਤੁ ਗੁਪਤ ਕਾ ਕਾਗਦੁ ਫਾਰਿਆ ਜਮਦੂਤਾ ਕਛੁ ਨ ਚਲੀ ॥
ਨਾਨਕੁ ਸਿਖ ਦੇਇ ਮਨ ਪ੍ਰੀਤਮ ਹਰਿ ਲਦੇ ਖੇਪ ਸਵਲੀ ॥

Chitar Gupt ka kaagad faareya jamdoota kachhu na challi.
Nanak sikh dei munn pritam Har ladday khep savalli.

चित्र गुपत का कागदु फारिआ जमदूता कछू न चली ॥
नानकु सिख देइ मन प्रीतम हरि लदे खेप सवली ॥

> The record of his *karam* with *Chitar Gupt* is torn away, the
> messenger of death has no way with him.
> Nanak advises the mind to love the Lord, because it is a
> profitable bargain.
>
> M5/79/16

As humans we are best suited to clear our bad *karam* the fastest. We must do everything in this life to earn maximum good. Ideally our deeds should lead us to salvation in this life only – which is possible. A cave that has been dark since ages doesn't take ages to light up. If light is taken inside, the darkness departs and the cave is lightened instantaneously. Similarly people even with bad *karam*, can also get enlightened quickly.

Ramakrishna Parmahansa, the revered Bengali mystic said, "He is born in vain who, having attained the human birth, so difficult to get, does not attempt to realize God in this very life."

Remember, your good deeds will earn more credit if these are done with good and honest intention. Whatever you do, always check your intention and motivation for doing it. For example, donations made to charity for earning praise and to feel proud, is not the same as donations given with clear intention of helping someone, without any expectation in return.

"Even he with the worst of karma who ceaselessly meditates on Me quickly loses the effects of his past bad actions. Becoming a high souled being, he soon attains perennial peace."

Bhagwat Gita (IX, 30-31)

CHAPTER 29

MEAT AND LIQUOR

ੴ

What does SGGS say on consumption of meat and liquor? This is a commonly asked question and people don't seem to get a clear answer. The debates on the issue often turn argumentative where verses from SGGS are misinterpreted and misquoted to suit one's personal beliefs and likings. I will analyze a few verses where I shall be as objective as possible.

Guru Nanak's following verse is often quoted to suggest that he is against eating meat:

> ਰਸੁ ਸੁਇਨਾ ਰਸੁ ਰੁਪਾ ਕਾਮਣਿ ਰਸੁ ਪਰਮਲ ਕੀ ਵਾਸੁ॥
> ਰਸੁ ਘੋੜੇ ਰਸੁ ਸੇਜਾ ਮੰਦਰ ਰਸੁ ਮੀਠਾ ਰਸੁ ਮਾਸੁ॥
> ਏਤੇ ਰਸ ਸਰੀਰ ਕੇ ਕੈ ਘਟਿ ਨਾਮ ਨਿਵਾਸੁ॥
>
> Ras soena ras roopa kaamin ras parmal ki vaas.
> Ras ghoray ras seja mandir ras meetha ras maas.
> Aitay ras sareer kay kai ghat naam nivaas.
>
> रसु सुइना रसु रुपा कामणि रसु परमल की वासु॥
> रसु घोड़े रसु सेजा मंदर रसु मीठा रसु मासु॥
> एते रस सरीर के कै घटि नाम निवासु॥

> (People indulge in) pleasure of gold & silver, of lust for
> women, pleasure of perfumes.
> Pleasure of horses, of thrones & beautiful buildings, of sweets
> and pleasure of eating meat.
> With so many pleasures of the body (to distract), how can
> God's name reside there?
>
> M1/15/12

Here Guru Nanak has mentioned several pleasures which keep the mind and body so occupied that there is little space for God. Since meat is one of those pleasures it is argued that Guru Nanak is against eating meat. If that be so then we must accept that Guru Nanak is against other pleasures too. We must therefore do away with gold, silver, women, perfumes, and buildings etc. Can we do that? Some of these things, at least in limited quantity, are essential for our sustenance, survival and progeneration. I feel what Guru Nanak is saying is, that we should not be over indulgent in these things which leaves us no time for worship of God and hinders our spiritual growth. We can have some material possessions but should remain detached from them, so that if tomorrow something is taken away we don't get unduly disturbed. Detachment is a mental state of not being overwhelmed with material things and doesn't necessarily mean physical riddance.

Here Guru Nanak says discussion on meat is not so relevant and there are more significant issues:

> ਮਾਸੁ ਮਾਸੁ ਕਰਿ ਮੂਰਖੁ ਝਗੜੇ ਗਿਆਨੁ ਧਿਆਨੁ ਨਹੀ ਜਾਣੈ ॥
> ਕਉਣੁ ਮਾਸੁ ਕਉਣੁ ਸਾਗੁ ਕਹਾਵੈ ਕਿਸੁ ਮਹਿ ਪਾਪ ਸਮਾਣੇ ॥
>
> Maas maas kar moorakh jhagray giyaan dhyaan nahi jaanai.
> Kaun maas kaun saag kahavai kis meh paap samaanay.

मासु मासु करि मूरखु झगड़े गिआनु धिआनु नही जाणै ॥
कउणु मासु कउणु सागु कहावै किसु महि पाप समाणे ॥

Foolish people fight over meat, while they have no
understanding of higher awareness and worship.
What is called meat and what is mustard leaf, (important
thing is) what has more sins hidden within?

M1/1289/15

We can therefore say, it would be wrong to eat even a
vegetable if it is taken from a poor and needy person by sinful
means; and eating meat may be acceptable in a situation
where nothing else is available and a person is starving to
death – as sometimes happens in a war situation.

Guru Arjan Dev's views on eating forbidden meat:

ਗੈਬਾਨ ਹੈਵਾਨ ਹਰਾਮ ਕੁਸਤਨੀ ਮੁਰਦਾਰ ਬਖੋਰਾਇ ॥
ਦਿਲ ਕਬਜ ਕਬਜਾ ਕਾਦਰੋ ਦੋਜਕ ਸਜਾਇ ॥

Gaibaan haivaan haraam kustani murdaar bakhoraaye.
Dil kabaj kabja kaadro dojak sajaaye.

गैबान हैवान हराम कुसतनी मुरदार बखोराइ ॥
दिल कबज कबजा कादरो दोजक सजाइ ॥

Like a beast they kill, and eat forbidden meat.
Control your urges or the Lord will punish you in hell.

M5/723/15

The interpretation here is that one should not eat meat
because it is forbidden. However, forbidden meat could
also refer to *halaal* type of meat which involves slow and
painful death of the bird or the animal. This kind of meat

is consumed by Muslims, but it is forbidden for Hindus and Sikhs. Hindus/Sikhs, who do eat meat, have the *jhatka* meat, in which the death of the animal/bird is sudden inflicting minimum pain. So the above verse could also mean *jhatka* is permitted but *halaal* is forbidden.

Let us now look at some of Bhagat Kabir's writings which suggest that meat should not be eaten. This verse below exposes those who have double standards of keeping fasts to please God, and then eat meat for their gastronomical pleasures:

> ਰੋਜਾ ਧਰੈ ਮਨਾਵੈ ਅਲਹੁ ਸੁਆਦਤਿ ਜੀਅ ਸੰਘਾਰੈ ॥
> ਆਪਾ ਦੇਖਿ ਅਵਰ ਨਹੀ ਦੇਖੈ ਕਾਹੇ ਕਉ ਝਖ ਮਾਰੈ ॥
>
> Roja dharai manavai Allah suaadat jia sanghaarai.
> Aapa dekh avar nahi dekhai kaahay kao jhakh maarai.
>
> रोजा धरै मनावै अलहु सुआदति जीअ संघारै ॥
> आपा देखि अवर नही देखै काहे कउ झख मारै ॥
>
> You keep fasts to please Allah, while you kill living beings to satisfy your own palate.
> You see your own selfish interests, not of others, why indulge in this meaningless banter?
>
> Kabir/483/5

Bhagat Kabir now questions those who believe God is in everything and yet they indulge in killing living beings:

> ਬੇਦ ਕਤੇਬ ਕਹਹੁ ਮਤ ਝੂਠੇ ਝੂਠਾ ਜੋ ਨ ਬਿਚਾਰੈ ॥
> ਜਉ ਸਭ ਮਹਿ ਏਕੁ ਖੁਦਾਇ ਕਹਤ ਹਉ ਤਉ ਕਿਉ ਮੁਰਗੀ ਮਾਰੈ ॥
>
> Ved kateb kahuh matt jhoothay jhootha jo na vichaarai.
> Jau sabh meh ek Khudaaye kahat hao tao kiu murgi maarai.

बेद कतेब कहहु मत झूठे झूठा जो न बिचारै॥
जउ सभ महि एकु खुदाइ कहत हउ तउ किउ मुरगी मारै॥

Do not say Vedas or Bible/Quran are false, false are those
who do not contemplate on them.
You say there is same one God in everything, then why do
you kill chicken?

Kabir/1350/5

Some people have translated the word 'matt' in the first line
of above quote as 'religious path' and the interpretation as,
"say that Vedas, and Bible/Quran are false religious paths",
quite the opposite meaning. Bhagat Kabir is unlikely to have
so severely denigrated other religions.

Here Bhagat Kabir cautions those who kill living beings
because they will be in a miserable condition when God asks
them to account for their deeds:

ਕਬੀਰ ਜੀਅ ਜੁ ਮਾਰਹਿ ਜੋਰੁ ਕਰਿ ਕਹਤੇ ਹਹਿ ਜੁ ਹਲਾਲੁ॥
ਦਫਤਰੁ ਦਈ ਜਬ ਕਾਢਿ ਹੈ ਹੋਇਗਾ ਕਉਨੁ ਹਵਾਲੁ॥

Kabir, jia ju maareh jor kar kahtay heh ju halaal.
Daftar dayee jab kaadh hai hoyega kaun havaal.

कबीर जीअ जु मारहि जोरु करि कहते हहि जु हलालु॥
दफतरु दई जब काढि है होइगा कउनु हवालु॥

Kabir says, people kill living beings by force and say the dead
has become *halaal* (fit for sacrifice).
When all-loving God asks them to account for their deeds,
what will their condition be?

Kabir/1375/5

Now some advice for the so-called pandits, whom Bhagat Kabir considers no better than butchers:

ਜੀਅ ਬਧਹੁ ਸੁ ਧਰਮੁ ਕਰਿ ਥਾਪਹੁ ਅਧਰਮੁ ਕਹਹੁ ਕਤ ਭਾਈ॥
ਆਪਸ ਕਉ ਮੁਨਿਵਰ ਕਰਿ ਥਾਪਹੁ ਕਾ ਕਉ ਕਹਹੁ ਕਸਾਈ॥

Jia badhahu su dharam kar thaapoh adharam kahaho
katt bhaayee.
Aapas kao munavar kar thaapoh ka kao kah-ho kasaayee.

जीअ बधहु सु धरमु करि थापहु अधरमु कहहु कत भाई॥
आपस कउ मुनिवर करि थापहु का कउ कहहु कसाई॥

(O pandit) you kill living beings (for sacrifice) and call it
righteous act, then what would you call an unrighteous act?
You call yourself a high priest, then who would you
call a butcher?

Kabir/1103/2

Bhagat Kabir's advice for those consuming cannabis, fish and liquor:

ਕਬੀਰ ਭਾਂਗ ਮਾਛੁਲੀ ਸੁਰਾ ਪਾਨਿ ਜੋ ਜੋ ਪ੍ਰਾਨੀ ਖਾਂਹਿ॥
ਤੀਰਥ ਬਰਤ ਨੇਮ ਕੀਏ ਤੇ ਸਭੈ ਰਸਾਤਲਿ ਜਾਂਹਿ॥

Kabir bhang machhuli sura paan jo jo pranee khaanhay.
Tirath barat naym keeyae te sabhai rasalat jaanhay.

कबीर भांग माछुली सुरा पानि जो जो प्रानी खांहि॥
तीरथ बरत नेम कीए ते सभै रसातलि जांहि॥

Kabir says, all those who consume cannabis, fish and liquor;
their pilgrimages, fasting, rituals all go waste.

Kabir/1377/2

Some interpret above advice to be specifically against consumption of cannabis, fish and liquor, while others say these are generic names and include all forms of narcotics, meats and intoxicating drinks.

Now Guru Amar Das on consumption of intoxicants:

ਜਿਤੁ ਪੀਤੈ ਮਤਿ ਦੂਰਿ ਹੋਇ ਬਰਲੁ ਪਵੈ ਵਿਚਿ ਆਇ ॥
ਆਪਣਾ ਪਰਾਇਆ ਨ ਪਛਾਣਈ ਖਸਮਹੁ ਧਕੇ ਖਾਇ ॥

Jit peetai mutt door hoye barul pavai vich aaye.
Aapna paraaya na pachhaanayee khasmaho dhakkay khaaye.

जितु पीतै मति दूरि होइ बरलु पवै विचि आइ ॥
आपणा पराइआ न पछाणई खसमहु धके खाइ ॥

By drinking (liquor) his wisdom departs and madness
enters his mind.
He cannot distinguish his own from the other, he is roughed
up by the Husband Lord.

ਜਿਤੁ ਪੀਤੈ ਖਸਮੁ ਵਿਸਰੈ ਦਰਗਹ ਮਿਲੈ ਸਜਾਇ ॥
ਝੂਠਾ ਮਦੁ ਮੂਲਿ ਨ ਪੀਚਈ ਜੇ ਕਾ ਪਾਰਿ ਵਸਾਇ ॥

Jit peetai khasam visrai dargah milai sajaaye.
Jhootha madh mool na peechayee jay ka paar vasaaye.

जितु पीतै खसमु विसरै दरगह मिलै सजाइ ॥
झूठा मदु मूलि न पीचई जे का पारि वसाइ ॥

If you drink that which separates you from your Husband
Lord, you will be punished in Lord's court.
If you can help it, do not drink such filthy liquor.

M3/554/14

To sum up, the overall impression one gets is that Sikh Gurus are not clearly for, or against, eating meat, while Bhagat Kabir is vehemently opposed to killing of birds and animals. Regarding liquor, there is a common view opposing it.

My own take is that if you are on a spiritual path you should avoid consuming both, non-vegetarian food as well as liquor. Eating meat involves killing birds or animals which are part of Oneness of the creation. Since you too are a part of the same Oneness, you would be killing something of your own.

However, killing living beings may be acceptable where they endanger a higher form of life. For example, controlled killing of rats, mosquitoes, rabid dogs etc. can be justified when they spread disease and endanger humanity.

Some argue that fruits, vegetables and plants are also living beings, so why eat them. The difference is that they don't have a nervous system/consciousness and when we cut and cook them they do not suffer pain or anguish like birds and animals do.

Physiologically humans are more like herbivorous (vegetarian) animals than carnivorous (meat eating ones). Here are some of the differences:

Carnivorous animals have two large teeth for biting flesh, and the other chewing teeth are also sharp, whereas herbivorous animals only have rounded teeth like humans.

Jaw movement of carnivorous animals is up and down only, while herbivorous animals move their jaw up and down, as well as sideways.

Meat eaters drink water with their tongue unlike non meat eaters which suck water with their breath, like humans.

Human digestive system is best suited for vegetarian diet which gets digested within 2-3 hours. Meat takes much longer.

Carnivorous' saliva does not have digestive enzymes, while humans as well as other herbivores have.

It is a myth that carnivorous animals are stronger than herbivores. Elephant, gorilla, horse, and bull etc. are all very strong despite being herbivorous.

More people are now becoming aware of benefits of vegetarian food and are switching over. Is meat an essential part of human diet? Harvard and Cornell Universities state that the optimum amount of meat in a healthy human diet is precisely zero.

Liquor consumption as such is clearly not advised, because it dulls the mind and is detrimental to spiritual growth. It makes one lose touch with reality and with true self.

"Nothing will benefit human health and increase the chances for survival of life on earth as much as the evolution to a vegetarian diet."

Albert Einstein (1879-1955)
American Scientist

CHAPTER 30

GRATITUDE

ੴ

Though this is the last chapter of this book, by no means is it the least - it contains one of the most empowering lessons. Let me start with this passage from the Bible, containing a Jesus parable:

> *"Whoever has will be given more, and he will have an abundance. Whoever does not have, even that he has will be taken from him."*
>
> (Matthew 13:12)

What does this mean? What is it that people who already have will be given more, and those who do not have, even what they have will be taken away? What is Jesus referring to? Many people have tried to solve this riddle and have come up with varied answers. Some believe it is faith he was talking about, others say he was referring to responsibility, yet others say he meant working ability and so on. Perhaps those who are closest to truth are the ones who believe what he meant was 'gratitude'. So those who have gratitude will be given more and those who don't have gratitude, even what they have will be taken away.

Quran has this to say about gratitude, "The Lord proclaimed, *'If you are grateful, I will surely increase you (in favour) but if you deny, indeed my punishment is severe.'"* (Surah Ibrahim 14:7)

What is gratitude? The word 'gratitude' is derived from Latin word *gratia*, which means graciousness, or gratefulness.

Gratitude is a thankful appreciation for what an individual receives, whether tangible or intangible.

Sincere expression of gratitude can bring about abundance in every aspect of your life - be it health, wealth, love or happiness. Ungratefulness on the other hand can make your life quite unrewarding.

SGGS urges us to be ever grateful to God for everything He has given. He has indeed given us bountiful. In the verse below, Guru Arjan Dev tells us that we must express our gratitude to the One who created us and has given everything:

ਜੀਉ ਪਾਇ ਪਿੰਡੁ ਜਿਨਿ ਸਾਜਿਆ ਦਿਤਾ ਪੈਨਣੁ ਖਾਣੁ ॥
ਅਪਨੇ ਦਾਸ ਕੀ ਆਪਿ ਪੈਜ ਰਾਖੀ ਨਾਨਕ ਸਦ ਕੁਰਬਾਣੁ ॥

Jiu paaye pind saajeya ditta painan khaan,
Apnay daas ki aap paij raakhi Nanak sadh kurbaan.

जीउ पाइ पिंडु जिनि साजिआ दिता पैनणु खाणु॥
अपणे दास की आपि पैज राखी नानक सद कुरबाणु॥

He who fashioned the body, put the soul within, gives food and clothing;
Who himself ensures honour of His servants, Nanak says, be ever ready to sacrifice your life unto Him
(be ever grateful to Him).

M5/619/19

There are two types of people in how they respond when they receive something. First, those who are ever thankful for whatever they receive, and second, those who are always complaining for what they have not received. When you appreciate what you have, you will always get more, and when you complain about what you don't have, you will always experience scarcity. That is the law of attraction - you bring to your life what you think

most of the time. If you are always grateful you will receive
ever more and if you keep complaining you could be deprived
of even what you already have. Gratitude gets you abundance
while complaining gets you paucity.

Guru Angad Dev says, we should appreciate and thank the
One who gives us sustenance:

ਜਿਸ ਦਾ ਦਿਤਾ ਖਾਵਣਾ ਤਿਸੁ ਕਹੀਐ ਸਾਬਾਸਿ ॥
ਨਾਨਕ ਹੁਕਮੁ ਨ ਚਲਈ ਨਾਲਿ ਖਸਮ ਚਲੈ ਅਰਦਾਸਿ ॥

Jis da ditta khaavana tis kaheeyai saabaas.
Nanak hukam na chal-ee naal Khasam chalai ardaas.

जिस दा दिता खावणा तिसु कहीऐ साबासि ॥
नानक हुकमु न चलई नालि खसम चलै अरदासि ॥

We must be grateful to the One who gives us everything
to consume.
Nanak says we cannot order our Husband Lord around,
the right thing to do is to pray and (be thankful)
to Him.

M2/474/18

Here is a beautiful verse from Guru Arjan Dev containing
some food for thought for the ungrateful people:

ਦਸ ਬਸਤੁ ਲੇ ਪਾਛੈ ਪਾਵੈ ॥ ਏਕ ਬਸਤੁ ਕਾਰਨਿ ਬਿਖੋਟਿ ਗਵਾਵੈ ॥
ਏਕ ਭੀ ਨ ਦੇਇ ਦਸ ਭੀ ਹਿਰਿ ਲੇਇ ॥ ਤਉ ਮੂੜਾ ਕਹੁ ਕਹਾ ਕਰੇਇ ॥

Dus bastu lay pachhai paavai; ek bast kaaran bikhot gavaavai.
Ek bhi na daye dus bhi Har laye; tau moorha kahu kaha karaye.

दस बसतु ले पाछै पावै ॥ एक बसतु कारनि बिखोटि गवावै ॥
एक भी न देइ दस भी हिरि लेइ ॥ तउ मूड़ा कहु कहा करेइ ॥

> He just forgets the ten gifts he has received, and loses faith
> for just one thing he doesn't get.
>
> What if the Lord doesn't give even that one thing, and takes
> away ten already given? What would the idiot do then?
>
> M5/268/6

We must not deny the fact that God has created everything and He is the one who has given us our life, our soul and everything else. We must therefore gracefully accept what we are given and be thankful to Him.

In the following verse Guru Arjan Dev asks us not to ever forget the Lord and then lists out what all He has given us:

> ਨਿਰਗੁਨੀਆਰ ਇਆਨਿਆ ਸੋ ਪ੍ਰਭੁ ਸਦਾ ਸਮਾਲਿ ॥
> ਜਿਨਿ ਕੀਆ ਤਿਸੁ ਚੀਤਿ ਰਖੁ ਨਾਨਕ ਨਿਬਹੀ ਨਾਲਿ ॥
>
> Nirguniyaar iaaneya so Prabh sadaa smaal;
> Jin keeya tis cheet rakh Nanak nib-hee naal.
>
> निरगुनीआर इआनिआ सो प्रभु सदा समालि ॥
> जिनि कीआ तिसु चीति रखु नानक निबही नालि ॥
>
> You virtue-less ignorant man, always remember that Lord;
> Who created you and will also see you through.
>
> M5/266/16

The above verse by Guru Arjan Dev continues as translated below reminding you of what all God has given, and is still giving. It includes:

Fashioned and adorned you, protected you from heat in the womb.

Arranged milk when you were a child, in youth gave you food, happiness and understanding.

In old age he arranges for the close ones to help and serve you.

You happily live on this earth, enjoying the company of children, siblings, friends and spouse.

Provides you with cool water, pleasing air and priceless fire.

With His grace you enjoy all the pleasures and necessities of life.

He gave you hands, feet, ears, eyes and tongue.

By serving Him you enjoy the nine treasures and earn honour in the Lord's court.

He is always close by and protects you throughout your life.

He gives delicacies to relish, perfumes to wear, beautiful homes to live, silk clothes to adorn, and a comfortable bed to sleep in.

God has given you so much, and if you look at your life more deeply, you will find He has given you far more than required. But you are not grateful to God. You promptly say 'thank you' to someone who hands over a piece of paper that you dropped; yet you say nothing to God, who has given you so much and continues to give ever more.

Guru Nanak here speaks of ungrateful people who are not liked by the Lord:

ਮਨਮੁਖ ਲੂਣ ਹਾਰਾਮ ਕਿਆ ਨ ਜਾਣਿਆ ॥ ਬਧੇ ਕਰਨਿ ਸਲਾਮ ਖਸਮ ਨ ਭਾਣਿਆ ॥
ਸਚੁ ਮਿਲੈ ਮੁਖਿ ਨਾਮੁ ਸਾਹਿਬ ਭਾਵਸੀ ॥ ਕਰਸਨਿ ਤਖਤਿ ਸਲਾਮੁ ਲਿਖਿਆ ਪਾਵਸੀ ॥

Manmukh loon haraam kiya na jaaneya,
badhay karan salaam Khasam na bhaaneya.
Such milai mukh naam Sahib bhaavasi,
karsan takhat slaam likhiya paavasi.

मनमुख लूण हाराम किआ न जाणिआ॥ बधे करनि सलाम खसम न भाणिआ॥
सचु मिलै मुखि नामु साहिब भावसी॥ करसनि तखति सलामु लिखिआ पावसी॥

The ungrateful self-oriented people do not recognize what
God has done for them. They make false salutations,
which are not appreciated by Him.
God likes those who have His name on their lips and have
found the Truth; people salute their high positions and
they receive as destined.

M1/143/4

In the following three verses Guru Arjan Dev also tells us
how ungrateful people suffer during their lifetime and continue
to remain in the cycle of death and rebirth:

ਨਰਕ ਘੋਰ ਬਹੁ ਦੁਖ ਘਨੇ ਅਕਿਰਤਘਣਾ ਕਾ ਥਾਨੁ॥
ਤਿਨਿ ਪ੍ਰਭਿ ਮਾਰੇ ਨਾਨਕਾ ਹੋਇ ਹੋਇ ਮੁਏ ਹਰਾਮੁ॥

Nark ghor boh dukh ghanay akirtghana ka thaan,
Tin Prabh maaray Nanaka hoye hoye mooye haraam.

नरक घोर बहु दुख घणे अकिरतघणा का थानु॥
तिनि प्रभि मारे नानका होइ होइ मुए हरामु॥

Hell with terrible pain, is the place for the ungrateful.
Nanak says, God brings about their death accompanied by
immense suffering.

M5/315/9

ਬੀਚੁ ਨ ਕੋਇ ਕਰੇ ਅਕ੍ਰਿਤਘਣੁ ਵਿਛੁੜਿ ਪਇਆ॥
ਆਏ ਖਰੇ ਕਠਿਨ ਜਮਕੰਕਰਿ ਪਕੜਿ ਲਇਆ॥

Beech na koye karay akritghan vichhar payeya.

Aaye kharay kathin jamkankar pakar layeya.

बीचु न कोइ करे अक्रितघणु विछुड़ि पइआ॥

आए खरे कठिन जमकंकरि पकड़ि लइआ॥

No one helps the ungrateful who get distanced from God.
They live miserably till finally caught by the messenger
of death.

M5/546/14

तुम्ह देवहु सभु किछु दइआ धारि हम अकिरतघनारे॥

लागि परे तेरे दान सिउ नह चिति खसमारे॥

Tum-h dayveho sabh kichh daya dhaar humm akritghanaaray.

Laag paray tayray daan siu nah chit Khasmaaray.

तुम्ह देवहु सभु किछु दइआ धारि हम अकिरतघनारे॥

लागि परे तेरे दान सिउ नह चिति खसमारे॥

Out of magnanimity You give us everything, though we
are ungrateful.
We remain busy with things You have given but do
not remember You.

M5/809/4

Do remember that God does not like false gratitude or empty praises. The expression of gratitude must be genuine and straight from the heart; without any expectation. Of course God amply rewards those who offer sincere thankfulness.

Guru Arjan Dev now says God looks after and forgives even the ungrateful:

ਦੇਖੈ ਸੁਨੈ ਹਦੂਰਿ ਸਦ ਘਟਿ ਘਟਿ ਬ੍ਰਹਮੁ ਰਵਿੰਦੁ ॥
ਅਕਿਰਤਘਣਾ ਨੋ ਪਾਲਦਾ ਪ੍ਰਭ ਨਾਨਕ ਸਦ ਬਖਸਿੰਦੁ ॥

Dekhai sunai hadoor sadh ghat ghat Brahm ravind,
Akritghana no paalda Prabh Nanak sadh bakhsind.

देखै सुणै हदूरि सद घटि घटि ब्रहमु रविंदु ॥
अकिरतघणा नो पालदा प्रभ नानक सद बखसिंदु ॥

The Lord is always close-by and watches and listens to us,
He resides in every heart.
He looks after even the ungrateful and is ever forgiving.
M5/47/6

So far we had seen that God punishes those who are ungrateful, but now in the above verse Guru Arjan Dev says He looks after and forgives even the ungrateful. How can He punish the ungrateful as well as look after them? The truth is, that God is always very loving, caring, compassionate, just, magnanimous and ever-ready to help anyone and everyone. The problem lies in our own thoughts and deeds. We invite punishment by generating bad thoughts and by indulging in sinful activities that create negative *karam*. God does not punish us, we punish ourselves when we violate His law - we are duly rewarded when we obey the law.

Gratitude is a tremendous quality to possess. It can transform your life remarkably by bringing about happiness and fulfillment. Learn to be grateful and say 'Thank You' to God for everything - big or small. Count your blessings everyday and thank God. When you start counting your blessings you will realize how blessed you indeed are.

Also thank people you come in contact with daily. Even if you have a negative experience with someone, thank God and thank that person for teaching you something.

Guru Gobind Singh had such a towering personality, yet see his humility and sense of gratitude towards his followers when he said:

"Inhi Ki Kirpa Say Sajay Hum Haen Nahi Mo So Gareeb Karor Paray."
(It is because of their benevolence that I stand glorified; otherwise there are millions of poor people like me.)

There are other benefits of gratitude too. Those who express gratitude heal faster and live longer. Also, grateful people are more positive and happy. When you are grateful there can be no negative thoughts in your mind. Try thanking God for something you have, and see how positive you feel. Now try complaining to God for something you don't have. You will notice how depressing the feeling is. Whenever you are feeling low, thank God for something, you will feel better. Thank You, Thank You, Thank You - let your whole day be filled with it.

Live your life with an attitude of gratitude.

"Gratitude is the healthiest of all human emotions. The more you express gratitude for what you have, the more likely you will have even more to express gratitude for."

Zig Ziglar (1926-2012)
American Author &
Motivational Speaker

CONCLUSION

ੴ

Over the last few centuries the world has made great progress. This progress has been backed by modern science and technology which has created immense material wealth. It was expected that this development would benefit people around the globe, particularly the poor and the needy. That has not happened. More wealth has been accumulated in the hands of those who were already rich, while sufferings of the poor have only increased.

This progress has not at all contributed towards making the society happy and satisfied. On the other hand it has created immense competition with resultant pressures, tensions and anxiety, which are taking their own toll. The have-nots are in pursuit of bare minimum necessities while the haves are not willing to share their wealth. Materialism, it can be concluded, does not hold the key to success and happiness. Look at Bhutan, a small Himalayan nation, with minimum wealth and least invested in science and technology, yet on the 'happiness' index of nations it holds number one position in the world.

People across the world, particularly those in the developed countries, have begun to accept that spiritualism is the answer to major problems of humanity. More and more people are pursuing spiritual living where material needs are minimal and happiness endless. Many doctors, scientists, professors and other well educated individuals, backed by scientific research, now believe that there is indeed 'spirit life' beyond the physical life, and that we reincarnate very many times - as also, that destiny in our future lives is created by our deeds of this life.

There is greater belief in God now, more so among the highly respected scientific community. Dr William D Philips, Nobel Prize winner in physics in 1997 said, "I believe in God because I can feel God's presence in my life, because I can see the evidence of God's goodness in the world, because I believe in Love and because I believe that God is Love."

There is a sure and steady spiritual evolution underway; though not very visible yet, but it is gaining momentum. We have to evolve, there is no other way. We evolved from rocks to plant life, from plant life to animals and from animals to human beings. The next stage is to get free from the shackles of our ego and our uncontrolled mind, so as to attain a higher level of consciousness/awareness. That is the stage where we attain God-realization, and where love & truth reign supreme.

Whatever little spiritual teaching took place in the past was done by the organized religion. Its main purpose was to exercise control over people's minds to make them more dependent on religion. It shackled them instead of setting them free. The current revolution is taking place outside the religion, which makes it free of any dogmas, meaningless rituals and faulty beliefs. Books, lectures, congregations, retreats, electronic-cum-social media, are the mainstay of this teaching. It is not dependent on religion or on formal system of education.

Spirituality teaches you to see the entire creation as One and to deal with every living being with love and care. SGGS is a holy book in which you find everything that is required for truthful living and spiritual growth. It is all about love, compassion, humility, worship, truthfulness, sharing and caring. It has nothing that promotes enmity, hatred, revenge etc. With God's grace SGGS would bring about enlightenment of more and more people that would lead to the next higher level of our evolution.

It is not enough to just acquire spiritual knowledge - the more important thing is to live by it.

Guru Nanak said:

> ਸਚਹੁ ਓਰੈ ਸਭੁ ਕੋ ਉਪਰਿ ਸਚੁ ਆਚਾਰੁ ॥
>
> Sachoh orai sabh ko upar sach aachaar.
>
> सचहु ओरै सभु को उपरि सचु आचारु॥
>
> **Truth is high, but even higher is truthful living.**
>
> M1/62/11

In this book I have taken out a few drops from the vast ocean of wisdom contained in *Shri Guru Granth Sahib* which I am sure will help bring more joy and peace in your lives.

Finally, a poem titled 'Fear' by Lebanese poet, Khalil Gibran (1883-1931):

It is said that before entering the sea
a river trembles with fear.

She looks back at the path she has traveled,
from the peaks of the mountains,
the long winding road crossing forests and villages.

And in front of her,
she sees an ocean so vast,
that to enter
there seems nothing more than to disappear forever.

But there is no other way.
The river cannot go back.

Nobody can go back.
To go back is impossible in existence.

The river needs to take the risk
of entering the ocean
because only then will fear disappear,
because that's where the river will know
it's not about disappearing into the ocean,
but of becoming the ocean.

We too are on a journey like the river. The river heads towards the mighty ocean to finally merge with it, while we are on a journey towards the mighty Almighty. Like the river, we too cannot go back, though there may be some temporary slippages. The river meanders off and on, so do we take detours here and there, but the destination is very clear; which is to awaken and merge with God.

"And the time came when the risk to remain tight in a bud was more painful than the risk it took to blossom".

Anais Nin (1903-1977)
French Author

Time has come for the flower in your heart to blossom forth.

AFTERWORD

ੴ

As I write this end note, the world has been going through immense suffering caused by revival waves of Corona pandemic. In some countries like India the situation has been extremely grim. There were far too many tragic and painful deaths happening every passing hour. Crematory fires could be seen burning all over the country, day and night. People found themselves helpless and frightened. Experts tell us that perhaps, the worst is yet to come.

Sikh volunteers have been in the forefront once again, saving hundreds of lives with all types of *seva*, including free supply of scarce oxygen - noble deeds indeed which will purify their souls.

On the other hand there were the unscrupulous people exploiting patients and their near ones in every possible way. Not only were they missing the chance to enrich their souls, they were actually impoverishing them.

In this dark hour, this is my prayer to *Waheguru* on behalf of all of us. It is from *gurbani* of Guru Amar Das:

ਜਗਤੁ ਜਲੰਦਾ ਰਖਿ ਲੈ ਆਪਣੀ ਕਿਰਪਾ ਧਾਰਿ ॥

(O God) please save this burning world with Your kind benevolence.

ਜਿਤੁ ਦੁਆਰੈ ਉਬਰੈ ਤਿਤੈ ਲੈਹੁ ਉਬਾਰਿ ॥

Whichever way it be done, please save the world.

M3/853/12

AUTHORS OF SHRI GURU GRANTH SAHIB

The Sikh Gurus (6)

	Guru At Age	Guru For No of Yrs	Hymns in SGGS
1st Guru Nanak Dev (1469-1539)	-	-	974
2nd Guru Angad Dev (1504-1552)	35	13	62
3rd Guru Amar Das (1479-1574)	73	22	907
4th Guru Ram Das (1534-1581)	40	7	679
5th Guru Arjan Dev (1563-1606)	18	25	2218
9th Guru Teg Bahadur (1621-1675)	44	10	116
10th Guru Gobind Singh (1675-1708)	9	33	1*

Holy Saints (15)

	Religion and Region	Hymns In SGGS
Sheikh Farid (1173-1266)	Muslim, Punjab	4
Bhagat Jai Dev (1201-1273)	Hindu, Bengal, Poet	2
Bhagat Trilochan (1267-1335)	Hindu Brahmin, Maharashtra	4
Bhagat Namdev (1270-1350)	Hindu, Maharashtra, Tailor	61
Bhagat Ramanand (1400-1467)	Hindu, UP	1
Bhagat Kabir (1448-1518)	Muslim, UP, Weaver	541

Bhagat Ravidas (1450-1520)	Hindu, UP, Shoe Maker	40
Bhagat Sain (1343-1440)	Hindu, Punjab, Barber	1
Bhagat Dhanna (1415-1475)	Hindu, Rajasthan, Farmer	4
Bhagat Peepa (1426-1562)	Hindu, Rajasthan/UP, King	1
Bhagat Parmanand (1483-1593)	Hindu, Maharashtra	1
Bhagat Surdas (1479-1580)	Hindu, UP, Poet	1
Bhagat Bhikhan (1480-1573)	Muslim, UP, Sufi Saint	2
Bhagat Sadhna (b. 1180)	Muslim, Sindh/Punjab Butcher	1
Bhagat Beni (Period not known)	Muslim, Punjab	3

Bhatts (11)

Bhatts were traditional poets and singers who eked out a living by eulogizing kings and other important people. When the influence of Sikh Gurus began they became followers of Sikhism and started writing and singing praises of the Gurus. Their writings appear in SGGS at pages from 1389 to 1409. There is some confusion about the exact number of Bhatts whose writings appear in SGGS because of some similar sounding names. However, there is a general belief that following eleven Bhatts contributed: Kalh/Kalhshaar, Jalap, Kirat, Bhikha, Salh, Bhalh, Nalh, Gayand, Mathura, Balh, and Harbans.

Other Contributors (4)

These are, Bhai Mardana (3), Baba Sundar (6), Bhai Satta (1) and Bhai Balwand (1).

* Guru Gobind Singh did not include his own poetry in SGGS. However, there is one couplet which was written by him which is mentioned as *Salok Mahalla 10* in some old

hand-written scripts of SGGS. In the present version the couplet is part of writings of his father Guru Teg Bahadur under *Salok Mahalla 9*.

When Guru Teg Bahadur was imprisoned by Aurangzeb in Delhi, and just before he was martyred for the cause of Kashmiri pandits, the Guru sent a couplet to his son to seek his response as a test of his readiness to take over *Guruship* from him. The couplet he sent in a letter was:

ਬਲੁ ਛੁਟਕਿਓ ਬੰਧਨ ਪਰੇ ਕਛੂ ਨ ਹੋਤ ਉਪਾਇ॥

ਕਹੁ ਨਾਨਕ ਅਬ ਓਟ ਹਰਿ ਗਜ ਜਿਉ ਹੋਹੁ ਸਹਾਇ॥

Bal chhutkeo bandhan paray kachhu na hoat upaaye.
Kahu Nanak abb oat Har gaj jehu hoho sahaaye.

बलु छुटकिओ बंधन परे कछू न होत उपाइ॥
कहु नानक अब ओट हरि गज जिउ होहु सहाइ॥

My strength is gone and I am shackled, there seems to be no way out.
Says Nanak, O Lord give me Your support and help me as You helped the elephant (from a story in the *Puraanas* in which God helped the elephant).

M9/1429/6

Then as a young boy of nine, Gobind Rai (later to become Guru Gobind Singh) replied:

ਬਲੁ ਹੋਆ ਬੰਧਨ ਛੁਟੇ ਸਭੁ ਕਿਛੁ ਹੋਤ ਉਪਾਇ॥

ਨਾਨਕ ਸਭੁ ਕਿਛੁ ਤੁਮਰੈ ਹਾਥ ਮੈ ਤੁਮ ਹੀ ਹੋਤ ਸਹਾਇ॥

Bal hoa bandhan chhutay sabh kichhu hoat upaaye.
Nanak, sabh kichhu tumrai haath mai tum hee hoat sahaaye.

बलु होआ बंधन छुटे सभु किछु होत उपाइ॥
नानक सभु किछु तुमरै हाथ मै तुम ही होत सहाइ॥

My strength is restored and my shackles removed, there is
always a way out.
Nanak says, everything is in Your control, O Lord,
only You can help.

M9/1429/7

Guru Teg Bahadur was very pleased with the reply and
approved his taking over *Guruship* after him.

APPENDIX B

QUOTES FROM SHRI GURU GRANTH SAHIB INCLUDED IN UN DOCUMENT

ੴ

Three quotations from SGGS have been included in the UN document titled '18 Commitments on Faith for Rights,' prepared under the office of the High Commissioner, UN Human Rights. There are about thirty quotations in all, taken from various religious texts, of which following three are from SGGS. The English translation given here is as mentioned in the UN document. Besides English, the original document also contains French and Arabic translation.

ਪੈ ਕੋਇ ਨ ਕਿਸੈ ਰਵਾਣਦਾ॥
ਸਭ ਸੁਖਾਲੀ ਵੁਠੀਆ ਇਹੁ ਹੋਆ ਹਲੇਮੀ ਰਾਜੁ ਜੀਉ॥

Pai koi na kissai ravaan-da;
Sabh sukhali vuthia ihu hoa halemi raj jio.

पै कोइ न किसै रञाणदा॥
सभ सुखाली वुठीआ इहु होआ हलेमी राजु जीउ॥

"No one shall coerce another; no one shall exploit another. Everyone, each individual, has the inalienable birth right to seek and pursue happiness and self-fulfillment. Love and persuasion is the only law of social coherence."

M5/74/3

ਭੰਡਹੁ ਹੋਵੈ ਦੋਸਤੀ ਭੰਡਹੁ ਚਲੈ ਰਾਹੁ ॥
ਸੋ ਕਿਉ ਮੰਦਾ ਆਖੀਐ ਜਿਤੁ ਜੰਮਹਿ ਰਾਜਾਨ ॥
ਭੰਡਹੁ ਹੀ ਭੰਡੁ ਉਪਜੈ ਭੰਡੈ ਬਾਝੁ ਨ ਕੋਇ ॥

Bhandoh hovai dosti bhandoh challai raaho.
So kiu manda aakheeyai jit jameh raajaan.
Bhandoh hi bhand oopjai bhandai baajh na koye.

भंडहु होवै दोसती भंडहु चलै राहु ॥
सो किउ मंदा आखीऐ जितु जमहि राजान ॥
भंडहु ही भंडु ऊपजै भंडै बाझु न कोइ ॥

"It is a woman who is a friend and partner for life. It is a
woman who keeps the race going.
How may we think low of her of whom are born the greatest.
From a woman a woman is born: none may exist without
a woman."

M1/473/8

ਬ੍ਰਹਮ ਗਿਆਨੀ ਸਦਾ ਨਿਰਦੋਖ ॥ ਜੈਸੇ ਸੂਰੁ ਸਰਬ ਕਉ ਸੋਖ ॥
ਬ੍ਰਹਮ ਗਿਆਨੀ ਕੈ ਦ੍ਰਿਸਟਿ ਸਮਾਨਿ ॥ ਜੈਸੇ ਰਾਜ ਰੰਕ ਕਉ ਲਾਗੈ ਤੁਲਿ ਪਵਾਨ ॥

Brahm giani sada nirdokh; jaisay soor sarab kau sokh.
Brahm giani kai drisht samaan; jaisay raj runk kau laagai
tul pavaan.

ब्रहम गिआनी सदा निरदोख ॥ जैसे सूरु सरब कउ सोख ॥
ब्रहम गिआनी कै द्रिसटि समानि ॥ जैसे राज रंक कउ लागै तुलि पवान ॥

"The God-conscious being is always unstained, like the sun,
which gives the comfort and warmth to all.
The God-conscious being looks upon all alike, like the wind,
which blows equally upon the king and the poor beggar."

M5/272/12

Printed in the USA
CPSIA information can be obtained
at www.ICGtesting.com
LVHW040314280923
759109LV00025B/255/J